Social Capital Online

Kane X. Faucher

Critical, Digital and Social Media Studies

Series Editor: Christian Fuchs

The peer-reviewed book series edited by Christian Fuchs publishes books that critically study the role of the internet and digital and social media in society. Titles analyse how power structures, digital capitalism, ideology and social struggles shape and are shaped by digital and social media. They use and develop critical theory discussing the political relevance and implications of studied topics. The series is a theoretical forum for internet and social media research for books using methods and theories that challenge digital positivism; it also seeks to explore digital media ethics grounded in critical social theories and philosophy.

Editorial Board

Published

Critical Theory of Communication: New Readings of Lukács, Adorno, Marcuse, Honneth and Habermas in the Age of the Internet
Christian Fuchs
https://doi.org/10.16997/book1

Knowledge in the Age of Digital Capitalism: An Introduction to Cognitive Materialism
Mariano Zukerfeld
https://doi.org/10.16997/book3

Politicizing Digital Space: Theory, the Internet, and Renewing Democracy
Trevor Garrison Smith
https://doi.org/10.16997/book5

Capital, State, Empire: The New American Way of Digital Warfare
Scott Timcke
https://doi.org/10.16997/book6

The Spectacle 2.0: Reading Debord in the Context of Digital Capitalism
Edited by *Marco Briziarelli* and *Emiliana Armano*
https://doi.org/10.16997/book11

The Big Data Agenda: Data Ethics and Critical Data Studies
Annika Richterich
https://doi.org/10.16997/book14

Forthcoming

The Propaganda Model Today: Filtering Perception and Awareness
Edited by Joan Pedro-Carañana, Daniel Broudy & Jeffery Klaehn

Critical Theory and Authoritarian Populism
Edited by Jeremiah Morelock

Social Capital Online: Alienation and Accumulation

Kane X. Faucher

University of Westminster Press
www.uwestminsterpress.co.uk

Acknowledgements

It would prove unwieldy to name everyone who has played a role in the formation of this book from concept to publication, but I owe a major debt to a few whose roles were absolutely essential. Firstly, to the diligent and eagle-eyed Press Manager at the University of Westminster Press, Andrew Lockett, without whom this process would have been derailed long ago. I would also like to extend my gratitude to the reviewers whose suggestions vastly improved this book and helped me achieve clarity. I thank my home unit, the Faculty of Information and Media Studies at Western University for affording me the opportunities to teach and further explore many of the concepts developed here. Also, to two defining influences on my thinking: Dr Nick Dyer-Witheford, whose friendship and fine-grained discussions on labour and political economy are entwined; and to James Chaffee, a fellow author whose insistence on precision never let me get away with anything I couldn't operationally define. Last on the list, but certainly top of mind, to my partner, Debra, who has been very patient with me taking time away on occasion for me to complete my textual labours.

Competing interests

The author declares that he has no competing interests in publishing this book.

Published by
University of Westminster Press
115 Cavendish Street
London W1W 6XH
www.uwestminsterpress.co.uk

First published 2018

Series cover concept: Mina Bach (minabach.co.uk)

Printed and bound by CPI Group (UK) Ltd, Croydon, CR0 4YY
Print and digital versions typeset by Siliconchips Services Ltd.

ISBN (Paperback): 978-1-911534-56-3
ISBN (PDF): 978-1-911534-57-0
ISBN (EPUB): 978-1-911534-58-7
ISBN (Kindle): 978-1-911534-59-4

DOI: https://doi.org/10.16997/book16

The full text of this book has been peer-reviewed to ensure high academic
standards. For full review policies, see: http://www.uwestminsterpress.co.uk/
site/publish/

To read the free, open access version of this book
online, visit https://doi.org/10.16997/book16 or
scan this QR code with your mobile device:

Contents

Introduction: What is Online Social Capital?

In 2014, Jonny Byrne, a 19 year old from Ireland, drowned in the River Barrow after participating in the NekNominate social media game: an online version of a chain letter style challenge to drink copious amounts of alcohol in perilous situations in an effort to gain 'likes.' This was followed by the death of Ross Cummins (22) of Dublin, who was also said to have taken up the challenge.

In the run-up to the US 2016 presidential election, Donald Trump made extensive use of Twitter to attack his political opponents, media companies, and various celebrities critical of him as a means of bolstering his base of supporters. As President, Trump has continued to make use of this medium, and on various occasions has pointed to his number of followers as proof of his popularity and political legitimacy.

In May of 2017, a Russian reporter recorded a few short videos of a sophisticated click farm in China where over 10,000 smartphones were placed in docks connected to a network with the single purpose of providing 'likes' and comments to social media content.

What these examples have in common is the subject of this book: the pursuit and accumulation of online social capital, and what implications these have for political economy and critical media studies. With the nearly ubiquitous presence of social media, there has also arisen a great deal of emphasis on online social capital. The number of articles on how to improve online branding strategies, the growing use of click farms, and orchestrated botnet campaigns to artificially inflate social proof are testament to the increasingly perceived importance of acquiring likes and followers on social media. What significantly differs from a time before digital social media is that popularity can now be better measured, as well as displayed as a form of status. And, despite the awareness that some of these numbers may be inflated by the use of automating features,

---

How to cite this book chapter:
Faucher, K. X. 2018. *Social Capital Online: Alienation and Accumulation*. Pp. xi–xxv. London: University of Westminster Press. DOI: https://doi.org/10.16997/book16.a. License: CC-BY-NC-ND 4.0

there may still be a sense of assuming the value of an individual online user via an appeal to the numbers associated with her or his profile. And for those who do not garner higher numbers, there is the risk that others will assume they have lesser value as social beings.

Beginning with the very personal and individual experience when using social media, I want you to picture yourself having posted an interesting piece of experiential content on your social media profile, such as photos of a recent vacation, notice of a new publication, or the birth of a nephew. A few hours pass and you decide to log back into the account. You are reasonably sure that many of the people in your network will have checked the newsfeed since then, and you are looking forward to comments and possibly seeing a few likes and comments. However, no one has interacted with your content. If you reflect on how you feel at that moment, it might vary from indifference to disappointment. So you log back off. Assume in this hypothetical example that one of your app-enabled digital devices is synced with your social media account, and that it is programmed to provide you an alert any time someone interacts with your content. A few more hours pass and you see a small '7' on the top right corner of the icon for your social media app. How would you describe how you feel? Excited with anticipation and eager to tap into your account to see what others have said? A few days pass, and using our hypothetical example, would it make a difference to your mood if there were 10 likes? 100 likes? 10,000 likes?

For some people, these numbers may not be important, whereas for others it is a reflection of personal value that may increase in making those numbers rise. Some will find ways of sharing their content more broadly in the hopes of garnering more likes, while others may even alter their online performance and content tailored to what will be perceived as more popular. Just as avid market watchers may gain gratification in watching their stock portfolios increase by large amounts, or be disappointed when the increase is lower than anticipated, it may be a similar situation for those who invest a great deal of value in these social media counters. If the pursuit of such numbers were unimportant, then we could ask why a Google search for 'how can I increase likes on Facebook' produces a result of over 427 million hits.

If this book were just about the individual and her or his accumulation of online social capital, it might not warrant lengthy treatment; however, the processes that occur behind the visible world of social media, the ideological implications of how online social capital is positioned as a deliberate strategy by major social media networks to encourage participation for profit, and the immiseration of labour on click farms *do* justify bracketing out online social capital for closer analysis.

What is online social capital? How does it differ from more traditional forms of social capital? Why does the term seem to enjoy some degree of consensus without an operational definition? What are the implications that arise from a focus on accumulating likes and leveraging our online profiles through acts of conspicuous display? Who essentially profits by these actions, and how do they do it? Where does online social capital fit in a broader context of capitalism? At this point, a provisional working definition may serve as a bridge toward a much closer analysis:

1) At the user-end, online social capital is a product of online exchanges that in many cases can be expressed in some numeric form, which may or may not be correlated with a perception of an online user's value in a digitally networked community. Online social capital becomes a kind of offering to the social marketplace when users attempt to leverage the quantifiable measures of friends, followers, views, and likes for some goal.
2) On the network owner's end, online social capital is the labour of users that can be mined as a data commodity and converted into profit, while also existing as a strategy to keep a digitally networked community active in providing their unpaid labour.

This statement (1) does not imply that *all* forms of online social capital have a numeric basis (likes, followers), as it may also include non-numeric forms (knowledge sharing, community building). The basis by which we furnish this provisional definition will become clearer as we proceed, particularly in unpacking the competing and complementary definitions of social capital in the first chapter, and later speaking directly to metrification,[1] the 'like economy', and platform capitalism in the chapters that follow.

As we delve deeper into this topic, a variety of other issues will arise that challenge some of the more basic assumptions we might hold as to what online social capital is, and how this intriguing 'like economy' functions. To this end, the book seeks to answer the four following questions:

1) How does the process of acquiring online social capital align with the goals of capitalist accumulation?
2) How does this process lead to alienation?
3) In what way does this process echo the goals of neoliberal capitalism specifically?
4) What ties this accumulation to some of the unfortunate by-products of social media, such as aggression and narcissism?

It is important to have some grounding in what social capital is, and how online social capital is both similar and different from it. In both instances, social capital involves *social networks*, with online social capital having the added dimension of residing within the structural ecosystem of digital networks. This is not to say that the affordances of digital networks does not permit considerable overlap between the two types of social capital, but that these digital networks upon which ever more social interaction occurs, manifest a whole new host of opportunities and problems that are unique to the nature of online interaction. Notwithstanding the pioneering work of those such as Pierre Bourdieu (1984),

James Coleman (1988), and Robert Putnam (2001) in particular on the concept of social capital (which we will cover in the first chapter), the rise of big data, commodified social networks, and platformisation has created new conditions through which we come to understand social capital.

In the past few decades, the concept of social capital has received a considerable amount of attention, expanding into the disciplines of the social sciences, critical media studies, history, economics, managerial literature, and as a policy instrument. Although its initial mention can be traced to Alexis de Tocqueville (1960 [1835]) and was later more popularly reprised in the 1960s by Jane Jacobs (1961) to signify the power of a social collective to spur change at the political level, social capital as a term has enjoyed a few surges of recent interest: in new public management theory, social theory and policy, and with respect to online social networks. In the common parlance of the day, social capital generally refers to two somewhat different, yet also similar, phenomena that relate to networks in general.

Three main theoretical approaches are used:

1) Social capital as a resource acquired and/or mobilized by social actors. This resources is derived through social relations and the creation or maintenance of social connections in some form of community (Putnam, Bourdieu).
2) Social capital as part of the broader system of capital and its inherent contradictions where labour is socialized, and the potential for exploitation and alienation arises (classical Marxism).
3) Social capital as the social product of immaterial labour that, in turn, (re) produces social relations (Autonomist Marxism).

For the purposes of this book, I define online social capital as wrapped up in an artificial economy, represented by numeric counters in a 'like' and 'attention' economy, facilitated by social buttons and operated by social media sites to encourage more participation for their own real economic interests (data collection, targeted advertising, and the exploitation of digital labour). Online social capital operates in such a way that it follows a market-based logic of instrumental rationality for the accumulation of a resource that cannot be directly converted into other forms of capital. It is an ideological product of neoliberal-informationism that champions competitive individualism rather than community-based collaboration within a broader network spectacle, fostering the conditions of conspicuous prosumption, status display, and a metric by which to falsely compare social value with other users. The social media site leverages users' pursuit of online social capital for exploitation, while also further alienating those users according to Marx's four main aspects of alienation.

My definition follows Marx's concept of capital, and views this pursuit of online social capital as part of the commodification of the online self through a form of digital labour on social media from which surplus value is extracted.

The definition deviates from Marx on the basis of the price relation between commodified selves as it does not lead to any reliable exchange. Online social capital operates as a false economy of conspicuous status display within a real economy, and it is for that reason Marxist insights will be appended to the insights of Veblen and Debord.

Definitional Problems

There is little consensus about social capital beyond a few assumptions: that it is relatively tangible, generally positive, that it can be associated to economics and rationalising the production performed on social networks, and that more of it is better than less (Mikiewicz 2011). In the hands of those promoting particular political and economic agendas, it becomes a somewhat nebulous motherhood statement with a positive cachet. The main cleavage of the term is whether it refers primarily to sociological or economic phenomena. Moreover, there is considerable debate as to whether or not social capital should be understood as either the result of our interpersonal relationships, or as an economic term. Those who favour the first interpretation (Robison et al. 2002) reject the capital(ist) metaphor.

If we abandon the metaphor of capital in the term of social capital, we may risk being blind to the underlying ideological and economic processes that condition online social capital as a form of accumulation and alienation, particularly through the reification of interpersonal communicative relations as a source for profit by network hosts, and the reality of a potentially infinite surplus value that may be extracted from these acts of communicative exchange – a point well covered in many of the works of those such as Christian Fuchs. As I will argue throughout this book, it is not possible to entirely separate social capital in its online context from the enclosure of capitalist ideology and the strategies of instrumental rationality particularly endemic to neoliberal capitalism. Online social capital and the environment in which it is accumulated and measured is inextricably bound up in many of the same assumptions that underpin capitalist accumulation. The pursuit of numeric social capital in our social media context – the 'like economy' – is built on a foundation of conflict minerals, super-exploited sweatshop labour, precarious ICT services labour, rampant commodification and exploitation of user-generated content, data extraction and sale. In other words, the pursuit of likes is not entirely benign.

Another sense of social capital as it is referred to in popular culture quickly degrades into a placeholder for ease or efficiency of connectivity and communication, and this largely resting on digital networks. Online social capital becomes a substance which may be measured in terms of number of friends/followers and approbation cues, such as likes and retweets, or on a more granular basis (especially among search engine optimization specialists and social media strategists, demographic reach and engagement). In this way, online social capital is something to be *built through strategies of accumulation*, ideally by means of reaching a critical digital mass whereby the capital increases autonomously with little intervention apart from an adjustment to a social media campaign, content refreshing, and incentives to other digital users to carry on the task of increasing capital (sharing, digital word-of-mouth, etc.).

Networks

It is important to consider the ecosystem in which it operates: networks, social buttons, and platforms. When we speak of networks, there are two senses by which we should understand them: as *structural* (digital network architecture) and *social* (human interaction, group dynamics, and – in the case of social media – computer-mediated communication).

The structural nature of digital networks facilitates the online functions of the social aspect of networking, but the structural nature is what appears to make the social 'measurable,' and thus of value to those who would seek to exploit networks for a wide variety of purposes.

Social networks in their own right became an object of study by the psychotherapist, Jacob L. Moreno (1934), particularly in developing a way to measure them using sociometry, out of which one could plot a visual diagram of a social network in what is called a 'sociogram'. Social network analysis (SNA) can show us how actors, nodes, or entities in social networks are connected; how information flow occurs in the affinities between nodes, as well as the particular affordances of each node pending placement within a network configuration; we can measure degrees of separation (or steps along a pathway) between nodes and their ability to transmit information; and we can determine if the ties between nodes are weak or strong, and what probable implications emerge from this. This bears some resemblance to other attempts to theorise and quantify networks in terms of systems theory, whereby we study objects (people, channels, procedures) that have attributes, and relationships in a broader environment (or a series of nested systems within systems). The holy grail of such approaches has been the promise, implicit or otherwise, that social relations can be measured, can be explained and possibly predicted in an analytic and objective way. This has opened up new vistas for potentially predicting behaviour, and has been used in areas as diverse as understanding group dynamics in organisational behaviour studies, the use of Game Theory during the Cold War, combatting terrorist networks, and to aid political and marketing decisions. In its more unfortunate applications, it has played a role in the use of racial and cultural profiling.

Since the earlier days of SNA (Moreno 1934, Barnes 1972, Granovetter, 1973, Krackhardt 1987) and actor-network theory (Law & Lodge 1984, Latour 1987, Latour 2005), more sophisticated approaches have integrated the use of probabilistic algorithms, whereby data collection and analysis can be rendered more automated and changes to a network can be deployed more efficiently in real-time. This has presented enormous benefits for social media platforms and their commercial partners. For example, even the use of loyalty cards provided by retail stores has permitted the collection of consumer data based on various inputs (geographical location, demographic information, and purchase data) in order to create a consumer profile for more effective targeted marketing in the form of coupons or email alerts recommending products that the algorithm 'predicts' will have a higher probability of resulting in appealing to a consumer's interests based on an algorithmically-constructed profile and past purchasing behaviour. Algorithms have also served in potentially identifying influencers who are more likely to adopt and disseminate political or consumerist messages through interpersonal persuasion. What began somewhat innocently with the use of SNA, the Mass Observation movement (Madge & Harrisson 1937), and focus groups would eventually become ever more efficient in delivering persuasive events by tracking individuals, social interactions, and social context. What remained was some way to 'eavesdrop' on these social interactions, if not also encourage more interaction so that the data could be obtained. The first step was to find a medium or venue where such social interactions could occur which would allow unobtrusive surveillance. The second step would be to harvest this data and find a means to analyse it efficiently and effectively using computers rather than rely on the slower and more labour intensive process of human beings. The last step was to develop a way to incentivise these social interactions without prodding, and this development would be actuated partially through the use of social buttons.

Social Buttons

The integration of social buttons on popular social media platforms such as Facebook has introduced a whole new dimension to online social interaction. Social buttons include a range of possible and prescribed interactions such as sharing content, commenting, voting, recommending, and various approbation cues such as likes, hearts, and stars. With the introduction of these buttons, these activities could be measured and, in some cases, result in the earning of digital badges to recognise a user's content as being popular or informative by a community. In the earlier days of Facebook, certain cues and push questions were used, such as asking 'what is going on?' in the status update field to encourage the user to supply that content, which would then be disseminated to that user's network. Since then, social buttons may include incremental features such as liking where each click adds one to a numeric counter. However, as Gerlitz and Helmond note, the use of social buttons is not innocuous as they provide a wealth of data to the social media platform for the purposes of data mining and the sale of this data to third-party entities. It was understood that '[u]ser activities are of economic value because they produce valuable user data that can enter multiple relations of exchange and are set up to multiply themselves' (Gerlitz and Helmond 2013, 1360). At the user level, the like economy of the social web functions to metrify and intensify user activity and engagement which perpetuates more activity and engagement, while on the back end these social media platforms have been successful in moving from a centralized data collection model to one that opts for decentralised flows (Gerlitz and Helmond 2013, 1361). This model for encouraging social participation quickly becomes user-perpetuated and feeds Big Data as the process becomes decentralised. This seems on the surface at odds with any dreams of command and control – the province of cybernetics. Yet, despite this decentralising process, data flows could still be subject to centralised processing, almost like a global scale feedback loop that would then be channelled to a number of other network systems for various purposes.

On the more technical and less social end of understanding networks, emerging out of statistical electrical systems, we might credit the rise of computing and cybernetics in the 1940s. Claude Shannon's (1948) mathematical theory of communication became a foundational model for the development of the first technical communication systems, while the work of cyberneticists such as Norbert Wiener (1948) began to have an appreciable impact on several other non-technical disciplines. The value of feedback systems could be seen in new ideas explored in the domains of anthropology, linguistics, biology, education, and management studies. We might even credit the earliest days of ecology – and the coining of the term 'ecosystem' – to the influence of cybernetics and its principles. Understanding networked systems as a kind of struggle between information as coherence and entropy as noise may be useful on its own, but it is far from the whole story.

Today when we speak of the rise of the network society, this generally refers to a span of time from the development of the personal computer, the internet, to the situation in which we find ourselves today where so much of the world's technical and economic processes depend exclusively on digital networks. And within this digital ecosystem resides our online social networks. If social capital itself applies to non-digital networks of our social relations, it must therefore exist wherever there are social relations in a digital context.

Platforms

Social media platforms shape the affordances of our online social lives not only by devolving the work of social media upon its users according to specific micro-tasks of 'liking' etc., but also function as a broker of our online communications. More perniciously, they structure and govern our online activity in less than visible ways. Benjamin H. Bratton describes platforms as something institutional, fixed, yet at the same time operating by a form of distributed control:

> It is important as well to recognize that 'platforms' are not only a technical architecture; they are also an institutional form. They centralize (like states), scaffolding the terms of participation according to rigid but universal protocols, even as they decentralize (like markets), coordinating economies not through the superimposition of fixed plans but through interoperable and emergent interaction. Next to states and markets, platforms are a third form, coordinating through fixed protocols while scattering free-range Users watched over in loving, if also disconcertingly omniscient, grace. (Bratton, 2014, n.p.)

Nick Srnicek tells us that platforms can be characterised:

> by providing the infrastructure to intermediate between different user groups, by displaying monopoly tendencies driven by network effects, by employing cross-subsidization to draw in different user groups, and by having a designed core architecture that governs the interaction possibilities. (Srnicek 2016, n.p.)

In other words, Srnicek points to how the new model of platform capitalism no longer requires the creation of a marketplace: it is simply the infrastructure upon which, say, users on a social network interact. The network effects facilitate the perpetual growth of a user-base, while direct costs need not be paid by users to access the service, due to cross-subsidisation which means money can be made in other areas (such as the sale of user data to other companies in the form of ad space).

The merger of network effects and new forms of digital capitalism can be said to function as an enclosure around our online social ecosystem. The integration of social buttons not only encourages more user participation with the promise of intangible, numeric reward, but is one of the most effective tools for social network platforms to extract data for the purposes of monetisation while still providing a 'free' service to its users who perform a kind of unwaged labour for the network. Gamifying the process through social buttons and their incremental counters does not banish the spectre of exploitation or eliminate alienation; it merely provides a venue for real accumulation for the platform and non-monetary accumulation for the user. The problem is that such data extraction for profit is masked by the incentive to 'play' the games of accumulation using these social buttons designed by the social network platforms. Unlike a traditional arcade game or pinball machine where players will insert a quarter in exchange for an experience and possibly achieve a high score for some social cachet, in this instance it is the arcade game that is 'free' for the user to play, but in exchange for having every one of her or his movements tracked, traced, recorded, and sold as data.

As we operate these 'machines' for social play, we obtain a kind of token currency. What is the nature of this currency? What we call online social capital is not isolated from other forms of social capital. How online social capital and traditional forms of social capital intersect creates the conditions of an interconnected problem.

Management and Accumulation of a Resource

We notice how the two senses treat of social capital as a resource. In management theory literature, it is an existing resource that needs to be properly managed, whereas in digital culture it is something to be aggregated or collected before it can be properly managed. The question then turns on how to understand online social capital. Should we define it as a resource that can be capitalised and thus part of an economy of exchange, or is it a process more aligned with building community? If we take the former view, it is not difficult to see how social capital becomes reduced to, and motivated by, an economic understanding. More to the point, the use value of social interaction becomes subordinate to the economic rationality of accumulation.

With the emergence of the internet, and specifically the participatory framework of Web 2.0 which allows users to produce and share content, the utopian ideal of an entirely decentralised network of media producers and consumers (or prosumers) has been lionised as an inclusive and democratising antidote to top-down, largely unilateral media hierarchies that dictate content to a passive audience on a one-to-many basis. However, this new media arrangement narrows options to ever fewer media conglomerates and hosting services that extract surplus value from our online participation. The idea that we can pursue our own rational-individual or collectivist agenda using an array of online tools, boosting our social capital, conceals the marketisation and privatisation of online social activity. The affordances of social media promise a kind of 'sovereignty' by our ability to create, connect, and build social capital anytime and anywhere, but the only sovereignty of social media appears to privilege consumption. While we pay the entrance fee for joining cheap or 'free' online social services by volunteering our personal data, which is then sold to advertisers for pinpoint marketing, ultimately the concept of social capital takes on a largely economic definition as most of what we share, produce, or say in the digital milieus is commodified, along with the social network user as a worker-commodity.[2]

Given the (techno-)optimistic excitement surrounding the notion of social capital as a source of liberation and self-actualisation that circumvents authoritarian controls, be those of the state, big business, or medical and educational institutions, subjecting the term to an appropriate interrogation and critical analysis has all but been drowned out by the chorus of those who praise the apparent benefits of increasing one's social capital almost as an end in itself.

The leveraging of social capital may be said to increase access to information and opportunities for collective social action (Ellison et al. 2007). We might note here that there is no guarantee that such outcomes will arise, but may be a function of several factors, including the current state of popular attention migration, content viability for an audience, network reach, effective persona and message management, and so forth. Yet what is overlooked in many attempts to describe the movement and accumulation of social capital is precisely the structures that enable, inhibit, and ultimately exert control over online social behaviours. Beyond being merely a concern for network analysts and social software engineering, we may grasp this control of data in terms of power, and the trade-off being a user's potential to accumulate social capital as one of the markers of status.

One of the central premises of Thorstein Veblen's (2010 [1899]) notion of conspicuous consumption involves the display of status as resulting in a proportionate increase in social preference. Arguably, online behaviour as a function of conspicuous consumption is indeed highly conspicuous in its nature, but also involves some degree of conspicuous production, especially with regard to the construction of the digital self as something 'unique' and ego-idealistic, at least insofar as there is an attempt to bracket off the digital self as something of a singularity that will 'stand out.' It is for this reason that we might revise Veblen's insights to speak of conspicuous *prosumption*, and how this factors in our current 'like economy' of social capital.

The very nature of the most popular online social networking sites seem to actively encourage a kind of entrepreneurial self-promotionalism in creating branded identities linked to consumer tastes that make it much easier to extract sellable data. The seeds of this shift – largely a blend of neoliberal economics and the rise of personal digital technologies – can be recognised in an article by Tom Peters who argues the one way with competing with large multinational companies is to become its 'micro-equivalent': 'We are CEOs of our own companies: Me Inc. To be in business today, our most important job is to be head marketer for the brand called You' (Peters, 1997, n.p.). Peters goes on to provide advice on how to make use of the affordances of the web at that time – website creation and emails – as a means by which to influence others to associate value with one's 'brand.' Peters declares that self-branding is an inevitable necessity in the future of work, and that one must be a mix of leader, teacher, visionary, and businessperson. One may note that such an argument speaks to a range of strategies of converting the non-commercial aspects of the self into something marketable and profitable. The self becomes the very locus of investment for the specific purposes of deriving profit, and it is the 'miracle' of digital technology to actualize this potential. It is in this way that neoliberalism perpetuates a major shift of the self as *Homo juridicus* (a legal entity of the state) to an economic subject where entrepreneurialism becomes key to this new relationship

(Read 2008, 28). This self-branding activity is part of the social factory, and this factory 'seeks to involve the worker's personality and subjectivity within the production of value' (Lazzarato 1996, 3) whilst there is 'the transformation of social human activities into directly productive work' (Morini, 2007, 45).

Inasmuch as self-branding in the pursuit of online social capital appears to appeal to the freedom of an entrepreneurial self, in true neoliberal fashion it is the downshifting of responsibility and risk-taking to the user, while profit is extracted by the social network platform from this labour. As Alison Hearn defines it, 'the branded self must be understood as a distinct kind of labour; involving an outer-directed process of highly stylized self-construction, directly tied to the promotional mechanisms of the post-Fordist market' (2008, 167).

We can already see how there are two forms of accumulation taking place: one at the site of the self-branded user operating within the affordances of the network structure to accumulate friends, followers and likes; and the second situated within the platform itself to have a ready searchable database of active online users performing the labour of broadcasting their consumer preferences for easier data accumulation and sale. As Hearn argues, the online user's push for accumulation of these resources is a mirror of post-Fordist capitalism:

> Arguably, these sites produce inventories of branded selves; their logic encourages users to see themselves and others as commodity-signs to be collected and consumed in the social marketplace. How else to understand the accumulation of hundreds of virtual 'friends' (usually people one barely knows) and the view that this constitutes 'popularity' than as the channelling of age-old human desires into the hollow, promotional terms of post-Fordist capitalist acquisition? (Hearn 2008, 177).

This exploitation also extends to those users who have no interest in accumulating more 'likes.' In clicking on these social buttons, this not only cross-syndicates content, but also functions as data for the algorithm to tailor and 'personalise' what content will be made available. The more we are encouraged to 'like' content, the more of our data is being collected and used to deliver related content, and the more of our data can be matched against advertising. Every click of a social button is a speech statement, and as social media users are encouraged to partake of ever more social interaction online, it is surely the social networking sites that profit from every exchange, be it in the production of new content to accumulate more likes, or in liking someone else's content.

Theoretical Approach

In taking a Marxist view, the wealth of social capital can be viewed as a historically developed form powered by circulation and nesting circuits. Marxist analysis will be the proper fit given the macro-level emphasis on class structure and the exploitation of labour in the creation of the surplus value on social networking sites. By contrast, an emphasis on human capital focuses on micro-level analyses of family, gender, etc., which speak to how these networks inform individual access and mobilisation of social capital. There will also be occasion to bring cultural capital into this discussion given that it also places emphasis on class divisions, in bringing the insights of Thorstein Veblen to discuss the nature of conspicuous forms of display as an instrument of socially reproducing status.

What remains is to examine the social relations that underpin social capital, and what sort of social relation it is when we speak of a distinctly *digital* form of social capital, and how this is situated in an encompassing framework of capitalism itself. Capital as accumulation is historically grounded in the circulation of commodities that lend themselves to the money relation; i.e., that which mediates the relation of *value* between commodities, but in such a way that the money relation leads to the purchase of some commodity for the purposes of selling it (such as, for example, someone who buys houses for the purpose of flipping them for profit). The apparent absence of any clear money relation to mediate social capital in the 'like economy' problematizes our return to Marx for guidance, and so it is incumbent upon us to reconstruct this newer relation.

What makes this task more challenging is rooted in the very term of social capital itself, and its numerous (sometimes contradictory) definitions. Social capital has no apparent quantifiable measure.[3] That is, how would one measure one's social capital on Facebook or Instagram? One might say that the number of connections, likes, comments, and other approbation cues have a numeric value, and thus represents social capital with a unit of measurement. However, there are a few problems with this view. Despite some services that claim to measure social capital or one's social media profile value, there is no consensus, with monetary values ranging from effectively zero to hundreds if not thousands of dollars. Recalling Marx's definition of capital, it is not an inert 'thing'; that is, simply totting up the number of connections or retweets associated with a user profile does not translate into capital *unless it is in circulation*. This signals a second major issue: in the acquisition of likes, followers, connections, etc., is there a direct line from this acquisition as an increase in capital toward the 'sale' of such things to increase profit? In other words, can one sell their accumulated 'social capital' to a buyer, and thus increase personal profit?

If there is a commodity relation to online social capital, it will not be necessarily determined by a numeric value indicating likes and such, but within the less visible sphere of data in the hands of the social network host. It is here that real circulation is exceedingly important, for the profit increases of many of the most popular social networks depends on their user bases: the number of users who join and actively participate and share content, when volunteering their time and personal information to these sites in exchange for access. An increase in the number of service subscribers is also an increase in data, which can be accumulated and curated, and then sold as a commodity to advertisers.

This increases revenue, and in the case of publicly traded companies such as Facebook and Twitter, potentially increases share price. What we might term a 'critical mass' of prosumers or the exploitation of a mass general intellect is well-suited to the business model of these social network sites that exploit users and exercise control to extract surplus value from users' labour.

Plan of This Book

If one could summarise the goal of this book, it would be that the *social networking sites by design may function as a bridge between accumulation of online social capital and alienation that results from this activity, and this is enabled by platform capitalism and the network spectacle.* The question of online social capital involves issues beyond user exploitation, as it also contends with alienation that is the result of this conspicuous form of accumulation. In order to achieve this objective it will be essential to ground the discussion by exploring the context of online social capital.

In chapter 1, I trace the contours of what is precisely social about online social capital, and how it compares to cultural capital. For this contextual chapter, it will be our goal to take stock of some of the movements within the literature of social capital itself, and what bearing this may have on better understanding online social capital. Due to the fact that social media is both a structural and social phenomenon, powered by digital network architecture with its affordances as well as a space of social interaction, beginning with what is social about these networked environments will provide us with a bridge between how social capital has been traditionally understood in the literature and how it compares to a distinctly online form of social capital.

In chapter 2, I pivot to understanding online social capital from a more economic standpoint as a 'capital' resource to prepare us for understanding how strategies of economic accumulation may seem to colour the social aspects of accumulation. There is certainly a precedent for this connection given how closely aligned economic and cultural considerations may be in the broader understanding of social capital and community.

In chapter 3, attention will be paid to how capital accumulation occurs in the process of acquiring online social capital. I explore the role communicative and platform capitalism plays as a bridge that unites the social and economic aspects of online social capital. This will function as a means to better assess such aspects as the mobile 'prosumer' and the system 'gaming' use of social buttons. What are the implications of capitalism's co-opting of social functions in the online social media environment?

In chapter 4 I determine how this process of accumulation is alienating by recourse to the works of Marx and Veblen. Both figures have a view of alienation that is in some ways similar, but differ in terms of the outcomes of increased alienation due to their respective views of capitalist society. The importance will be stressing how the pursuit of online social capital can not only be considered a form of work, but that there are consequences to such a pursuit as it may increase our alienation from each other, ourselves, other workers, and the world.

In chapter 5, I follow this line of alienation to explore some of the less savoury consequences of a highly competitive social media environment, spotlighting two major strains that seem emblematic of a pursuit of online social capital: the narcissistic turn, and a potential increase in online aggression. By exploring some of the foundational work in narcissism, it will be important to stress that social media may enable more *apparent* narcissistic behaviours, but it may not be the case that users are generally more narcissistic. Instead, the nature of online social capital competition may appear to compel users to adopt a more narcissistic form of content production as might be expected from this environment. In terms of aggression, I will explore some – but not all – disinhibition effects that can be considered aggressive and hostile, and how it is linked with an increasing perception of needing to be heard on social media in order to accumulate more stake in the online attention economy.

In chapter 6, I delineate how the specific form of online social capital and its transactional framework resides within what one might call the network spectacle, allowing us to revisit many of the insights of Guy Debord's *Society of the Spectacle*. In some ways, there is something far more literal about this form of spectacle. If Debord's description of the spectacle says it is all encompassing, and that any attempt to critique the spectacle must rely on the language of the spectacle, what can be said of a *network* spectacle? Is it all-encompassing – an enclosed social ecosystem with its echo chamber effects where *what* we are permitted to say (prescribed by the affordances of the social media platform) is conditioned by the language of this network spectacle? Would the gamifying aspects of social buttons prove somewhat reductive of our social interactive capabilities, economising communication in such a way that social exchange is Taylorised for easier and more efficiently channelled data extraction? Is what we as users see just the wide mouth of the funnel, while the platform can incrementally narrow our social exchanges into those that fit the requirements of this network spectacle? How does our pursuit of online social capital, enabled and surreptitiously used as an instrument of profit and control, serve the ends of a network spectacle, which is to grow in perpetuity?

In the concluding chapter, I explore some of the more urgent implications of where the process from online social capital accumulation to alienation can lead us as researchers, advocates, and critical users of social media. It is not simply a case of 'unplugging' from social media, nor of simply adopting wholesale the optimistic rhetoric surrounding social media usage as emancipatory. Instead, it will be of the utmost importance that we continue to be diligent and critical on a go-forward basis and continue finding new ways of resisting capitalist appropriation of what perhaps ought to be our shared, global, public commons.

CHAPTER 1

Online Social Capital as Social

Let's start with an example: The Fossil Forum (www.thefossilforum.com) is a discussion board-based global forum that specialises in the collection, study, and appreciation of fossils. With nearly 25,000 members from around the world, the forum serves the function of uniting an otherwise disparate group according to a passion for palaeontology – professional and avocational. Registered members will have varying degrees of expertise, from amateurs to established researchers. The forum does not rely on advertising revenue, and instead funds its operations through direct donations and member-created auctions. The forum also prohibits the posting of commercial links, and does not provide commercial appraisal of fossils. Members have the opportunity to post their finds for the community to assist in proper identification, engage in a wide range of fossil-related topics, exchange advice on preparation and collecting, share open access documents, and allows members to post personal galleries. In terms of online social capital, the only visible metric is the accumulation of 'informative points' awarded by the community when a member posts content that is considered informative. The non-metric forms of online social capital in this community can be considered the shared assets of expertise, experience, and informative resources. In addition, members who initially met on this forum have organised collecting trips offline. Members can be awarded forum badges for being 'member of the month' (decided by staff), 'fossil of the month' (chosen among several competitors by community voting), and 'paleo partner' (awarded to any member who has contributed meaningfully to palaeontology, such as publishing an article, volunteering at a museum or donating a specimen of scientific significance).

Like many social media sites, The Fossil Forum is a high-trust network. Its narrow focus affords greater consensus on vision, mission, and values. New members are not granted immediate access to some features until a number of posts of substance have been made. The community is moderated by a team of volunteers to prevent spammers, provide positive encouragement to new members and ensure that the forum's policies are enforced. A forum such as

How to cite this book chapter:
Faucher, K. X. 2018. *Social Capital Online: Alienation and Accumulation*. Pp. 1–12.
London: University of Westminster Press. DOI: https://doi.org/10.16997/book16.b.
License: CC-BY-NC-ND 4.0

this serves as an example of an ideal form of social capital whereby it is the development and sharing of social assets for community benefit.

In adopting a critical stance with respect to online social capital, it would be folly to simply focus on the negative, as there are several examples like the one discussed above where online social capital does align with individual and community empowerment. Of note would be groups that have been unfairly marginalised who can congregate in a virtual space to organise, mobilise, and provide mutual support. In addition, if we consider the Autonomist Marxist tradition, social media can function as a tool for breaking down barriers between otherwise disparate groups to form new alliances along shared lines. However, even before considering the matter of online social capital as part of – or as a possible resistance to – the circuits of capitalism, it will prove beneficial to backtrack and consider the core concept of social capital. This chapter explores the foundations of social capital and moves toward identifying some of the more problematic aspects that arise in its migration to an online context.

Social Capital and Cultural Capital

The word 'social' is liable to conjure up many associations that speak to our condition as 'social beings,' the collaborative benefits of community, and potential for self-expression. However, when left on its own, the term may leave one gasping for more precision; namely, when we use the word social are we referring to sociality? Social interaction? Media in general (as all media is a form of social exchange and are techno-social systems)? It may serve us better to adopt a neutral understanding of what is considered social exchange rather than assume one that is positive or negative given that social interactions have the potential to be constructive or non-constructive.

We can credit Pierre Bourdieu (1997) with identifying four types of capital: economic, cultural, symbolic, and social. By separating these forms of capital, it is not as though Bourdieu was setting up a cordon between them, for he understood that there were interrelated dynamics that would influence the abilities and opportunities of social agents to gain and distribute different forms of capital. Bourdieu defines social capital as:

> [T]he aggregate of the actual or potential resources which are linked to possession of a durable network of more or less institutionalized relationships of mutual acquaintance and recognition – or in other words, to membership in a group – which provides each of its members with the backing of the collectivity-owned capital, a 'credential' which entitles them to credit, in the various senses of the word. (51)

Bourdieu further explains that the volume of social capital is dependent upon some conditions, such as network size, effective use of connections, and the volume of other forms of capital each of the individuals in the network possesses (1997, 51). In other words, social capital does not generate itself independently of its relations with other forms of capital: the economic, symbolic and cultural are entwined. Moreover, maintaining or increasing one's social capital requires considerable and perpetual effort as it has a tendency to devalue over time. What Bourdieu's definition implies is that other forms of capital have the potential to be converted into social capital, but what may be missing here is how the relation of labour features in the production of social capital in the first place and the effort required to convert one form into another. We might here consider an illustrative example of energy and effort required to convert one form of capital into another, a form of exchange where there is some form of investment to make this conversion possible. For instance, assuming some individual of financial means (economic capital) wished to create name recognition in a bid to run for a city council position, that person would need to leverage his or her standing in the community as well as invest in political campaign specialists. The candidate would likely 'press the flesh' at various events, canvass voters, launch a social media campaign, schedule media appearances and so forth to create more awareness of the candidate and her or his viability for office. In this process, the candidate may have to leverage other human assets to obtain endorsements from those whose standing in the community is respected. In this instance, economic capital is used to gain political capital.

Instead of providing an optimistic definition of social capital, Bourdieu includes it as part of a worldview where capital is the totality of all social existence that plays a role in reproducing inequality while preserving dominance and class hierarchies. Social capital has little to do with open inclusion: it is an instrument of exclusion, to build walls not bridges. For example, a country club may use membership fees to exclude those without significant wealth from joining, excluding certain people that are statistically less likely to possess the financial means; a political party's anti-immigrant message may function as a barrier to entry by those who may wish to dispute those values; stakeholder influence in a community may be negatively impacted for those whose precarious employment situations may mean frequent job-changes and uprooting to new communities for employment, if not also the lack of financial security to afford home ownership; and even specialist language by technical professionals and academics can be an insurmountable obstacle for those not specifically trained in those disciplines. Bourdieu claims that these are the given facts of our social reality that govern who can join particular networks.

Bourdieu's view is more aligned with that of cultural capital; namely, that capitalisation is a process of social reproduction, with the most institutionalised form being education whereby 'objective' culture is internalised and reproduced by social actors. What appears to emerge as consensus, such as norms and values, are the product of social training via respected institutions. If there is 'profit' to be gained by this form of cultural capital participation, it is a measure of how well an individual conforms to the established norms and values of a society in order to obtain its opportunities and benefits. If we were to map this on to social media, there are implicit values and norms there as well; for instance, proper forms of netiquette that allow for the use of web-specific acronyms, the value of reciprocity in liking and following, the 'taboo' of using all capital letters as akin to shouting, and so forth. What may be considered socially reproduced also results in the creation of divisions on the basis of age, class, and even language.

It is worth remarking that Bourdieu's valuable contributions to our understanding of social capital were written prior to the rise of mainstream social media. Although the internet at the time did possess affordances for some online for and email, arguably a great deal of social networking and the accumulation of social capital was still being done in more traditional, analogue ways. The exploitation of distinctly digital social networks had yet to become a more viable option, and the eventual arrival of such networked forms of communication would have an appreciable effect on social relations. In some cases, the emergence of popular social media served to break down barriers of distance and class, yet at the same time social media would serve to exacerbate differences of class, ethnicity, ideology, gender and income. I do not view Bourdieu's conception of social capital as no longer viable, but that instead there are several aspects of his analysis that can be retained or modified in what would otherwise be considered a new social situation of network effects that are tied to acceleration and scale.

A contemporary of Bourdieu, James Coleman (1988), provides a definition of social capital that is less conditioned by economics and class structure, and instead provides potential for empowerment – particularly for marginalised, disenfranchised groups. For Coleman, we ought not to consider social existence simply one of economic conditioning whereby we are selfish beings of instrumental rationality, but that social aspects on their own merit much more focus. Coleman critiques the purely economic understanding of social capital:

> The economic stream [...] flies in the face of empirical reality: persons' actions are shaped, redirected, constrained by the social context; norms, interpersonal trust, social networks, and social organization are important in the functioning not only of the society but also of the economy. (96)

It is not that Coleman entirely disregards the importance of economic considerations in social organisation, but that over-emphasis on this point would imply that human beings are but passive beings whose agency is determined exclusively by economic capital. This might be the case under particular conditions, but I take the slightly more pessimistic view that the digital network structures themselves cater more to the creation of passive consumers and producers of content on these platforms, implicitly encouraged by the broader ideological apparatus of social media to simply accept its affordances as 'good' without question. That so much social interaction becomes more dependent on valuing through actual metrics as a kind of 'reward', or that interaction is prompted by a series of incessant notifications, speaks more to a kind of reactive and passive form of social activity that is based on digital stimulus and pseudo-economic reward.

In Coleman's interpretation, social capital is not something that is privately owned like property, but is instead an available resource that emerges as the by-product of social relationships. Coleman's understanding of social capital opened the way to viewing it as something not unlike a property held in common by a community, akin to other forms such as heritage assets and the idea of the tightly knit neighbourhood community. Under this view, the ideal for maximising the volume of social capital as a shared asset might be a small town given the closer and long-standing ties the community may possess.[4] In sociology, the term *Gemeinschaft* refers to this kind of kinship structure and unity that arises from such a scenario, as opposed to *Gesellschaft*, which refers to individuals tied to larger structures in a more vertical, less horizontal, model. What engaged thinkers such as Ferdinand Tönnies (2002 [1887]) – who adopted the terms of *Gemeinschaft* and *Gesellschaft* in his pioneering work, – resonates ever more strongly today with the decline of rural communities at the expense of increased (sub)urbanisation, the ideological emphasis on the individual as an economic rather than social actor, and the rise of social media. The net result of these changes in the way community-mindedness has given way to an increase in individualisation is a view advanced by Robert Putnam in his book, *Bowling Alone*.

With this newer focus on social capital as a community asset, we find Robert Putnam taking up the baton in exploring this in more detail. For him, social capital involves trust, reciprocity, information, the possibilities for collective action and the transition from individualist identity to a community identity. In his most influential work, *Bowling Alone* (2001), Putnam identifies the threats to social capital and community engagement – be it the stealthy hijacking of social capital by financial capital, indifference to community and civic engagement, a decline in volunteer service group memberships, and changes in the techno-social systems of media. Although Putnam does seem to sound a note of optimism that computer-mediated communication may somehow renew the value of social capital, this is in no way guaranteed. Phenomena such as slacktivism (Christensen 2011, Morozov 2012), for example, may only provide the token appearance of deeper engagement. And, although some barriers to entry have been lowered for many in the formation of communities and access, class divisions are in many ways still reproduced in a digital form: the urban-rural split with respect to reliable access to digital networks and the heavy representation of those with wealth and status still dominate the social web.

Putnam's view suggests the growth of online social networks may better facilitate more bridging social capital, and that these digital networks will increase our exposure – and possibly create more incentive – in developing social relations with those who hold very different views. Bonding social capital relies more on homophily and preferential attachment: our tendency to group with those who are like us. Being exposed to a multiple variety of viewpoints and perspectives seems to present a very real benefit, but this is jeopardised by selective exposure to content, algorithmic sorting at the network end, and the ability for users to customise their relations according to homophily.

The Dark Side of Social Capital

There are unintended negative consequences in the application of social capital. For example, Putnam references the Oklahoma City Bomber, Timothy McVeigh, who actively networked in discussing tactics with other radical right-wing conspirators (2001, 21–2). For Putnam, the concept of social capital itself is benign (and can be beneficial), but there is a possibility that others may use their cooperative social linkages for malevolent purposes – which may include strengthening hate groups, engaging in astroturfing campaigns or in committing crimes. Furthermore, the use of social capital among certain groups can exacerbate cliquish behaviours, marginalise or exclude outsiders, and thus promote rather than eliminate inequalities. Unscrupulous corporations or politicians, hate groups, and so forth are just as capable of leveraging social capital in their networks for their own collective gain at the expense of – or the explicit goal of harming – the interests of others.

Francis Fukuyama (1995) also acknowledges the potential abuse of social capital in producing these kinds of negative externalities, but he introduces the notion of broadening the radius of trust among all actors: the wider the radius, the more others will gain access to the benefits of those social capital resources. However, we might ask what happens in the event of there being a large reserve of trust among several actors, while surreptitious forms of covert surveillance, exploitation, and a 'profit over people' model is still in place. A corporately run digital social network like Facebook would be a prime example of a high-trust culture that engages in practices that may not be in the best interests of its users.[5] And, just as social capital has the capacity to increase trust as per Putnam and Fukuyama's respective understanding, it has the capacity to increase distrust – particularly of out-groups or in networks where internal competitive values can foster suspicion or sabotage in an effort to gain advantage.

The one clear way bridging social capital is endangered in online social networks is precisely what is made visible by the algorithm used by the platform to deliver content. This 'filter bubble' – a term coined by Eli Pariser (2012) – speaks to how our use of the web delivers ever more 'personalised' experiences that will conform to our interests and values while limiting exposure to alternative viewpoints. And it is not just on social media where this occurs. In five experiments conducted by Epstein and Robertson (2014) to track how voting preferences can be manipulated by the use of search engines. SEME – search engine manipulation effect – was shown to have an appreciable impact on how internet users' opinions are shaped by what the search engine results produce, and that a higher value is attributed by these users overall to those search results that are higher ranked. When we contrast this against Putnam's view of increased bridging social capital, it would appear that there are significant obstacles thrown up by the very platforms we use. Already, there has been a profusion of fake news outlets who are able to capitalise on narrowcasting to niche groups. For instance, the rise of Breitbart and Alex Jones' Infowars have been able to unify various far-right extremist groups in the proliferation of conspiracy theories such as claiming the tragic Sandy Hook shootings were a staged false flag event orchestrated by the Obama administration to take away citizens' guns, and Pizzagate which claimed that the Clinton campaign was engaged in running a paedophile ring out of a pizzeria. As more people would click on these stories, the more similar stories would appear in their newsfeeds.

As concern has mounted over the impact of filter bubbles in creating a warped world scenario in manipulating our perceptions through algorithmic sorting, more studies have been done to trace the causes and implications of social media content filtration. Such filters on visible content may be said to contribute to a kind of digital tribalism, hostile divisiveness, and an outright 'balkanization' of the social web. In his farewell address, then-President Barack Obama pointed to the threat these filter bubbles presented to democracy when people retreat into these polarising bubbles:

> […] especially our social media feeds, surrounded by people who look like us and share the same political outlook and never challenge our assumptions. The rise of naked partisanship, and increasing economic and regional stratification, the splintering of our media into a channel for every taste — all this makes this great sorting seem natural, even inevitable. And increasingly we become so secure in our bubbles that we start accepting only information, whether it's true or not, that fits our opinions, instead of basing our opinions on the evidence that is out there (Obama 2017)

We may turn to other more recent examples of how the impact of social media can increase social capital for malevolent purposes. The terrorist organisation ISIS has been remarkably effective in their use of social media for the use of recruitment and branding:

> The Islamic State maximized its reach by exploiting a variety of platforms: social media networks such as Twitter and Facebook, peer-to-peer messaging apps like Telegram and Surespot, and content sharing systems like JustPaste.it. More important, it decentralized its media operations, keeping its feeds flush with content made by autonomous production units from West Africa to the Caucasus—a geographical

range that illustrates why it is no longer accurate to refer to the group merely as the Islamic State of Iraq and al-Sham (ISIS), a moniker that undersells its current breadth (Koerner 2016).

As much as Western media has focused on how ISIS has broadcast its atrocities on social media, this only makes up a small part of its social media branding activity. Propagandistic content indexed on infrastructure improvement and economic development are used to portray the positive benefits of ISIS' activities. Moreover, ISIS' use of social media is quick to capitalise on current events to target marginalised groups for recruitment.

A second example originates largely from the uncensored social media platform, 4Chan, a successor to Something Awful. The causes of the rise of the alt-right is still a matter of speculation but we might credit 4Chan and various subreddits in essentially playing a prank with its long history of the community's sometimes cynical or controversial embrace of various movements such as Occupy, Anonymous and as the origin of the infamous Gamergate scandal. It would only be later adopted by various far-right groups as a symbol of unity against political correctness, globalisation, and multiculturalism. Sparked, in part, by economic conditions and a surge of refugees, the alt-right movement, which focuses on a kind of retrograde nationalism, protectionism and xenophobia, surged. But it was 4Chan and the co-opting of a cartoon frog, Pepe – created by Matt Furie in his *Boy's Club* and never intended as a symbol of hate – that precipitated the spread of a now recognisable meme (memes being one of the preferred methods of 4Chan). As Dale Beran writes,

> Pepe symbolizes embracing your loserdom, owning it. That is to say, it is what all the millions of forum-goers of 4chan met to commune about. It is, in other words, a value system, one revelling in deplorableness and being pridefully dispossessed. It is a culture of hopelessness, of knowing 'the system is rigged'. But instead of fight the response is flight, knowing you're trapped in your circumstances is cause to celebrate. For these young men, voting Trump is not a solution, but a new spiteful prank (Beran, 2017).

Subsequent memes circulated throughout the 2016 US presidential campaign. In one instance, Democrat candidate Hilary Clinton denounced Trump supporters as 'deplorable,' which then resulted in the creation and proliferation of memes by alt-right supporters embracing the term as a badge of honour. Memes making use of Pepe and the term 'deplorables' became a rallying point for alt-right, neo-Nazi and other white nationalist groups, being used in a variety of contexts, including supporters of UKIP, the Dutch Party for Freedom under Geert Wilders, Marine Le Pen's National Front, and the populist Alternative for Germany (AfD) party. It has also been brandished in response to any criticisms of extremist nationalist views, and against political moderates. This has been joined by other associated epithets such as 'librul tears,' 'deep state,' 'cultural Marxism,' and 'cuck' (short for cuckold, and in reference to the cuckold pornographic genre where the narrative clearly defines 'alpha' and 'beta' males – terms employed frequently by the alt-right and originating on 4Chan).

On the other side of the political divide would be the efforts of #Resist, a proliferation of Twitter accounts functioning as subversive alt-government agency operatives, and antifa. The result has been an increasing polarisation along the ideological axis of far left and far right. Examples such as these underscore the negative forms of online social capital.

Such efforts at extreme polarisation seek to escalate discord and instability. What is needed is to re-appropriate the tools of social media to insist on civil discourse, dialling down hostilities.

Online Social Capital: Measurement

As social capital can be considered a resource that is generated, accumulated and distributed in a social network, it is important to keep in mind the networked environment in which the exchange of social capital occurs. Given the networked communicative capitalist aspects of social media, with its goals of extracting surplus value, exploiting free labour, and in automating social functions for data and profit with the smokescreen of 'customisation,' these characteristics will have serious implications for the prospect of what social capital means in a digitally networked environment.

Operating behind the social aspects of social networks is the ongoing engine of generating profit from user sharing and participation, and this through advertising (John 2013). The appearance of the social functions as a kind of shell around a mechanistic, almost cybernetic process by merging the technical with the social, creating a form of social engineering (van Dijck 2013). Moreover, various theorists have found evidence and made compelling arguments that the real outcome of online social activity tends toward extracting the surplus value from creative activities (Fuchs 2008), and to thus perpetuate a cycle of exploitation of free labour (Terranova 2000, 2004). These acts of exploitation by large, corporately owned and controlled social media render moot many of the supposed empowering benefits of social media usage.

There is no shortage of those, such as Clay Shirky (2008) or danah boyd (2007) who will sing the praises of social media as being an empowering force for those who might not otherwise have as many social opportunities in offline life.[6] What unites many of these ideas in their more optimistic portrayal of social media in terms of its affordances, opportunities and benefits is an emphasis on its social character, largely at the exclusion of a critical political economy perspective. Yet at the same time, it will not serve to be dismissive of the empowering effects of social media. As the example of The Fossil Forum at the beginning of this chapter demonstrates, it is possible to create and participate in digital spaces that are community-centred and empowering rather than exploitative and alienating.

In smaller networks that do not make use of social buttons for the purpose of accumulating likes, online social capital may operate differently. Rather than numeric markers, social capital may be gained in a more narrative form such as repeated demonstration of expertise about a subject, kindness, reciprocity and sharing. In such cases it is difficult to apply a numeric measurement to the online social capital that is generated in communicative interactions.

When it comes to online social capital, some industries and organisations prefer to have something more tangible they can measure, and possibly exploit for the purposes of manipulation. Those who seek to invest in strategies and tactics to optimise online social capital growth as linked with human capital (particularly in management studies) may prefer to have an empirical basis upon which to base their decisions. The relational perspective in social scientific research attempts to bridge the gap between understanding the social dynamics of a community and in having usable and rigorous empirical tools to map, measure and apply predictions to any changes in social structure and develop new mechanisms or methods to improve connectedness, and enhance trust within a community. However, even a more empirical approach still banks on several assumptions, not least of which being if social capital is itself amenable to measurement at all. What needs to be asked at every instance is how online social capital is measured, and why. If online social capital can be measured, then there is a basis upon which it might be managed. The use of metrics provides a tool for optimising strategies for the accumulation of online social capital.

If social capital is a resource embedded in our social relations that can be mobilised, the ease and speed by which developing connections and sharing information occurs in these networks may very well result in a larger volume of social capital resources from which to draw upon and mobilise. A greater return on temporal investment can potentially be realised due to the viral nature of some forms of content sharing.

Online Social Capital: Ownership

Who has ownership of online social capital as a resource? Is it held by individuals, in the relations between individuals, or collectively held in common? Is online social capital simply a synonym for the influence one can exert as a function of one's status, and thus aligned with a discourse on class and power? If so, we are back at the foot of the circle whereby social capital's economic power subsumes that of the social, and that the social is purely an instrumentalist means of preserving or increasing power.

> The social is precisely what it pretends to be: a calculated opportunity in times of distributed communication. In the end, the social turns out to

be a graph, a more or less random collection of contacts on your screen that blabber on and on—until you intervene and put your own statement out there. (Lovink 2012, n.p)

Geert Lovink castigates those who have propped up an overly idealistic definition of the social in social media when it has simply been an effort to inject some humanistic notions in something that is properly cybernetic. The challenge he presents us is not to expand the number of digital humanities programs, multiply the number of tools or fall back into a nostalgic form of soft deconstruction, but to place critical theorists at the helm of enormous technological programs. Lovink's bold proposal has considerable merit as it would make it possible to address ethical issues right at the design stage, but the realities seem to mitigate against this as it would mean a relinquishing of control by those whose pecuniary interests govern the creation and maintenance of our social media network platforms.

In order to better address these questions, it will be necessary to consider the other side of the term: social capital from an economic standpoint. From there, we will be able to view social capital as part of a nuanced economic and social system as social capitalism.

A Social Tool or Numbers Game?

Bourdieu's definition of social capital is indexed on the social reproduction of inequality, set in the broader context of all other forms of capital, whereas for Coleman social capital is an available non-financial resource that empowers individual agency. Operating between the two definitions would be Putnam, who also notes some of the unintended consequences of social capital, particularly among those who have malevolent designs.

As Bourdieu argues, social capital exists in a broader context of other forms of capital, but there is now the additional aspect of how *online* social capital operates differently due to the affordances of a digital network structure owned and operated by corporate interests. The nature of the online environment does seem to allow for a more accelerated accumulation of social capital resources due to wider audience reach and the way online social capital can be facilitated by social buttons, and in being able to measure our online 'performance'.

Social media sites have an appreciable impact on what types of online social capital we accumulate, and how much. Through algorithms that deliver content on the basis of a proprietary formula, there is cause for concern that we are being served with a very selective worldview based on our interactions in these spaces, a form of selective exposure that narrows and filters our perspectives. Moreover, where the accumulation of online social capital becomes an end in itself through the pursuit of more friends, followers, retweets, and likes, it seems to be less about the social aspects and more about playing a numbers game, competing with others to obtain a high score as proof of popularity and social value.

The use of visible metrics obscures the more substantive value of online social capital as a truly cooperative and collaborative shared social asset. By ignoring – or insisting – on removing the numeric bias, focus might be restored to the truly social benefits of interaction and participation by shifting the importance away from individuals and back unto a community.

Main Points

- Pierre Bourdieu's understanding of social capital is closely aligned with cultural capital, and its function is as an instrument of exclusion given its connection to economics, and an agent of social reproduction through education and broader cultural forces.
- James Coleman's definition of social capital places less emphasis on economics, and more on the prospects for community empowerment.
- Both Robert Putnam and Francis Fukuyama indicate where social capital can have negative aspects due particularly to groups who disseminate hate and exclusion.
- The algorithmic sorting of our online information on social media sites would appear to exacerbate the creation of cliques, as well as produce the conditions for selective exposure.
- Online social capital seems to tend toward quantizing our social relations while social media sites continue to extract surplus value from these exchanges. This presents a parallel series of economic circuits: the online social interactions resembling a model of capitalist accumulation, while the social media sites that own user content are able to capitalise on these user interactions.
- Although some traditional theories of social capital focus on non-economic forms of capital, such as trust and reciprocity, online social capital makes those secondary to economic relations.

CHAPTER 2

Online Social Capital as Capital

What is the monetary value of a 'like', and how does this factor in our discussion of online social capital? In this chapter we examine the economic dimension of online social capital and address this issue through the lens of the circuits of capitalism.

In Nikolai Gogol's *Dead Souls,* the main character Chichikov traverses the Russian countryside and offers to buy up the deeds to serfs who had died since the last census. Given that the census only occurred every five years, the feudal landowners were expected to pay a property tax on the number of serfs they owned. Whether or not the serfs lived during those five intervening years, the tax was to be paid according to what was reported in the last census. Chichikov, who seeks to wed above his social station, lacks sufficient land to win the hand of the woman he has chosen. To rectify that situation, he concocts a scheme to purchase the deeds to the deceased serfs at a discounted rate and to assume the tax obligation. From a purely financial perspective, this makes a lot of sense to the landowners who would gladly be rid of the tax burden on deceased property. Chichikov's plan meets some resistance from landowners who find the request odd, but eventually he acquires enough virtual property to approach a bank and use it to secure a loan to purchase land. What Chichikov has done is to leverage artificial wealth to obtain real wealth.

If we were to adapt Gogol's classic novel for the digital age, Chichikov might be in the market for purchasing the services of a sophisticated botnet or click farms to boost his online status similar to someone who has many supportive followers and numerous likes. Today, click farms are a booming business for those seeking to get automated high volume web traffic and click-throughs on ad banners. Click Monkeys, a Ukrainian company, specialises in running a service that they claim cannot be detected by DoubleClick or Google, and boasting a workforce of about 20,000 who work in four shifts of 5,000, 24 hours a day, producing over 84 million page views or clicks.

How to cite this book chapter:
Faucher, K. X. 2018. *Social Capital Online: Alienation and Accumulation.* Pp. 13–37.
London: University of Westminster Press. DOI: https://doi.org/10.16997/book16.c.
License: CC-BY-NC-ND 4.0

Click Monkeys, operating from a tanker ship, claim their services are legal: 'the giant tanker ship click farm we have stationed just outside U.S. waters off the coast of San Francisco is registered at a Ukrainian berth so we're not subject to any U.S. laws!' This is but one of hundreds of click farm services, including iBuyFans, BoostLikes and Buy Cheap Social. However, with more sophisticated detection software, click farms could not as easily rely on computer automated clicking, and so resort to using low-paid human labour in major click farm hubs in the Philippines, Malaysia, China, India, Bangladesh and Pakistan. A random name generator (RNG) produces a list for social media account creation, and the workers are given their orders for the day, be it to click on a particular Facebook business page, boost the number of followers of a candidate running for office or post comments on popular news sites in large numbers to sway public opinion. An article in the *Guardian* paints a dire portrait of the real human cost of purchasing click farming services:

> For the workers, though, it is miserable work, sitting at screens in dingy rooms facing a blank wall, with windows covered by bars, and sometimes working through the night. For that, they could have to generate 1,000 likes or follow 1,000 people on Twitter to earn a single US dollar (Arthur 2013).

The amount of money generated by click farms globally is not accurately known given that many of these farms operate outside of the law and may be paid in untraceable cryptocurrency transactions, but the amount would not be trivial.

In an updated regulatory filing in 2012, Facebook reported that 83 million – or 8.7 per cent of its then-955 million users – were fake or surplus accounts (United States Securities and Exchange Commission 2012).[7] Not only does this potentially point to a rise in the number of services and size of operations in managing fake accounts, but it has an impact on Facebook's credibility in terms of selling advertising space. If a certain percentage of Facebook accounts are fake, then advertisers may have doubts about the effectiveness of purchasing Facebook's services. Moreover, with the ease by which one can acquire artificial followers and likes, this places inflationary pressure on the value of these numbers in a 'like economy'.

As ever more businesses and individuals seek to increase profit, status, and brand positioning using social media, the competition for likes, followers and an abundance of five-star ratings has become a necessity. It is almost unthinkable for a business not to operate one or several social media accounts to directly connect with customers and conduct its business in the rapidly expanding e-commerce market. Moreover, the need to maintain online presence becomes ever more an apparent necessity for artists, musicians, videographers, designers, and for attaining some degree of social popularity. Our

Chichikov might acquire a million new (fake) followers, which may attract the attention of other users to consider Chichikov someone worthy of following. Once Chichikov has achieved his critical mass of followers – many similar to the dead serfs purchased in the original novel – he could leverage this artificial wealth to become a paid influencer to endorse products and services as a source of real wealth.

Fungibility: What is the Exchange Rate on a 'Like'?

When focusing on the 'capital' aspect of social capital, in one form or another reference is made to an economic understanding of the term. With respect to capital, there is always some form of fungibility: the means by which capital has a element to be transferred between entities as part of the social relation involving exchange. According to Marx, with reference to commodities, the conversion takes place courtesy of the underlying 'guarantee' of the money relation. Every commodity has an exchange value (set by its material and labour costs plus a margin of profit, part of which is cycled back into production as capital). The problem, identified by James Coleman, would be that some instances of *social* capital do not lend themselves to equivalence; for example, a skilled professional in one field cannot be exchanged for a skilled professional in another (1994, 302). Moreover, insisting on the word capital from a political economy perspective may serve to commit us to an understanding of the term as a relation that is mediated by money, and involves the creation of surplus value through production.

The argument against this approach may be in the risk of adopting too rigid a definition of capital. However, this leaves open a criticism that in order for the term to have any definitional value for its operationalisation, we must insist on precision. The very term 'capital' is an open invitation for political economists to take it under serious analytical consideration – and with good cause, given the capitalist nature of most social media. Ideally, there ought to be some things that should not be considered commodities, and thus not reducible to the money relation, such as the subjective qualities of human beings. This, however, is facing a major test in the online world where ever more social media users are caught up in self-commodification, such that the content they produce (and the personal data they furnish) is a form of commodity for the social media network platform, and as there is widespread selling of experiences-as-commodities. 'Labour produces not only commodities: it produces itself and the worker as a commodity–and does so in the proportion in which it produces commodities generally' (Marx 1972 [1844], 69). What is the commodity in the online 'playbour' of the networker where there is no clear employer? Is the commodity the individual actively reproducing her or himself as a digital product? Is it the data that is generated through every interaction?

Three Forms of Exchange: User-As-Commodity, User-Generated Commodity, and 'Rent'

In online social environments, there are three forms of commodity that enter into some form of exchange: the user-as-commodity, the user-generated commodity and the 'rent' paid by companies for advertising space. Much more than simply enabling the production of content that becomes part of social circulation and exchange online, the producer becomes a digital 'object' of continual production.

Social media profiles and their connections may be considered a form of virtuosic score. That these social media profiles will be in most cases piloted by actual network users also means these users are performing a kind of production by furnishing new content and acting as cross-syndicators who distribute the content of others over the network. The posting and sharing of one's creative productions, knowledge, opinion, and experience may all be classed within the general intellect of the social networkers who participate in the social networking 'hive.' As such, the users are virtuosos who produce and distribute content without being paid a wage to do so. Paolo Virno describes virtuosity in this way:

> Virtuosic performance, which never gives rise to a finished work, in this case cannot even presuppose it. It consists in making Intellect resonate precisely as attitude. Its only 'score' is, as such, the condition of possibility of all 'scores.' This virtuosity is nothing unusual, nor does it require some special talent. One need only think of the process whereby someone who speaks draws on the inexhaustible potential of language (the opposite of a defined 'work') to create an utterance that is entirely of the moment and unrepeatable (Virno 2006, 189).

Enticed to make frequent declarative statements with status updates, explicit or implicit endorsements of products and services etc., the user both produces the content necessary for the social environment as well as producing the self as a perpetual work-in-progress product. To the extent that the user and the user's content production become commodities, there is some form of value attributed to each by the social network host for the purposes of selling advertising. The work need not ever be complete, as the network host can draw value from each action a social network user makes – be it the clicking on content or its production – for it all feeds directly into the system as usable and saleable data. As a social network user develops or changes over time, so too does the accumulation of data in building a better data profile of each user, courtesy of being able to automate the detection of trends or patterns in user behaviour. Even the non-work component of a social media user's profile has value: when an adolescent comes of university age, relocated to a different country, or become middle-aged, said users can be placed in different 'buckets' and targeted with demographic-specific advertising. The user is a user-as-commodity as data can be obtained and refined for surveillance and marketing purposes. The state at which the user engages in production and consumption then adds the second aspect, the user-generated commodity. Both of these may be considered the market-facing aspect of social media environments, conducted in full view of the social network's users. The more hidden and proprietary aspects occur 'under the hood' or behind closed doors, such as in the sifting and sorting of data, in the algorithmic visibility of content, and through the sale of data to third party advertisers.

'Rent' in virtual spaces is paid by two main 'tenants' to the social networking service: (i) the user through their abstract social labour, who can make use of the service to have a unique profile and interact with others and, (ii) businesses and marketing firms who purchase advertising space on the site, tailored to data matching between the users' data and the desired market segment. For the second kind of 'tenant,' there may be a tier structure whereby a company may purchase increased exposure, better targeted demographics, or premium analytic tracking tools for an increased rate.

The relationship social networking services have with the two 'tenant' groups does not qualify as rent if by rent we mean a piece of property that is leased by a rentier. What problematises the rent model is partly the nature of fixed capital associated with rent: a property owner has a fixed number of physical properties, or a car rental service has only so many vehicles in its fleet. Major social networking companies may have some form of finite space, but server space expansion is not a significant barrier, particularly when an almost infinite surplus value can be extracted from a large user base.

Among several reasons why large social networking services like Facebook cannot be characterised as rentiers, Fuchs tells us:

> Facebook invests money into production and constantly lets users produce data commodities in order to sell ever more advertisements and accumulate ever more capital. Facebook is first and foremost an advertising company: it lets its users produce ever more data and ever more commodities in order to accumulate ever more capital. Such a dynamic process of accumulation of use-values, surplus-labour, surplus-products, commodities and money capital cannot be found in the case of a rentier. (2015a, 35)

Fuchs (2010, 190) points out that the content generated by users (informational content) is a commodity produced by user labour that has an exchange value for the social networking service. However, even the issue of whether users are performing labour at all is still in contention, given the nature of the 'goods' produced by users that can be reproduced without the further labour of the user.

Rigi and Prey (2015, 398) disagree with Fuchs' formulation because the exchange value of informational content is not a factor since the nature of digital information has replicability, and can be transported at a negligible cost. The labour time involved in the initial production of informational content may be considerable, but its reproduction is not if it can be done easily and will not require any additional social labour time by the user. Rigi and Prey argue that there can be no exchange value for informational content because it is not a commodity in its initial produced state, and no surplus value can therefore be extracted. They do, however, admit that it is possible that such information can be converted into a commodity with an exchange value when processed and sold to advertisers, but that this takes the form of a service rather than a good such as information. The automated means of obtaining, sifting and sorting that information permits large social networking services like Facebook to generate surplus value in the form of profit. In sum, the surplus value is generated from the processing of information, not in the raw material form of information produced by user labour. Moreover, Rigi and Prey argue that the exchange values involved in technological and labour inputs to produce the informational content do not appear in the final reproduced product, and so there is no exchange value to speak of.

Firstly, this may present a slippery slope insofar as it may also come to justify the exploitation of any number of content producers – be the content apps, digital books, online newspapers or digital music – as digital piracy partially operates on the premise that it is not theft, given that the material costs for replicability are negligible and not directly exploitative.

Secondly, although Rigi and Prey's critique of Fuchs appears to short-circuit any claim to the generation of surplus value contingent upon the exploitation of online prosumers since the informational content has no exchange value, we might refer to Fuchs and Sevignani (2013) who speak of the inverse commodity whereby the commodity itself (data) remains largely concealed from the user behind the notions of gift reciprocity and 'the social' that these social media sites extol for its users as a means to encourage content production and participation, which ultimately increases the ability of social media sites to engage in acts of accumulation.

Thirdly, as Fuchs (2015b, 119) says, the major blindspot in this debate about whether or not digital labour is being exploited is understanding the key differences Marx himself makes between different forms of labour as productive or unproductive. To gain a better foothold on what is at stake in this debate, Fuchs draws from a careful reading of Marx three types of productive labour: labour that produces use-values, labour that produces both capital and surplus-value and collective labour that also produces both capital and surplus-value. Perhaps one of the more telling fragments, most amenable as an analogy to social media users' (un)productive labour, would be what Marx says of actors:

> Actors are productive workers, not in so far as they produce a play, but
> in so far as they increase their employer's wealth. But what sort of labour

takes place, hence in what form labour materializes itself, is absolutely irrelevant for this relation.(Marx, *Theory of Surplus Labour* 1857/8, 328–9, qtd. in Fuchs 2015a, 136)

There is an analogical link between actors, performers and buskers to that of social media users as virtuosos. Although the social media site does not dictate the script (beyond proscribing some actions and expressions identified in the terms of service) it owns the stage, the content; it can advertise and modify for whatever reasons it deems fit, and charge admission. The admission in this case is two-fold: a 'free' admission to other users to view the content and produce their own, and a kind of 'backstage pass' to third-party advertisers in the form of curated network data. However, unlike a theatre owner and actors, the latter of whom will be paid a wage from the proceeds of the admission price, the users on social media are not paid a wage and would qualify in Marx's rendering as self-employed individuals. Even if there may be a debate over whether social media users' content production and participation (both of which involve labour time) is productive or unproductive *for the users*, it still generates a surplus value for the social media site that takes the use value of the users themselves (data) and transforms it into a commodity, and thus can be considered exploitative (of both individual and collective labour on these networks). What is highly problematic in this debate on productive versus unproductive labour is the amorphous character of production, consumption and distribution in the age of networked, neoliberal capitalism as opposed to the more straightforward relations in industrial capitalism.

It could be argued that the user is 'paid' for her or his labour by being granted access to the service in exchange for granting the network exclusive license to use and distribute all content as the network sees fit. Is it not the case that the social media service provides ample opportunity for play and leisure? In such a case, there is no justification for any user to demand a percentage of the proceeds generated from the selling of data or the time spent in leisure as a 'licensing fee' or royalty is being paid in the form of a service for being social in an online context, with a wide range of tools and affordances to facilitate it. Moreover, as major social media sites operate according to a business model, they are indexed on profit, but also need to generate sufficient revenue to pay employees and make improvements to the service.

There are problems with this view. One of the most significant is the steady blurring of the lines between labour and leisure. Trebor Scholz (2013) uses the term 'playbour' to describe this merger. Although many users on social media may view their actions – everything from clicking on content, to producing content for others to consume – as a form of leisure, it is a form of additional (rather than necessary) labour time. Such forms of digital play have become entrenched and normalised to such an extent that it may not trigger awareness among many users that their actions are being transformed into a data commodity to which they gain no remuneration. For those with the material advantages to participate in online leisure activities such as these, it may not seem like work, but still arguably qualifies as such. This blurring occurs when 'knowledgeable consumption of culture is translated into excess productive activities that are pleasurably embraced and at the same time often shamelessly exploited' (Terranova 2013, 37).

Not all social media use is play, or even playbour. Perhaps less acknowledged would be that class of workers who use social media as part of *necessary* labour time where social media becomes a site of labour for those who are employed to manage a company's social media account. If these same people also operate their own personal social media accounts during their leisure hours, these sites become a source for two avenues of potential exploitation. When an employee of a company is tasked with the company's social media accounts, there is considerable labour that takes place, including the development of new content, managing the account, and interacting with other users.

The user's productive labour power consumed by the network platform leads to a discrepancy between that expended power and that of the value or price that is derived from that labour: surplus value. As there is no wage paid to the user, the costs of production in terms of variable capital expenditure is limited to those who are directly employed by the social media company. On one hand, the user may participate in the enjoyment of her or his production, as well as that of others, just so long as access to the devices and services remain affordable. In other words, the user can produce and consume the product of her or his labour as opposed to not being able to afford to do so. However, on the other hand, the product of this labour does not belong to the user, but to the SNS company.

It is important to reiterate Fuchs and Sevignani's point that the relationship in this circuit (users, social media company and advertisers) is not one of rent. We might instead employ the more apt term of *factorage*. The role of the factor during the colonial period in the US and Britain differs from commission or rent whereby the factor would own the goods to be sold without revealing the principal. A site like Facebook owns the content and the data they derive from users, and sells the data to the purchaser (advertiser) without revealing the identities of the users from which the data was obtained. In return, Facebook uses its platform to target the advertising to the users.

Circuits and Circulation

Nick Dyer-Witheford identifies four main segments along capitalism's circuit, effectively refurbishing Marx's concept: production itself, the reproduction of labour power, reproduction of nature and circulation (1999, 92). The smooth flow of capital depends on a heavier reliance on digital networks to better integrate each of these segments, and it does so through a variety of means, be it the proselytising of digital networks, market-intensification, concealing productive labour behind the veil of play, or the further despoliation of nature in the resource extraction, manufacturing and disassembly of digital devices. The focus here will be to read online social capital through these circuits and its position in the process of circulation.

If online social capital is something that is produced through circulation, what is being circulated? The short answer would be to state that online social capital is the circulation of virtual (intangible) goods in terms of an exchange, and that one or both parties in that exchange may gain an advantage. Something is being exchanged here in terms of heterogeneous goods that may or may not come under the unifying index of *price*. If online social capital is the raw virtual *profit* gained by an exchange, we may ask how it is reinvested, or if there is a standard or fluctuating price associated with content. This may be highly circumstantial, for a user whose content receives n number of likes or retweets may derive a different 'sum' of online social capital than another user who receives the same n. We would also have to factor in the labour in the production of the content, however minimal; for example, the up-votes on a video by a user playing Bach on a pipe organ would have to factor in the time, training and money involved in becoming adept at the pipe organ, whereas a video with the same up-votes featuring a squirrel chasing a cat is a serendipitous capture of an event uploaded to a site, not involving a tremendous amount of labour or training cost. Factoring on the production cost of the event alone, the pipe organist may have had to rent a music hall to perform Bach, and the other user was simply walking through a public park.

In the second volume of *Capital*, Marx identifies the three-stage process of capital circulation. In the first stage, the capitalist converts money into commodities (M–C); in the second the capitalist puts the commodities into the production process, thereby creating commodities of a higher value (P); and finally the capitalist converts the new commodities into money (C'–M'), from which the cycle begins again. The intervening step in this process is both the purchase of labour power and the means of production, both of which are necessary for the conversion of the commodity (C) into a higher value commodity (C'), where the net gain of profit is derived from the surplus value generated in this conversion.

This formula (M–C > L / MP) is entirely suited to the conditions of industrial capitalism, but will differ in a social media environment where each user may simultaneously be the commodity and the labour power. The circuit begins with the social media platform and the initial investment in the purchase of labour power (L) in the form of software specialists and the means of production (MP) in the form of hardware, offices, services, etc. This resembles the industrial capitalist circuit. In the end, the value-enhanced commodity is the social network itself (C'). However, what has been built is the virtual infrastructure, the factory space for what will be the *additional* phase of this circuit: the 'purchase' of the labour power in the form of new users to produce the content for this network. Until then, the network itself is an empty frame devoid of content. The means of production is partially supplied by the network in the form of the actual network space and user interface, but not entirely: users still need to purchase the digital devices and the connection services via an internet service provider even to access this virtual factory, just as a worker might have to purchase a vehicle to commute to work. The users produce with their labour (L') the next commodity, which is content. However, in this process the network is converted into a partial means of production for the users who will ultimately supply the final commodity in the chain: data. This data is then sold by the network platform and converted into the money form.

The network as commodity form is two-faced insofar as, on the one hand, it becomes a partial means of production for user labour, but it is also a commodity in its own right as what it sells to the user (in this case, a prosumer of content) is the services related to the network 'experience.' In this simplified formulation, there are two levels of labour power: the cognitive labour of computing professionals to create the network, and the creative-cognitive labour of users to populate the network with content.

$$M - C < \overset{L}{\underset{MP}{—}} - C' < \overset{L}{\underset{MP'}{—}} - C''$$

M = Money Form; C = Commodity Form; L = Labour Power (cognitive labour of the designers, engineers, et al); MP = Means of production (hardware such as servers, software, offices, etc.); C' = Network Infrastructure; L' = Cognitive and creative labour of users; MP' = Means of production among users (network infrastructure + devices and internet service provider); C'' = user-generated content converted into data and sold to advertisers.

In this formulation, the commodity form sold directly to advertisers is represented by matching the data against available advertising space on the network. However, there are another two levels that speak to how this circuit operates. As users generally do not pay a subscription fee to use the social media network's services, the trade-off is user data, which takes the place of the money form in this relation. In exchange, the consumption of the service may be marketed as 'experience.' Experience is sold back to the users by way of targeted advertising whereby the users are invited to purchase an object or service as something to enhance their own experience according to expressed consumer tastes. The final stage occurs within this circuit from the user-end, and involves online social capital and its generation. Users may seek to convert their offline experiences (for example, travel) and labour (cognitive and creative) into online social capital, generally expressed numerically through counters and facilitated by the use of social buttons. The generation of social capital can involve increasing the size of one's personal network, which can be considered a benefit to the social media network as it may enrich the data being produced and facilitate cross-syndication; the user can produce new content of interest to other users (creative, experiential, cognitive), which in the process of its being published on the social network grants the social network ownership of that production – insofar as the terms of service dictate that they have the right to distribute, market, alter and modify it in any way they so choose. The symbolic aspect of social capital generation takes the form of numeric counters whereby, for example, a user's content on Facebook is paid in the form of likes by other users. These represent a token wage that has no exchange value with any other currency, yet it is still a form of work. For the social media network and the advertiser, the economic values are indexed more on the *volume* of activity – both as a sum of all network user production and participation, and the sum of each user's production and participation. Value in this instance is obtained through a mass general intellect, a sum total of all users' creative and cognitive labour in the production and cross-syndication of content. In this exchange, rather than the traditional formula whereby the labourer sells her or his labour power in exchange for a wage (L–M), the user sells the raw commodity (user-generated labour, experience, and data) in exchange for the benefits of the network service. As a 'value-added' perk, the user's production of the self as commodity can result in the gain of online social capital, which should not be mistaken for the money form (wage or profit). Occupying the space and not regularly contributing and participating in the network (interacting with other users, producing content) may result in quickly diminishing returns as the algorithm that populates each user's newsfeed may become populated with more active users. Given the fast-paced nature of content creation from a large user base, one's content can quickly fall 'below the fold' whereby the relevance of the content becomes determined by its visibility. This will have an impact on one's online social capital, and so an increase in user-generated production and participation is a sufficient condition for increasing online social capital. The sufficient condition may also be contingent upon a variety of strategies and tactics that can be employed to increase online social capital. Why we do not claim that production and participation is a necessary condition might be on account of one's offline forms of gaining social capital and popularity, some of which may generate conversation on social networks by other users. An Olympic medallist may not have to take a selfie or broadcast a win if other users are making mention of it on the social network.

In order for the social network to be profitable, the initial money that was invested at the beginning of the cycle must not only be recouped in the sale of the commodity, but that the commodity form will be of a higher value due to productive labour. The labour must have produced surplus value, or $C' = C + c$ (where c = the surplus value extracted from the productive labour). In the ideal circumstances, a portion of the surplus value is reinvested in the circuit of productive capital, and may include–in the case of a social media network – better hardware, software, data curation methods, marketing and optimising user interface for both ease of use and more efficient data capture. Data, furnished by users through their productive labour and self-commodifying activities, is the commodity that is sold and converted into money. This is very much in line with the traditional formula; however, the difference is the second step of production after the in-house labour, that of users whose labour is unwaged and thus has a surplus value delimited by the size of the network, the connections on that network, and the participation and production of its user base.

The users provide two specific enhancements to the network commodity through their activity. The first is in supplying content, which creates the 'substance' within the network's framework. The second occurs when users comply with ever more invasive yet innocuous-seeming requests for data. For example, when Facebook introduced its timeline feature in 2012, ostensibly marketed to users as a means of curating their own content and posting items known as 'Life Events.' Users could then fill in significant events that may have occurred prior to their subscribing to Facebook. Apart from the possibly disturbing question of slotting one's pre-Facebook life events into the neatly arranged timeline interface, it provides an immense trove of data for Facebook where it can produce a much more refined data profile of the user based on a longer timeline to use for predictive purposes. What may seem innocuous, such as posting a pleasant memory from the distant past, becomes valid data for marketing.

The social media user is positioned in this case as a kind of entrepreneur who, as part of the circuit of capital, reinvests earned online social capital *without there being an obvious equivalence between these numeric forms of online social capital and money-capital*. Encouraging more participation and devising means by which to entice users to provide more personal data are profitable inputs into the social network's capitalist circuit. The lure at the user-end may partly be the promise of increasing online social capital, as it may seem to engage in a game of probabilities: producing more content might increase the chance of that content becoming visible to other users, and thus a higher chance of receiving coveted likes. A larger investment of labour time spent on social media might increase the odds of larger returns.

What remains problematic is that this online social capital, as capital, cannot be reinvested according to the traditional circuit of capital. However, let us assume for the sake of argument that online social capital, expressed numerically through volume via the use of social buttons, is its own distinct micro-economy of accumulation. We already know that this micro-economy is plugged into the actual economy of the social media platform's generation of capital as discussed above. If we take these numeric expressions as the money form, it is evident that 'more is better' with respect to accumulation.

Online Symbolic Capital

Online social capital shares a border with symbolic capital and how it gets reinvested. The nature of symbolic capital is convertible; that is, earning prestige in one area may be converted to another area. An accomplished athlete may leverage this renown to become a popular public figure to endorse a product, a highly regarded astronaut may run for public office, and even a popular YouTuber may make the leap to becoming a reality TV show star. In following on from Max Weber's analysis of status, Thorstein Veblen (2010 [1899]) explored the intersection of class and status, and in particular the habits of the wealthy elite to display that status through conspicuous consumption. Pierre Bourdieu (1984) argued that class differences are expressed as symbolic differences, thus perpetuating inequality. Depending on the social space, these forms of capital will be distributed differently. The old models of class still prevail on social media as established celebrities and other public figures maintain a presence there with numerous followers and considerable attention, but given the 'democratisation' of the web, this has contributed to a softening or shifting of regard for traditional authorities so that it is not just the experts and elites who hold sway in public discourse. Although this may represent a significant change, divisions online still exist along class, gender, race and linguistic lines.

Considering the symbolic capital differences on social media along the lines of online social capital, those who already have wealth and status have an easier time acquiring more online social capital due to their being popular or well regarded. Popular figures such as Justin Bieber, Katy Perry or Donald Trump can very easily acquire new followers, retweets, likes and favourites. However, if we consider an 'average user,' their accumulation of online social capital may also signal an opportunity to leverage this for other purposes, although there is no clear line between gaining likes and followers, and achieving a higher status in another field. In some cases, this does occur, such as in the case of microcelebrities on social media who are able to leverage their popularity on social media to endorse products and services for money.

Metrics such as likes and followers are a form of currency by which one user can be compared to another. If it is a form of currency, it is certainly one that can be manipulated, such as in the use of click farms. How many likes are 'enough' on a post to be viewed as having value, according to those who will rely on these measures as being equivalent to value? What of inflationary pressures on this currency? User X produces an interesting post with an associated album on Facebook regarding her vacation to Jamaica. It is her hope that, in converting the experience into a digital format, it will be of interest to her network. She has successfully converted her class-based symbolic capital in being able to afford a luxury vacation to her online social advantage. The network users connected to User X respond with likes and comments, and this may drive popularity as it appears in more users' newsfeeds courtesy of the proprietary algorithm. User X accumulates, say, 1,000 likes and is now more prominently featured in the newsfeed of other users in the network. Let us now assume two scenarios: in the first, the activity the post has generated attracts the attention of a celebrity who also visits and likes the posting, the result of which generates an even higher volume of likes. In the second scenario, User X feels 1,000 likes is insufficient attention for the post and so opts to purchase the services of a company that will auto-generate them using either bots or actual persons who are hired to promote content. In the first case, it is less about the intrinsic value of the post that merited the surge in 'likes,' but the influence of a well-known person created the conditions of a social herding effect, not unlike a celebrity endorsement of a product or service. In the second scenario, User X has purchased what are effectively counterfeit forms of social currency. The second scenario may be more pernicious in terms of inflationary pressure on the individual value of each 'like'. Moreover, it also demonstrates another avenue by which online social capital plugs into the actual economy through the development and purchasing of services to artificially generate online social capital. If social capital, numerically expressed, can be seen as a competition to acquire a large quantity, we have only to recall Marx's warning that the creation of surplus value will inevitably lead to inequalities. In the games of social capital, there are clear 'winners and losers.' As competition over this value may increase, so too may less savoury social strategies be employed to gain the advantage, such as aggressive forms of competition for attention.

The depreciation effect of online social capital numerically expressed is also part of the economic relation. A piece of content from a year ago that may have garnered a large number of likes does not retain its initial value. Unlike a piece of machinery that will depreciate in value from use, the content does not undergo any physical depreciation: someone's tweet or Facebook post is not subject to wear and tear over time. Its value diminishes for a variety of reasons, which may include relevance, but also its availability for immediacy and exposure in a large social graph. Even if the content is 'yesterday's news,' it may still be relevant.[8] However, what is unique to online social capital would be the fact that the apparent numeric value does not go down, nor is its value diminished in relation to new content that has more or less likes. At the point the content is no longer accessed, that numeric value remains identical for as long as it is data housed on a server and still technically accessible by others. It may be a more useful analogy in considering the numeric value like a video game score, particularly of the older arcade variety where the prize for achieving a certain score is simply being afforded the opportunity to keep playing. And, just like a top score, the number itself does not diminish, but instead raises the bar for a bare minimum to be achieved in order to be on the leaderboard.

The content's numeric value cannot be exchanged for some other content. A thousand likes is not like a thousand units that can be converted in a typical currency market. One cannot convert it, insure it like property, or leverage a certain amount to obtain a loan like our friend Chichikov. Instead, it becomes a static numeric value that has no explicit monetary exchange value. It may, however, be 'resurrected' value in the case of politics where a muckraker may retrieve an old tweet by a political candidate for purposes of embarrassment or sabotage. In that case, there is no additional value added to the original content except as secondary reference.

The numeric markers for online social capital seem to exist outside the laws of supply and demand. There is no serious issue with supply. Given that there is a finite number of human beings on earth, a percentage of which have access or interest to 'like' a piece of content as a means of conferring a value upon it, then supply is technically finite. However, the creation of multiple accounts and the processes by which the system can be gamed using automated 'liking' services such as click farms allows for gaming the system and inflating supply. When some websites claim to peg a value on each 'like', ranging from zero to hundreds of dollars, we must question how they might have arrived at those values given the potentially unlimited supply available, and if the value arrived at is applicable to all content regardless of how old it might be.[9]

In terms of 'exchange', one's online social capital 'score' does present at least an indirect convertible value for those who work in social media marketing, public relations, or in the ICT sector where some applicants may be asked to provide proof of their social media skills by including their Klout score.

With a profusion of services for marketers and influencers, the use of scores and rankings will generally measure audience reach, follower engagement and cross-syndication. How these rankings are calculated is not always very clear, relying on proprietary algorithms. For instance, klout.com describes its calculation method in this way:

> We measure multiple pieces of data from several social networks, and also real world data from places like Bing and Wikipedia. Then we apply them to our Klout Score algorithm, and then show the resulting number on your profile. The higher your Klout Score, the tougher it becomes to increase. (klout.com).

Other sites, such as Webfluential, go as far as to put a dollar figure on the value of each post. The methodology for calculating this value remains within a black box, ostensibly to dissuade gaming the system unfairly.

What is meant by these monetary values given that one cannot simply exchange the content (as commodity) for money? To be charitable, it may refer to the increase in potential financial advantage in selling products or services: a person with a million followers may be able to maximise her or his audience if said user publishes a book or an album. This does not speak to the supply side of this question, and the potential availability of infinite likes may be akin to printing money, and yet there seems to be no runaway inflationary pressures on the value of each 'like' given that their designated value (by these websites) appears to assume a common value for each 'like', not taking into consideration other factors that exert influence over the value, such as novelty effect, exposure, etc.

The supply of likes is potentially infinite, and so is the demand. However, the question of value remains. Given that numerically expressed online social capital can succumb to over-accumulation, and a lack of opportunities for reinvesting it, this is likely to result in the ultimate devaluation of that capital. How does one remobilise online social capital in order to acquire more?

Monetary deals are occasionally brokered between users with a high numeric value of social capital and the host network. The more commonly known example would be YouTube which offers content creators with a high view rate based on CPM (cost per thousand impressions).

How this works is that advertising is matched to content, and the content producer gets a percentage – but only if the viewer clicks on the ad or watches the entire ad. If a viewer clicks 'skip this ad', the content producer does not get paid. The CPM is paid by the advertiser, but YouTube takes a 45 per cent cut, leaving the content producer with RPM (revenue per thousand impressions). This is calculated as follows: earnings divided by monetised playbacks multiplied by 1,000. However, the CPM can vary according to type of content and viewer demographic, resulting in a range of fifty cents to ten dollars. So, let us assume a $1.00 CPM rate on a piece of video content receiving a million views. Assume further that only 10 per cent of those viewers engage the ad content with a click or watch the entire ad. That leaves a CPM rate of 100,000. At a dollar each, we are left with $100. Deduct YouTube's 45 per cent cut, and the content producer is left with $55 for a million views. If we were to treat each view of the content (not the advertisement) as an 'admission price', the content producer has received 5.5/1000th of a cent for each view. It then becomes the responsibility of the content producer to encourage watching or clicking on the ad, not the content.

Compare this with major Hollywood productions. With any potential blockbuster there are very significant upfront costs for development, production (including pre- and post), crew wages, the cast and directors (generally calculated on speculation based on contingent compensation pending how well the film grosses). There are also print costs, marketing, residuals and different revenue inputs (theatre, pay-per-view, DVDs, streaming licenses, etc). According to Stephen Follows (2016), just as many blockbusters make a modest profit as those that fail. The major difference, apart from an economy of scale, would be that the average YouTube content producer may not have such upfront costs and so might technically be able to derive a bit more profit. However, it is not the case that there is a 50 per cent success rate on profit for YouTubers, and that profit percentages do not resemble those of Hollywood successes. Ten million viewers of one's YouTube clip do not net the same profit (adjusted against lower costs) than ten million viewers of a Hollywood blockbuster.

The accumulation of online social capital through numeric counters reproduces the mechanics of capitalism's instrumentalist and rational self-interest mindset as one might find in many popular video games indexed on character-levelling and loot accumulation. Moreover, these mechanics are reproduced across social media space, be it in the unpaid labour of the YouTube's Heroes Program where users are given points to 'level up' in performing crowdsourced activities for flagging content, Yahoo!'s comment section on news items with its reputation scoring system, or similar crowdsourced services where badges or other social tokens take the place of a wage for performing forum-based labour. Levelling up, earning social 'prestige' by numerically based accumulation, digital 'badges,' and so forth point to the gamification of online social interaction, but also the exploitation of unwaged labour.

Do accumulators of online social capital benefit from some form of compounding interest? Yes and no. Someone who has accumulated a large number of followers, and has a recognised track record of producing content others enjoy *and* benefits from the algorithm by which the user's new content appears in other users' social feed, can potentially leverage these for an increase on future reinvestment. It is no secret that the socially rich get richer, putting paid to the optimistic notion that those who are less popular in offline environments will have an almost guaranteed surge in popularity online as many of the offline barriers such as appearance, location or ethnicity can be lifted. Despite numerous exceptions, those who possess the skills for social popularity tend to migrate those skills to the online environment.

But what drives those in pursuit of social capital? Why do they not simply repose in the numerically-assigned figure of their online social capital and 'retire'? Firstly, there is no cash-out mechanism; one cannot simply exchange the number of Facebook likes or connections for money. Secondly, reinvestment of social capital to gain more increases apparent social power in ways that cannot be expressed in other forms. As David Harvey points out, 'the very rich cannot own billions of yachts or MacMansions. But there is no inherent limit to the billions of dollars an individual can command' (2011, 43).

There is a curious stability to online social capital due to the 'long tail'. Unlike certain sectors dominated by oligopolies in telecommunications, auto-manufacturing or banking, the failure of the most popular nodes in the network does not imperil the network to failure. In this social 'market', if extremely successful users like Justin Bieber or Kim Kardashian were to vanish from online social networks, others would fill the attention vacuum. In this way, social media networks are largely insulated from the failure of individual users, just so long as there is a steady supply of users continuing to produce content and provide data that can be commodified.

Rise of the Micro-Celebrity

If we calculate a social media user's specific labour in the production of a marketable identity to be 'sold' to other users and attract attention, it might be better distinguished as a form of self-branding. A brand uniquely identifies a product or service as distinct from other similar products and services. The branding narrative capitalises on what is unique about the product or service, while either explicitly or implicitly inviting comparison with similar products and services. In the case of those users who actively seek to create and maintain their digital representation as a form of branding, we might ask what they receive in return. There is an apparent use-value to the construction and ongoing reputation management of one's social profile, as it is the online social 'face' of the individual. However, brands generally operate by legal protective mechanisms such as trademarks, copyright, and similar forms of property. The use of the brand by other entities might entail the paying of licensing fees. In the case of online users as brands, there is really no mechanism by which the brand 'holder' can legally exert that it is under their ownership given that real ownership is held by the social networking service. Instead, the act of self-branding makes the leap from simple use value to an exchange value by participating in a social market, the abstract unifying relation that mediates the different brands on offer being a different form of price – the numeric counters of social buttons as a symbol, for example – in an economy controlled by the social networking service.

Despite questions of ownership, this has not dissuaded a number of social media users to leverage online social capital to become micro-celebrities. This new phenomenon, which appears to shift the creation of celebrity status to an achievable end for regular users, is defined as 'a new style of online performance that involves people 'amping up' their popularity over the Web using technologies like video, blogs and social networking sites' (Senft 2008, 25). A new category of influencers has emerged on social media that are able to capitalise on their following to endorse products and services in exchange for money. Emerging out of 'lifestyle blogging,' Crystal Abidin has traced the rise of the microcelebrity influencers, defining them as,

> [E]veryday, ordinary Internet users who accumulate a relatively large following on blogs and social media through the textual and visual narration of their personal lives and lifestyles, engage with their following in 'digital' and 'physical' spaces, and monetize their following by integrating 'advertorials' into their blogs or social media posts and making physical paid-guest appearances at events (2016, 3).

With Instagram being one of the most popular platforms for this kind of advertorial method, Abidin further traces the connection between the use of selfies and influencing behaviour as a form of subversive frivolity that capitalises on online social connections as an entrepreneurial means to market both the self and the product to establish a branding presence. Various companies have taken notice of how successful online influencers can be for marketing purposes, and influencer management agencies have emerged to act as brokers between influencers and companies.

With media exposure on the success of influencers in making considerable sums of money, this has generated interest among those who seek to monetise their social media activity. Even so, the media availability heuristic will mostly focus on stories of success as opposed to numerous failures – a situation not dissimilar to the excitement generated by producing stories about 'appillion-aires', where the focus on a few wildly successful entrepreneurial app developers conceals the majority of developers who did not succeed.

There is considerable labour in the process of being an influencer, as it involves successfully integrating and embedding the endorsement of a product or service with the carefully curated posting of a selfie. Conspicuous product placement, product demonstration, photo editing and the like must be conducted in a way that is aesthetically pleasing to an audience as well as maintaining trust in the individual who is posting the content. What may seem an effortless and casual selfie-taking is usually the result of a great deal of preparation and post-production editing. This labour may also be highly gendered and ageist work, with young women between the ages of 18–24 earning more than men, and potentially relying on stereotypical conceptions of beauty.

The issue of self-branding is part of a broader post-Fordist and neoliberal ideology of valorising the entrepreneur (Hearn 2008; Read 2008; Khamis et al. 2017). Although the issue of selfies-as-reflexivity and self-branding deserve their own specific and more extensive treatment, the purpose here is to signal how self-branding in particular plugs into the capitalist circuit of production. In the case of influencers, sponsored posts can be considered a form of contract labour. In this process, the influencer transforms the image of the self into a saleable commodity by exploiting the high-trust nature of online social networks. It is not enough for a social media influencer (SMI) to have a large follower base, but to continually grow it using an array of social media marketing strategies. On the one hand, the SMI has some degree of freedom to design his or her own content, but must be mindful that the client receives a good return on investment. On the other hand, the SMI will have to absorb the up-front costs associated with the branding activity, including the labour time involved in product staging, enhancing images and growing their follower base.

If one of the ideals of social media is to truly emphasise social interaction between people as a kind of digital public sphere, the advent of *social* marketing colonises the space, blurring the lines between a user and a brand, while also normalising the objectification and commodification of the self.

Liking and the Online Social 'Market' – Tracking and Tracing

Social networking services create the conditions of a 'free' social market. The currency of numeric social capital is not printed by the social networking service as if it were a treasury or mint, but it has set up the social currency system and manages it in different ways. The stability of this social market is partially underwritten by diversification so that if the individual with the most numeric social capital vanishes, there are plenty of others who can occupy that prime position. Moreover, the social market is buttressed by the collective transactions of social capital of most of its users, engaged in an act of online social capital exchange.

It is questionable if the social buttons feature, whether active or not, would have a significant bearing on the real economic conditions social networking services operate within: they would still sell advertising space, promote their own features, grow their user/prosumer base and likely continue to cycle capital into reinvestment into making improvements as well as expanding their reach. However, the addition of the social buttons feature might be an incentive for those who seek some numeric basis to engage in accumulation. In some cases, the numeric accumulation might be leveraged for monetary gain, as in the case of celebrities who might enter into agreements with companies to endorse products or services. Moreover, the addition of such social buttons has been part of an active strategy by companies like Facebook to multiply interactions, and to better track and trace interactivity for the purposes of increasing participation and potential profits.

As Roosendaal (2010) notes, Facebook uses its social buttons to track and to trace users by placing cookies on the user's browser, and this occurs even if the user does not interact with the button. Moreover, visitors without a Facebook account will also have a cookie placed on their browser, strongly implying that Facebook's data collection goes beyond just its users. This arguably invasive use of data collection appears to present a boon to not only corporate interests, but furnishes researchers with larger volumes of online behavioural data, a process of datafication:

> a legitimate means to access, understand and monitor people's behaviour is becoming a leading principle, not just amongst techno-adepts, but also amongst scholars who see datafication as a revolutionary research opportunity to investigate human conduct (van Dijck, 2014, 198).

What is unique about the metrification of user engagement through social buttons and what Gerlitz and Helmond (2013) dub the 'like economy', is that user intention is not what is being counted, only the end result of engagement. The social context of communicative intention, such as liking 'ironically', substantively or superficially, as an obligation of minimum reciprocity, points to a pared down sociality where our ability to decode communicative intent is left either to inference or explicit references should the user qualify by adding a comment to a post. Gerlitz and Helmond (2013) identify three ways these counters have an impact on social media interactions. Firstly, the act of liking has a multiplier effect in terms of traffic and engagement, particularly as receiving and giving likes is likely to perpetuate social activity; secondly, the social economy can be scaled (or customised) to each user, but operates across several social formations via newsfeeds, etc.; and thirdly, cross-syndication of content facilitates content matching through the affordances of the user-recommender model of content flow.

Apart from the serious privacy implications of such track and trace measures being employed by social media sites, it also sets up a kind of artificial social stock market that uses some degree of cybernetic mechanisms to measure activity, filter data, and sell these data as commodities. While the users are 'selling' their data to social media sites in exchange for opportunities to engage in online social activity, such activity is being measured and factored into predictive models to better refine advertising methods.

The motivation for why users participate in the behaviour of liking – a digital signal of endorsement, approval, approbation, reciprocity or social obligation – runs a very wide gamut. When Facebook initially introduced the liking feature, there was only the single explicit option of liking the content or not recording a 'like' at all. Some users complained that there was no 'dislike' button, but the addition of such a feature would diminish the positive experience Facebook was trying to promote. It was only recently, in 2016, that Facebook introduced the ability to add an emoji to better qualify one's emotional reaction to content. Although this provides more options to qualify our communicative intentions, it also strengthens the algorithm in better refining data.

In a survey conducted by Brandtzaeg and Haugstveit (2014), a useful typology underpinning the kinds of liking behaviours on Facebook were identified, including socially responsible liking, emotional liking, informational liking, social performative liking, low-cost liking and routine liking. In each of these cases, however, the user is conferring a value on another user's content (or a brand) for others to see. In some cases, this is done strategically: some users are politely soliciting the 'liked' user to reciprocate out of obligation or flattery, while others do so as a status or value statement such as wishing other users in the network to see that some user X takes a positive view of some product or cause. There are several strategic reasons users may have to confer value through social buttons, with some expecting one-to-one reciprocity while others seek to be associated with a popular user or popular content that they did not produce.

Aggregate Social Capital

In the second volume of *Capital*, Marx focuses his analysis on how the sphere of circulation moves to the sphere of production and then back to that of circulation. By the eighteenth chapter, he considers aggregate social capital, which is the sum of all capitals and their relations. Each individual capital circuit is but one moving piece in a larger complex of circulation involving both the reproduction of capitalist processes in production and that of the capitalist class. It is here, however, that we come to a terminological difficulty: the way in which social capital has been employed in the sociological literature of the twentieth and twenty-first century deviates substantially from how Marx uses it. At best, we may point to Bourdieu, who understood that the different forms of capital are interrelated, but the emphasis is not necessarily on production. If there is 'reproduction' of social capital in the literature, it is more the reproduction of social norms, sanctions, and opportunities afforded by wealth and status. This may satisfy to some extent the Marxist idea of the reproduction of the capitalist class and its interests, but does not address the production process from the standpoint of labour.

Instead of focusing on the immiseration of labour, much of the literature on social capital focuses on the correlative development of human capital (skills, education, etc.), which appears to simply assume that the capitalist process is a natural one, and that focus is better directed to ways by which one can measure and improve social capital in order to obtain benefits in occupational opportunities for advancement, which would then have a potential knock-on effect for an increase in social status and wealth.

Online labour itself becomes ever more fragmented and concealed by the very working tools employed with an almost fetishistic importance and imbued with an almost talismanic power. Although a potentially infinite surplus value is still extracted in this scenario from a mass cognitive intellect that becomes increasingly global, of equal concern is the extraction of surplus data from these computer mediated social interactions or exchanges whereby it is the capitalist market with all its powerful corporate interests that are the primary beneficiaries. That individual users who more resemble consumers than citizens may 'profit' by a more extensive degree of access to choices for new or better products and services, or may play a part in their redevelopment through online feedback processes that companies may monitor, these choices are gridded according to consumerism rather than self-actualisation. The profit motive did not simply vanish in the informationalisation of society. Despite the utopian claims that increased reliance on ICTs would shift the focus away from profit toward producing the social and public good, profit still remains the primary motive regardless of how it is dressed up in the appearance of sociality. The profit motive becomes embedded on social media, but is also sold as a benefit to individual users to function as entrepreneurs to exploit these networks in seeking their own profit. In some ways, this resembles something of a pyramid scheme. Whereas the promise takes on the appearance of distributing profit potential across all the nodes in a network, it is the concentration of wealth in fewer hands continuing unabated from the time of the captains of industry; in today's case, the captains of industry are the network giants who have discovered novel ways of augmenting the producer-consumer relationship whereby the consumer is also the producer who assumes the majority of the labour and the risk.

Information society proponents such as Alvin Toffler (1991) claimed that the knowledge economy, powered by computers and digital networks, would dematerialise labour in such a way that it would be transformed from the factory floor's routine drudgery and immiseration into better and more cognitively intensive labour, fails to appreciate the reality of much outsourced labour that is still largely routinised even with the integration of digital technologies.

That is, the nature of the toil has changed. Whereas ever more of the factory work may have dissolved away in increasing deindustrialisation and deskilling in once prosperous industrial manufacturing areas such as Detroit's automobile sector or the industrial heartland of Eastern Germany, we find new forms of routinised labour in places such as China, Bangladesh, the Philippines and India, where workers assemble digital components for the next wave of digital devices, or underpaid workers toil in boiler room working conditions and spend long shifts in click farms increasing the number of likes or 'level grind' for Western gamers who have the money to pay others to farm gold on *World of Warcraft*. Even in developed nations there is a surfeit of low-skill, routinised, poorly paid jobs that involve digital networks, such as those paid to create false and appealing accounts for dating website services.

Rather than dispensing with routinised labour of an industrial age, such labour has been reconfigured so that it may be the employment situation itself ceases to have any guaranteed routine; that is, the increasing precarity of employment on short or zero-hours contracts that make up ever more of the labour market. Still, when we consider how routine itself has changed, and the extraction of surplus labour, the routines become rituals associated with constant feedback and connection – the office worker who must respond to a flood of emails via his or her handheld device during vacation or any time outside of regular working hours just to remain on top of workload. In this way, some workers find their leisure time colonised by the demands – implicit or explicit – of labour, blurring the line between labour and leisure time. On one hand, the routine of the punch-clock may be on the decline for these workers, while on the other hand a new routine emerges of constantly checking in and managing workload outside of regular office time. In many respects, Taylorist scientific management has not vanished with the spread of the information age, but has been embedded as an intrinsic feature.

Even if we retain the largely functionalist definition of social capital as having nested structures involving trust, reciprocity and goodwill, there may still be inequality. As Bob Edwards points out, '[a]ccess to social capital depends on the social location of the specific individuals or groups attempting to appropriate it in much the same way that other forms of capital are differentially available' (Edwards and Foley 1997, 677). When ported to digital social networks, the question of location takes on less of a physical, geographic meaning and more of the order of location within a specific network, the flow of information between those network actors, and the in- and outbound reach of content from other self-selecting networks. Where issues of geography still come into play may be in terms of access to the network, particularly the differences of internet service coverage and speed between rural and urban areas with the former having less, and thus may have an impact on differential availability of online social capital.

In assessing the motivations that give rise to the development of social capital, off- or online, Portes (1998) identifies these as either consummatory or instrumental; consummatory insofar as they reflect deeply embedded social norms, and instrumental insofar as they involve the more economic aspects of rational action theory by which individuals perform actions with a view to gain advantage or profit. It might be considered more common that those engaged in the active, explicit pursuit of increasing social capital do so for instrumental reasons and thus for their own benefit (De Graaf and Flap 1988; Burt 1992). Rational action and rational choice theory are in themselves essential components to the economic theories that underpin neoliberalism, mostly pioneered by the Austrian School and later Chicago School of economics. Emblematic of this view are the axiomatic foundations of praxeology that assume in advance that all human action is rational (von Mises 1963, 18–21), and so it follows from this that the function of choice for the individual seeks at the outset an advantage on the basis of a rational calculation.

It is under these conditions, garlanded by the continued adoption of some cybernetic principles in our network age, where the inward turn to the self becomes ever more a placeholder for traditional forms of community and social capital; instead, online communities and self-selecting networks as promoted by social media are largely decorative in nature. With a keenness on marketing to the self-as-brand, a new crop of social media individualists and cyber-libertarians can appropriate what is meant as social capital as a rational, self-calculating instrument to ultimately promote individual values.

Main Points

- The capital aspect of online social capital can be expressed in Marxist terms as an exchange rate guaranteed by a unifying 'price' due to metrification of social relations.
- The use value of social interaction is subordinated to the exchange value presented by online social capital and its reliance on standardised measurement
- There are three forms of online social capital exchange: (i) The user-as-commodity where the user is a source of data that can be capitalised by the social network owner; (ii) The user-generated commodity that involves everything social media users create or share, and; (iii) 'Rent' whereby the social network host 'leases' space to users to perform abstract social labour, and 'leases' the data produced to advertisers.
- Online social capital differs from symbolic capital insofar as the former does not lend itself to being directly converted. Although there are a number of services that claim to be able to put a dollar value on social capital, their methodologies differ widely and remain unclear.
- Users who choose to commodify their social connections and online social capital may choose to leverage these to become social media influencers and micro-celebrities, converting their digital production of the self on

social media into a profitable venture of creating advertorials for products, which thus sees capitalism colonise online social space yet further.

- Social media sites make use of social buttons and the pursuit of online social capital to better track and trace its users, capturing data, increasing participation and refining the data that is used by algorithms as a predictive marketing tool.

CHAPTER 3

Capitalism and the Ideologies of the Social

The question now turns toward how the use value of online social communication gets converted to a kind of exchange value. The first step will be to discuss the theoretical frontiers of capitalism as it pertains to social media, and to drill down to some specific strategic examples.

The normalisation of social media is expressed by its ubiquity and apparent necessity. To abstain from social media might be considered by some as proof of abnormality and a cause for suspicion. Hiring firms may pass over a candidate if said person does not use social media. In some cases, employers have flouted labour laws in demanding password access to social media accounts of prospective employees to invasively see who they 'really are' – a significantly more overt yet no less disturbing trend reminiscent of Henry Ford's penchant for sending agents to covertly surveil workers in their off-hours to report back on various behaviours, such as alcohol consumption. With the thickening of the US and Canadian border, the US Department of Homeland Security has refused entry to those travellers who do not hand over full password access to their social media accounts, or who may be put under additional scrutiny for not having any social media accounts at all. In less severe cases, some people may become inadvertently excluded from social functions that are organised solely on Facebook, based on the assumption that everyone has an account there. For others, there simply little choice but to engage in social media as part of the requirements of work due to how much social media has become integrated as part of a communications strategy for everything from marketing products and services, to the daily operations of local governments.

Just as there are more opportunities for social inputs using social media, a rise in apparent necessity in their use has been capitalised by social network owners as providing ever more economic inputs for profit generation. As more social competition may become manifest on social media in attempting to

---

How to cite this book chapter:
Faucher, K. X. 2018. *Social Capital Online: Alienation and Accumulation*. Pp. 39–59.
    London: University of Westminster Press. DOI: https://doi.org/10.16997/book16.d.
    License: CC-BY-NC-ND 4.0

accumulate a larger share of the attention economy, it may be fair to say that capitalism itself has become embodied in social and communicative activities, encouraging a competitive pursuit of online social capital.

Capitalism's colonisation of social time is not entirely new, but yet another of its integrated components aided in part by the ubiquity of social media, the latter's apparent necessity in both labour and leisure contexts and affordances for the automation of data extraction and cross-syndication of content. As such, it shares a border with other forms in the typology of capitalism: communicative capitalism, financialisation capitalism and neoliberalist-informationist capitalism. However, social capitalism in this instance operates within a kind of encapsulated social fishbowl – and to the fish, the world is an ocean. The same functions of capitalist accumulation seem to operate within the social media domain among users, but in ways that adopt capitalist ideology and apply it to the social. There are also still significant and real connections to real capital, yet our focus is on how the social on social media becomes ever more reminiscent of capitalism, and thus seems to operate as its own 'fantasy economy.'

We can define this 'fantasy economy' as the less visible means by which social interactions are not only exploited as data for social media companies, but also how capitalism itself becomes more normalised and embedded in online social media through the use of paid or sponsored content, and in the curious pursuit of obtaining some profit by the accumulation of incremental values associated with social buttons. Problematically, social relations have become ever more quantified and industrialised, right down to the means by which we can manage our connections and rely on ready metrics to engage in value comparison. Likes and other social metrics of this type become a form of standardised currency, to such an extent that for some it becomes a *sine qua non* of online popularity and opportunity. A curious new circuit has taken shape in many online social interactions where reciprocity becomes coded as a form of exchange that is underwritten by the like economy in the unifying form of a 'price' that can be calculated.

Communicative Capitalism

Luc Boltanski and Eve Chiapello (2005) characterise capitalism as a kind of spiritual exercise that aims to radically shift social values. Capitalism in its current form has discovered a means by which to better optimise forms of circulation as the key to accumulation. Whether it be through modifications to supply chain management in favour of just-in-time production, crowdsourcing, automation, and the development of more efficient networked systems for the extraction and curation of user-supplied data, the rate of circulation continues to increase.

In response to the high-flying promises of how increasingly networked communications would create more informed choice and true democratic engagement,

Jodi Dean identifies a new outcome: 'instead of leading to more equitable distributions of wealth and influence, instead of enabling the emergence of a richer variety in modes of living and practices of freedom, the deluge of screens and spectacles undermines political opportunity and efficacy for most of the world's peoples' (2005, 55). And, as our content can continue to circulate faster, on more networks, more efficiently and receive more inputs from more users, the same unity-in-diversity that was extolled as being the result of such networks has led to more inequalities and certainly more exploitation by those who own these networks. Whether enmeshed in what one might call a kind of fetish or a spectacle, more communication has meant less individual value in communication and more profit to be gained by ever tightening circuits of capital.

The 'ideal' of this social capitalism is predicated upon the idea that free and equal individuals, with free and equal access to the digital tools and opportunities, can pursue their desires online for the purpose of personal wealth enrichment gained through their own immaterial labour. The ultimate goal is to transcend equality via competitive strategies whereby the lucky, Darwinistic few will accumulate a larger share of the attention economy. Just as in capitalism overall, the contradiction is to vigorously promote individual freedoms where said freedoms are legally guaranteed as equally accessible by all, and then to pursue a program whereby disparity and inequality is the end goal. That is, everyone is said to be on the same starting line, but the winners will pull ahead by their own initiative and work ethic.

Neoliberal capitalism has a particularly problematic relationship with notions of the internal and external. According to its broader, macroeconomic goals, deregulated and borderless free trade plus direct foreign investment appears to efface the boundaries of the trade-zone inside and outside. When there are crises and failures, the preachers of neoliberalism will claim that external agents – terrorists, socialists, anti-capitalist fringe groups, which may be irresponsibly lumped together as all characterised as 'opposed' to the neoliberal idea of freedom – it is the fault of something 'external' to the system. When markets fail, responsibility is redistributed to such an abstract degree, which contradicts the extreme gospel of taking personal responsibility (preached to the non-wealthy as the means to wealth), and the laws of competitive, quasi-Darwinistic capitalism are temporarily suspended to permit corporate bailouts. Interestingly enough, the division between neoliberal capitalism and the more socialist or progressive ideologies is in where to pin blame for failure. The more left-of-centre perspective is to consider the citizen as part of a broader system or structure composed of forces – not all of which the individual can control. So, for example, lingering racial narratives may have a knock-on effect on crime, poverty and limits on opportunity as part of broader structural constraints. For the neoliberal, there are no structural constraints as such, for the heroic consumer can adopt a strong work ethic and simply choose to work his or her way out of poverty, discrimination and depressed wages by aggressively pursuing an almost libertarian objective of personal free enterprise. Of course, choosing unionisation would be rejected as a correct choice since that would be to prioritise cooperation over competition. When people find themselves in dire financial straits due to low-wage jobs, the neoliberal response is to say that said individuals simply made bad choices, and that they should make better choices in the future. This 'tough love' pragmatism is wilfully blind to any of the external factors that may have limited the individual's choices, and will not give a hearing to the context behind certain choices made or very real systemic limitations on opportunity that neoliberalism is complicit in upholding.

The lionisation of the individual as free-floating and self-determining is not only an essential piece of the neoliberal ideology, but also in the gospel of online social capital. This occurs despite the reality that these individual nodes (as they are networked) are not free-floating radicals simply pursuing their own unfettered pathways, but are instead locked-in monads. Individuals can choose their pathways and practices online from what appear to be an endless array of choices without visible obstruction, but more choice does not necessarily equate to actual freedom, particularly when what is made visible and 'personalised' for the user is structured by social media algorithms. Even search engine results on Google will favour businesses.

If communicative capitalism is little more than the circulation of content (Dean 2009, 22), a monologue staged by a multitude without much substantive engagement or subsequent offline action that could not be considered politically progressive.[10] It is akin to a village where everyone speaks and so few listen. And those who should be listening – governments and corporations with the economic power and control of assets to make responsive changes – will generally contribute to the dialogue with their own canned or talking point content, adding more circulating content to the monologue of the many. Or, worse still, tap into the conversation as a means of surveillance and as a strategic starting point for manipulation, persuasion and other tactics to further ideological agendas.

What Dean and others point to is a dilution of individual voices, ever more problematised by the convergence aspect of social media. Unlike previous forms of media that were communicative channels designed to inform and entertain, the number of purposes social media is put to creates a multiple divergence of uses, not only diluting voice, but functions. Such potential dangers of mass communication means were already considered even with the rise in popularity of the radio, pointing to a kind of rise of pettiness, banality and tribalism:

> Only after the human voice had been transmitted around the world with the speed of light did it become plain that the words so widely disseminated might still be the same words one could hear from the village gossip or the village idiot or the village clown or the village hoodlum. (Mumford 1944, 395)

John Stuart Mill's 'marketplace of ideas' takes on a more economic interpretation of market in terms of finance and commodification. Instead of ideas, we might witness more of a clearinghouse of half-digested, reactive rather than reflective, redundant, frivolous sentiments and opinions that either valorise corporate brands, prop up hate-based beliefs, traffic in mis- and disinformation, disseminate propaganda, or provide the data fodder for advertisers to embed their story-branding via targeted advertising on privatised social networks. David Harvey (2005) points to this absorption of human social interaction into the digital domain of networked culture, and it is Gilles Deleuze's prescient 'Postscript' (1995) that tells us that this turn to a largely cybernetics-inspired communication-control feedback technology creates *dividuals* and data blocs that are easier to predict and control because all behaviour and choice in that milieu is prescribed.[11] Possibilities on these networks are limited to what the network architecture permits. Ultimately, participation is a necessary but not sufficient condition of engagement and constructive action; however, participation in the network functions as a support and uncritical celebration of the network spectacle itself.

Just as classical capitalism succeeded in the abstraction of labour power from previous forms of labour, so too does digital communicative capitalism now succeed in abstracting social power as something derivative, quantifiable and imbued with the promise of exchange value. The user becomes the site of a new production, just as much as a member of the social factory performing 'socialised' immaterial labour. Even though the material advantage that may be gained by accumulating social capital may appear promising for many, it is still largely a process of alchemy, a transmutation experiment indexed on producing the more prosperous, popular future self. A life dedicated to accumulating social capital through promiscuous connectivity to increase the odds of receiving validation for one's online content production loses its intrinsic, experiential, social value. Taking pride in one's accomplishments, travels, personal benchmarks, and life events without feeling obliged to broadcast them on social media as a guiding means to validate experience is much more in alignment with our status as social beings as opposed to leveraging such events in the seeking of profit. Or, to apply a homily by William Bruce Cameron, '[n]ot everything that counts can be counted, and not everything that can be counted counts' (1963, 13).

The idea of social media as a kind of social factory aligns with the idea of the user as the site of production. The role communicative capitalism plays in the colonising of social life outside of work blurs the once static boundary between labour and leisure. At issue is the very ontological status of the social media user given the level of exploitation employed to extract ever more surplus value from those who produce content. The incentives to participate, and to do so often, with the subtext of remaining socially valid or relevant is caught up in the circuit of purchasing the means of production (hardware devices and software services), making it a 'pay to play' phenomenon. More importantly, it is the ontological question that speaks directly to how alienation emerges as a by-product of the circuits of digital communicative capitalism and the degree of importance attached to contused notions of social capital as a site of accumulation.

Participation on social media is voluntary for most, although there is ever more ambient pressure to subscribe or potentially lose out on reaping the social, cultural and professional opportunities afforded by such large networked spaces. Although social media participation in no way compares to forced or sweatshop labour (Hesmondhalgh, 2010), Dyer-Witheford rightly points out the parasitism of this shadowy capitalist world in which people are organised and mobilised according to the needs of the network:

> [Facebook posting] does not replace the 'normal' structures of daily class exploitation at work and home, but is added to and superimposed upon them, to constitute a regime in which the user is habituated, on pain of exclusion from social worlds, to surrendering the elements of their personality—identity, creativity, sociality—to enhance the circulation of capital. (Dyer-Witheford 2015, 93)

The grim appearance of necessity here is reinforced according to the ubiquity of social media, influential pressure from peers, and the shift in information being posted on these sites for various opportunities. This heavy degree of normalisation of social media is not without its risks, particularly as this normalisation favours the private sector owners of social media (and, subsequently, the shareholders) as it was this group who were the main beneficiaries of heavy financial investment after the dot-com crisis of the early 2000s.

In everyday terms, social media becomes yet another task to manage, another obligation to fulfil, on top of one's already existing obligations. The apparent necessity, buttressed by normalisation, begins to colonise both home and work, at times effectively blurring the distinction. However, it may not be recognised as such due to a view that socialising is not typically considered work. This does not take into account the very real conditions of labour time involved in online socialising activity, nor the fact that such leisure activities are being driven toward ever more 'eyeballs on ads':

> The more time a user spends on Facebook, the more profile, browsing, communication, behavioural, content data s/he generates that is offered as a commodity to advertising clients. The more time a user spends online, the more targeted ads can be presented to her/him. (Fuchs 2015a, 27)

Such advertising need not simply be what one sees in a social media site's sidebar or as sponsored content, but can also be entwined with the production of desire by other users, colonising the high-trust culture of networks and indirect word-of-mouth marketing:

> As social media allows us to be more open about our desires, we produce our own ontologies and metadata on such sites as Facebook: Sam

is a friend of Sue; Sue is a fan of BMW. When Sue 'likes' the latest BMW model, her desire is pushed out in the social stream. (Gehl 2014, 106)

Another aspect of increasing alienation might be the artificial creation of 'needs.' Although it may be hyperbole to accept the premise that if one is not on social media, one doesn't exist, there is an existing pressure to join. This happens in a context where some users will claim that it is justified along the lines of being the only way to view the lives of distant relatives or in not being excluded from social plans. The aspect of FOMO (fear of missing out) indicates the anxiety someone may feel in not being connected, and thus subscribing to these social media sites becomes more identified as a social necessity.

This necessity extends beyond the social, as some job recruiters have been reported of not hiring applicants because there was no social media history to better assess the character of the applicant. Refusal to join, and thus refusal to work for, a popular social media site can lead to diminished employment opportunities. Refusal to join may be construed as being in bad faith. Abraham Maslow's famous hierarchy of needs does indeed identify the social function as one of the human requirements, and social media has provided an additional space where this may occur, promising self-actualisation while reaping profit.

The Fourth Fantasy

When it comes to the role of communicative capitalism in the use of social media, Jodi Dean identifies three main fantasies: the Fantasy of Abundance, the Fantasy of Participation and the Fantasy of Wholeness (2005).

In the Fantasy of Abundance, Dean references the heady, dot-com years with all its optimism about how the information age would lead to moving away from economies of scarcity and toward an economy of abundance due to the affordances of new digital technologies in being able to manage larger volumes and faster speeds facilitating more efficient transactions (2005, 58). This idea of abundance has helped propel the alliance of neoliberalism-informationism (Neubauer 2011), allowing for the kind of creative destruction that has seen the shift between roll-back neoliberalism during the Reagan/Thatcher years to a modified, market-centric form of 'state-building' of roll-out neoliberalism in legitimising flexible labour markets, constant skills upgrading and the creation of a 'knowledge economy' (Peck and Tickell, 2002) while developing nations took on the burden of intensive industrialisation as Western nations became increasingly deindustrialised. Abundance is also associated with the reproduction of data and knowledge in ways that are not apparently tied to finite materials; i.e., the near infinite replicability of digital data as opposed to a limited print run of a book. However, there are very real-world finite limits, such as the materials that are required to manufacture the devices that access the online world (such as 'conflict minerals') and limits to energy in order to power and sustain the networks upon which more people depend.[12] Yet it is this fantasy of abundance at the broader economic scale of demand and supply that may have arguably presented a boon to major corporations that would have otherwise fallen victim to Marx's law of the falling rate of profit as certain forms of both fixed and variable capital costs can be reduced (or devolved to consumers).

Dean's treatment of this fantasy of abundance concerns communication, and that the 'exchange value of messages overtakes their use value' (2005, 58). All that matters is circulation of data: the message, the sender, the receiver, are all irrelevant or at least secondary to the circulation itself. As more users contribute content, the less value each instance of communication has, which then may precipitate a need or desire to be more shocking, outrageous, offensive and extreme in order to garner attention. So, with the abundance of messages we can send over social media, the more this becomes devalued as just contributions to data flow and circulation.

In the Fantasy of Participation, Dean speaks of the registration effect (2005, 60), which is the belief that our opinions and contributions online matter on their intrinsic merits, that they have a value more than simply contributing to circulation. On social media we are presented with numerous opportunities and prompts to contribute, be it a suggestion by the site to provide a status update, a reminder that one has not logged in recently to view what one has 'missed', to rate one's experience using a hotel booking service, to connect with a number of people harvested from one's email contact list, and so forth. Added to this would be forms of clicktivism and slacktivism associated with various causes whereby merely clicking a button replaces more substantive action and engagement. When we apply this to online social capital accumulation, we may also feel an obligation to 'like' the content of someone we like, which may prove much more convenient than writing a more substantive response, or as a form of obligatory reciprocity because said person has 'liked' our content. The notion that our contributions are significant is undermined by the fact that social media users are encouraged to participate more, but that content matters little beyond cross-syndicating the content and in providing ready fodder for keyword analysis performed by algorithms to deliver content and targeted advertising.

In the Fantasy of Wholeness, Dean points up the myth that the internet is a democratised, smooth space of unity, a true marketplace of ideas (2005, 67). The fantasy may put one in mind of the ideal that John Rawls (2005) speaks of in terms of political liberalism; namely, that prejudices and hierarchical considerations can be hung like hats by the door prior to meeting together as equals objectively discussing political conceptions of justice. In reality, communities on the internet are not commonly a McLuhan-style global village, but fragmented, composed of ideological tribes, and exacerbated further by algorithmic sorting that empowers filter bubbles that deliver content that conforms to the respective worldview of each user on social media. The algorithm's role in deselecting visible content maintains the social media space as a mostly positive one free of conflict, yet also free of the diversity one would expect of a truly globalised public that could ostensibly achieve a unity of differences.

Given these three main fantasies that Dean speaks of, I would append a fourth that may also conform to her idea of communicative capitalism, and perhaps overlap with each of the three fantasies: the *Fantasy of Equivalence and Conversion*. There may be a belief among users who actively seek to increase the visible numbers on their social counters that said efforts can be converted into actual capital, or that one's numeric online social capital is equivalent to some other stable value upon which one's personal or social value is based. If there is a belief that the like economy is somehow directly equivalent to a unifying price, there is an attendant belief in the conversion of contribution labour into a kind of payoff. This fantasy occurs in the most blatant and misleading way on sites that peg dollar values on social media accounts on the basis of followers, likes, retweets, etc., such as Klout et al. It may not matter if the content we contribute to the overall circulation of data is understood, just so long as it accumulates measurable attention in terms of likes, retweets and possibly increasing the number of followers as a function of network exposure.

Social Capitalist Strategies

There is no shortage of thinkers who continue to extoll the virtues of building digital social capital. One notable early example may be B.J. Fogg (2008) who lauds the affordances of Social Networking Services (SNS), particularly Facebook and its launch of its API, as a means of employing what he calls 'mass interpersonal persuasion' (MIP). The huge social graph provides access to much larger and better-organised audiences for targeting purposes by those micro-entrepreneurs looking to develop popular apps, while the automated structure allows for the proliferation of an app by effectively 'ghosting' a user's account in enticing others to join. The rapid feedback system also allows for quick and ongoing customisation of the app or its marketing and advanced analytics provide ample data for measuring app adoption rates and various pre-set demographic criteria such as browsers, geographical location, etc. Fogg lauds these affordances, and although he does briefly acknowledge the potential dangers of MIP in the wrong hands, he is overall optimistic about its prospects.

B.J. Fogg's model for mass interpersonal persuasion (MIP) is of some utility in exploring what is effectively *mass impersonal persuasion* (MIP2). Many of the mechanisms he cites such as *persuasive experience, automated structure, social distribution, rapid cycle, huge social graph* and *measured impact* may equally apply to strategies aimed at building online social capital. Despite Fogg's more optimistic conclusion that MIP decentralises authority in media from the top-down or hypodermic model to a recentralisation of power in the empowered[13] individual who can engage in a more open and participatory model of communication, even the grassroots bottom-up model can be co-opted by powerful entities to give the illusion of popular support. The very same mechanisms that allow for online anonymity or screen nonymity and mass participatory inclusion for expression also allow lobbying groups to leverage these mechanisms to construct an opaque image of a grassroots crowd using a variety of tools to create an artificial public.

Mass impersonal persuasion possesses the possible means of producing a persuasive experience without requiring a human entity to author each communication instance. By coupling an automated message delivery method with persona management solutions, contemporary astroturfing and botnet campaigns can be self-generating and self-renewing, adapting to different social communication requirements through the use of computerised linguistic analysis and textual production. One of the other distinct advantages of mass impersonal persuasion using advanced botnet methods is in increasing the volume and presence of messages that would, if operated by a human entity, be much slower and decrease the probability of broader social distribution.

In Fogg's six-point platform for mass interpersonal persuasion (MIP), each of these are indexed on experiential observations, measures, and effects. Fogg defines a persuasive experience as one that 'is created to change attitudes, behaviours or both' (2008, 4). The close alignment between viral effects and rapid cycle seem to operate according to a similar mechanism for distribution of persuasive experiences via web technology. However, more importantly, the use of online traffic metrics such as Google Analytics allow campaign managers to monitor and measure the success, attrition, or adoption rates of a particular campaign component or meme; and other analytical tools further allow campaign managers to monitor traffic on issues according to hashtags as a means of coordinating the campaign for optimal effect on those social media platforms that make extensive use of hashtags.

Since Fogg's study, the huge social graph has also seen significant changes, especially in the touted features of Open Graph (Facebook 2013) whereby a robust API allows for deeper app integration to maximise the 'Facebook experience,' facilitating cross-platform interaction between app content and Facebook status updates. For example, by adopting the Goodreads app, any action a user makes on Goodreads site such as starting or finishing a book can be automatically updated on the user's Facebook page for broadcast to that user's network. This form of automated message delivery, akin to Fogg's automated structure for message dissemination and successful adoption, minimises on the user being left to construct a message to persuade other users to adopt the app, and instead allows the Open Graph app to write the 'story' on behalf of the user. This form of digital surrogacy takes control of the central promotional message without relying on the user-host to promote the product or service.

Automated methods are vital to the operations and procedures of digital astroturfing and botnet campaigns. Fogg's discussion of how automated structure benefits MIP serves two functions:

> First, software can deliver a persuasive experience over and over. The computer code doesn't take a vacation or go on coffee breaks; the machine keeps working [...] The second point is that the automation makes it easier for people to share the experience with others. (5–6)

Fogg's focus is on the instrumental value of MIP; however, this may conceal some of the dangers that deserve more reflection, such as the potential to exacerbate alienation, the nature of unpaid work, a networked capitalist system that relies on app entrepreneurs shouldering the burden of risk and responsibility, and possibly events Fogg did not anticipate such as the rise of digital astroturfing with the use of sophisticated botnets. Fogg is not alone in seeing the potential advantages of building or accumulating online social capital, with a large number of primers, blogs, and how-to manuals on the subject that all take the accumulation of online social capital as inherently good. The danger of assuming this would be that it obscures the ideological aspects whereby these practices strengthen the hand of capitalist exploitation at the expense of the non-pecuniary online community, if not also the immiseration of workers who toil in click farms or the precarity of the app-development market.

The pursuit of online social capital appears to provide a solution in search of a problem. It certainly provides a solution to a very concrete and practical problem for capitalists seeking to increase markets and to seek ways of cutting costs by devolving marketing efforts to the consumers themselves in ways that consumers will actively participate behind the veil of play. However, for the average user seeking to increase likes and number of followers, being caught up in this kind of economy is also to be caught up in a kind of myth. Apparent social needs are magically provided by the social media space, and the metrification of that space provides the appearance of objective, measurable 'proof'. The emergence of social buttons and a metric for online social capital is enveloped within the myths and metaphors that have developed with cyberspace, but also the neoliberal value system where competition and greed are seen as good. The pursuit and accumulation of measurable online social capital emulates the pursuit and accumulation of actual capital, but there are little to no tangible profits to be made by those who pursue it. The pursuit itself is seen as good, as part of the digital sublime Vincent Mosco (2004) speaks of.

Gaming the System of Social Capital

If there were not a potential economic benefit to online social capital, there would not be a burgeoning cottage industry either promising clients to increase their social capital through services or instructional blogs. Some of these services involve arguably unethical practices such as purchasing bogus positive reviews (or negative reviews in an act of sabotage against a competitor), like-farms and the use of botnets. If online social capital is reduced to a kind of video game style high-score on a publicly available leaderboard, as many multiplayer game apps have as a feature, there must be a way to 'game the system.' This becomes much easier when we consider the affordances of social digital media, as opposed to in-person networking.

Some of the services provided may include digital manipulation of code to increase likes, friends, followers etc. This would involve exploiting or hacking the server, or in deploying automated software where the bots can follow a program script to sign up for the site to 'like' a Facebook page. Or, these might rely on more sophisticated programming to create convincing 'users' with a personality drawn from a list of options tied to geography and other criteria. This latter was exposed by George Monbiot (2011) in a proposal issued by the US Air Force for such services, and is backed by a patent on how this can be done. Generating fake audiences to build one's social capital only requires paying a fee for service to one of a series of providers.

The more labour-consuming practice has been to provide these services using real people, run by exploitative individuals in boiler room situations in the developing world. A worker may be paid by the account, or volume of likes, and quite poorly. AshleyMadison.com, a site which specialises in providing discreet services for those interested in extramarital affairs, endured two major scandals. The most recent of these involved a major hacking incident that revealed the identities of several users, some of whom were prominent public figures.[14] The scandal which received less media coverage was a series of claims that the website was making use of bots to populate the site with more female accounts so as to attract more male subscribers. These claims were initially denied by the parent company, AvidLife (now rebranded as Ruby), and then later admitted. The strategic use of bots to set up female accounts, and possibly associated images peeled from the web, was to serve to even out the gender ratio which was seen to be have a much heavier preponderance of male users. Closely aligned with this scandal was a claim by an employee in the US who was suing the company for injuries sustained working long hours creating fake accounts in preparation for the company's expansion into the Brazilian market.

Other forms may include political trolling where individuals are hired to promote or condemn a political candidate. In other cases, it might be a promotion of government policies, such as China's '50 Cent Party,' a group of bloggers so named because they were paid the equivalent of 50¢ for every blog post that praised or defended the government. Pay-to-tweet services have begun to emerge in the political sphere. A service called @robertsrooms, associated with the Blak political action committee (BlakPAC) in the US and founded by self-proclaimed 'citizen patriots' Robert Shelton and Anita White, promises to deliver conservative candidates electoral success by mobilizing 10 million 'social media warriors.' They have claimed to have helped in getting Donald Trump elected while also 'out-tweeting' Hillary Clinton's supporters. Their pay-to-tweet model compensates users on Twitter to retweet content or create new content under the direction of the service. Unlike the creation of sophisticated botnets that work clandestinely, this method of social media mobilisation operates out in the open and is ostensibly run by grass-roots supporters who are willing to sell their services to prospective political candidates of the same ideological view. The service runs multiple rooms where supporters can be coordinated in the posting or reposting of short videos, messages, memes and other content on social media in support of a candidate. At other times, these rooms may be coordinated to attack non-conservative candidates and their supporters.

In other cases, there may be direct manipulation using reward. A well-known rum company appeared at a bar that is popular with students, and offered a free drink only if they signed into their Facebook account and 'liked' the company's Facebook page. In order to avoid unfulfilled promises from thirsty patrons, the representatives had on hand a device upon which the patron would sign into his or her Facebook and 'like' the page in the representative's presence. There are many reasons why this aggressive practice can be considered objectionable, including pressuring patrons to publicly endorse a product prior to receiving it, but also the potential for violations of privacy.

In other games of online social capital, the pursuit of positive reviews for products and services is its own special industry, sometimes courting mercenary tactics of planting fake bad reviews of competitors or hiring out for fake positive reviews. Due to the high-trust culture of the web, it may be the case that a site visitor may trust a random user's review much more than the official word of the company being reviewed. In the arts of persuasion, it was Lazarsfeld et al. (1948) who discovered that word-of-mouth through one's peer group has a much more effective impact on decision making than official messages from mass media, but that 'forbidden fruit' (i.e., reporting on what has overheard) can be even more effective.

One of the common features of the online environment is the strong appeal to quantity considerations as a basis for making decisions and assigning value, and this has already been demonstrated to work in what is called 'social herding' (Huang and Chen 2006). Social proof mechanisms may prove more significant in a semi-democratic setting of mass participation since no individual user may have the time or inclination to inspect the claims of each individual user. In addition, given the screen-based (a)nonymity of many users, tracing a message to the profiles of users and comparing these views to those made by the same user on other sites under a different screen name frustrates attempts to construct a comparative picture of the user and may not permit a measurement for credibility across different sites. The use of numerical considerations under herding is simply a quantified version of bandwagon effect. Online social capital has already been naturalised in terms of granting value to certain users and content on the basis of recorded number of likes or comments associated with that user. It is possible, under certain conditions, to 'game' the system such that a large surge in likes may be picked up by the algorithm and thus cause more visibility of the content for more users. Although social media algorithms are likely more sophisticated in flagging sudden surges to prevent like-spamming, click- or like-farming is still a booming industry. Such operations may rely on outsourced labour, such as in Dhaka, Bangladesh, where click farms hire people to click likes on content. It is not just small companies trying to gain a foothold who might purchases services such as these; it was reported that the US State Department spent an estimated $630,000 on these services in 2013 before the Inspector General criticised this expenditure (Associated Press 2014). The use of human labour (or what is marketed as 'organic likes') was a response to social media companies being able to filter out suspected automated software attempts to artificially increase followers, likes, and views. However, the use of automated software to generate inflated social media scores and fake reviews is not over; more sophisticated software is being developed that can bypass social media filters.

Microburst Gratification and Mobile Prosumers

Personal validation through numeric markers is not unique to social media sites, nor does it have its origin there. A focus on quantitative considerations as being linked to value has taken many forms, from the number of possessions owned, number of home runs, pinball machine scores and bank account balances, to name only a few. However, it is with social media that users can assess their social value via the numeric counters of likes, friends, followers and comments in a synchronous communication environment. This real-time affordance of the network allows for instant notification of any increase in these numeric values, like a stock market ticker. Moreover, these notifications may induce in the user a small burst of gratification akin to a dopamine hit. One anecdotal way of testing this was through an experiment I repeated in several iterations of my social networking course over the last six years. The 'digital detox' experiment asked students to voluntarily remove the use of social media for three days,[15] and to report in diary form what they were feeling in their own words. In order to encourage honesty, reporting on relapses when they occurred was encouraged, and the diaries were anonymised. Of the recurring reported sentiments across several non-linked student cohorts, were narratives closely resembling that of addiction, withdrawal, and feelings of relief during relapse. In other cases, relapses were rationalised in much the same fashion as one might expect among some of those who return to the use of an addictive substance. What was of note was how often it was reported that notification services became the most common trigger for relapse. Some diarists described with some reflection on how responding to the notification provided an immediate sensation of pleasure and relief, an intensity shortly followed by a return to normal, a pattern resembling that of the chemical reward of the dopamine system.

Such conditioning to stimuli is not new in itself: prior to the internet, there may have been a similar dopamine-like response to the ringing of a telephone or finding a letter in a mailbox. But if there is a chemical incentive to the activity of increasing one's online social capital, it may be strongly linked to both the system of real-time notifications, as well as the psychological attachment to seeing an increase in numeric counters that are 'proof' of increasing value. Such an increase in quantitative values may be mistakenly correlated to an increase in social or personal value of the user in the similar way some may mistake an increase in personal wealth as an increase in personal and societal value. The acquisition of higher numerical values does not necessarily always correspond to an increase in effort. To reuse the video game metaphor, one of the more popular mobile game genres would be the 'idle' variety where the numeric values of a character, the time-based production of some building, or the accumulation of the in-game currency will occur while the player is not actively logged into the game. This sets up both a feeling of surprise and satisfies a feeling of progress and growth. In sum, validation and accomplishment through a process of accumulation, and the largely capitalist notion of growth for growth's sake.

Inasmuch as practices of accumulation, growth for growth's sake, is part of the constellatory ideological framework of neoliberal capitalism, so too is the notion of mobility. Invocations of mobility will generally tend toward understanding in terms of spatiality and temporality. One is considered mobile if one is not rooted or fixed in a particular location, with a freedom to be migratory or nomadic. When taken in a positive register, this mobility is by choice (rather than, say, a forced migration due to civil war or natural disaster). In terms of temporality, mobility refers to the ability to access content and services at any time. The social aspects of mobility, understood in more corporeal terms, is enabled by a distinctly *mobile* technology that is portable and can access content on a global scale. As opposed to improvements in transportation technologies in the last two centuries, mobility shifts into a distinctly cognitive and person-centred concept whereby one can be nomadic in the virtual domain while remaining rooted or fixed in place. Mobility, then, comes to signify technological mediation of content on demand anytime, anywhere. Perry et al. (2001) critique the 'anytime, anywhere' rhetoric of mobility as it still emerges out of the implications of hardware and software design. These proprietary forms of hardware and software commit the user to develop or access content through very specific channels. This fits comfortably within the principles of neoliberalism whereby choice is trumpeted yet restricted to a pre-set list of options it sanctions: 'neoliberal logic is best conceptualised not as a standardized universal apparatus, but a migratory technology of governing that interacts with situated sets of elements and circumstances' (Ong 2007, 5). What is of note is that *digital* mobility – no longer necessarily tied to time and space – is spoken in almost the same breath as flexibility, and thus granting some form of convenience and 'power' to the individual user.

Such mobility and its closely related virtue-word of flexibility is already witnessed in many workplaces where the worker's subjectivity is cultivated through constants skills upgrading to make them employable in a competitive global market, but this apparent empowerment acts as a cover for lack of job security (Moore 2010). Despite claims of self-expressive empowerment, the down-shifting responsibilisation of users does not come with actual power. In fact, power is retained within the network while risk is distributed to the user-base. What we see is 'a shift from exchange to competition in the principle of the market' based on inequality rather than equivalence (Foucault 2008, 118). This is little more than a part of the fundamental shift from Fordism to flexible production regimes, packaged in the seemingly positive idea of the creative economy. What we see is an actual retrenchment strategy perpetrated by social networks that seek to enhance their own centralised control over data collection and distribution.

No longer strictly a disciplinary society, but one of control, the mechanisms that carry out control practices aligned with neoliberal economic thought govern and steer what content is visible, and how it is to be distributed, to guard against the kind of a feeling of ataxia – a loss of genuine control – that might cause users to reflect and question the very tools and principles upon which these platforms rely. It is no longer acceptable in some circles to critique social media and what it may mean ideologically, but to either acquiesce in a spirit of resignation or to wilfully embrace the Joyful Science that marks the techno-optimist drive. The digital model for social interaction, when it is packaged as inevitable or simply necessary to realise the goals of the network's desire to expand into larger markets, leaves very little choice for users but to comply and thus conform to the new model if they wish to participate. The digital model then serves the double function of enforcing compliance among users with the terms of service they agree to, in addition to extracting surplus value from them.

One of the possibly hidden dangers of relying more on social media may be in how these are aligned with aspects of new managerialist-style tactics of surveillance and 'quality control' in terms of principal-agent relations. In the latter situation, content visibility and distribution, user interface changes, and shifts in how data is collected, becomes packaged as a benefit providing more quality and efficiency for users. The power of these increasingly cybernetic networks to surveil (or work with other entities to provide surveillance data), and channel select content, does not seem to speak favourably to user-empowerment. Instead, users are in effect data-farmed as inputs in a feedback system that will restrain choice and possibly shape their behaviour through what the platform decides to make visible. The discursive shaping of the term 'platform' has implications on how the information is distributed and made available, steering a middle course between what is:

> socially and financially valuable, between niche and wide appeal. And, as with broadcasting and publishing, their choices about what can appear, how it is organized, how it is monetized, what can be removed and why, and what the technical architecture allows and prohibits, are all real and substantive interventions into the contours of public discourse. (Gillespie 2010, 359)

Social media sites are not identical in form or function to the industrial sites of confinement where production took place, but instead a new dispersive instrument delegates tasks via digital controls, prompts to contribute content such as a status update, to respond to new content, etc. Social media sites may not be accurately classed as sites of production, and may have entered into the phase of metaproduction where what 'it seeks to sell is services, and what it seeks to buy, activities. It's a capitalism no longer directed toward production but toward products, that is, toward sales and markets' (Deleuze 1995, 181). The product in this case – user-generated content – is not produced as much as it is transformed, and it is achieved through the digital medium of its collection and delivery. The automation that goes along with this shift in data collection and algorithmic distribution opens up the mass of users and their content to global economic flows, possibly leveraged as branding instruments by social media sites to take control of new potential markets, and thus balance the two functions of *marketing* to its 'outside' and *monitoring* on its 'inside.'

When users of social media are restricted in terms of their choice to use the proprietary social software available, there is in this way a very clear command and control mechanism by which there is a push for standardisation and centralisation of online experience and the goal of content generation with more data capture. The transformation of organic social exchange into a social delivery *system* turns away from the species-being of human communication and social fulfilment through interaction and towards executability, predictability and back-end profitability.

> Spurious 'technological' developments [...] are those which are encapsulated by a ceremonial power system whose main concern is to control the use, direction, and consequences of that development while simultaneously serving as the institutional vehicle for defining the limits and boundaries upon that technology through special domination efforts of the legal system, the property system, and the information system (Junker 1980, n.p.)

It is this 'ceremonialist' hangover whereby social networks solidify power and wield the instruments (social software) to increase it, while it simultaneously re-inscribes the values of the elite. When it comes to the power of the users of the digital technologies, they can be said to surrender their labour to the functions dictated by the implications of social software design: 'The message behind the neutrality of screens is not that we are the organization. The real message, to be grasped, is that without the organization, we are nothing' (Thiry-Cherques 715).

The ongoing aestheticisation of social media technologies is packed behind the optimistic and glittering generality of what is one of neoliberalism's most favoured terms: innovation. Despite its frequent invocation, the term innovation is rarely precisely defined, nor are its implications addressed. Innovation can be seen as largely part of a discursive formation whereby certain assumptions on value are put forth and aligned with positive associations of (linear) progress, change, and novelty. A survey of the vast literature that touts innovation demonstrates inconsistency in its application, pending context, and attempts have been made to arrive at a unified consensus as to what innovation means, or how it is to be measured (Adams et al. 2006, 22). Attempts to construct a universal definition have taken the form of extensive literature reviews on the subject, and parsing out specific attributes such as the nature, type, stages, social context, means and aim of innovation (Baregeh et al. 2009, 1331–2). Inasmuch as procedural and attributional clarifications may assist in better operationalising efforts in the domain of innovation, left untouched are the assumptions that innovation in itself is positive. As Emma Jeanes (2006) rightly argues with an appeal to Deleuze on what is and is not 'creativity', the mantra of 'innovate or else' is uncritical and the champions of innovation rhetoric staunchly resist criticism. The 'innovation theology' seems inextricably bound to accountancy principles of finding efficient ways to reduce costs and leverage human capital in a perceived threatening, Darwinised economic environment of global hyper-competitiveness.

Accumulation and Time: 'Time is Money'

One of the goals of capitalism is to increase the rate of production over shorter spans of time by seeking efficiencies and rationalising production. During the rise of industrialisation, several techniques were introduced to achieve this end, be it through Babbage's idea of the division of labour into functional specification, standardisation of labour toward mass production, increasing mechanisation, and the application of Taylor's theory of scientific management. Furthermore, the conquering of space through the development of transportation networks such as the railways and communication through the telegraph enabled shorter time intervals for the exchange of goods, services, and information. Today, a global network of shipping routes by land and sea, in addition to methods of just-in-time production to decrease speculation and inventory costs, increased automation, and even the proposed use of drone technologies for the delivery of goods, has shortened the time in the production process as well as bringing a host of goods and services to market much faster. Speed and efficiency in supply chain management, for instance, are generally the hallmarks of a neoliberal economy. However, in the shadow of these gains is increasing reliance on super-exploited sweatshop labour, environmental damage and a growing pool of precarious labour while other types of jobs have been eliminated due to automation.

Capitalism relies on acceleration as its strategy to increase accumulation, and this is no different in the domain of social media where a growth of subscribers to whom will be crowdsourced the tasks of the subscriber base is part of the strategy for social media's financial success. With respect to social media, users are sold *experiences* via the services of the social media site, while advertisers are sold *space* according to the processed data of users' labour time and personal information. If the goal is to accelerate the rate at which commodities are sold in shorter time frames, refined tactics have been used such as algorithmic sorting and the outsourcing of the function of the commodification of experience to the users who depend on the social media service. These flexible arrangements for more efficient forms of accumulation becomes an embedded practice in neoliberal capitalism (Harvey 2005).

Accumulation of real capital through the extraction of surplus value from digital labour functions at the heart of large social media corporations, but the question turns to how this practice has migrated in a new form into a cultural norm online where users compete and adopt strategies to accumulate more social capital faster, seeking means by which the returns on labour time investment can be higher. Robert Hassan's (2009) concept of network time identifies behaviours that seem patterned by the economic aspects of prevailing neoliberal capitalism. Our social time ever more becomes colonised by digital labour time, and so social time becomes another segment in the chain of production so that it even becomes (socially) produced in line with the speed and expectations of the social media upon which it may be experienced. Various associated behaviours may follow, possibly explained by this patterning by a dominant neoliberal capitalist ethos that is already embedded in the social media network architecture itself. One may then cue the instrumentalist, pragmatic forms of social capital accumulation as yet another form of flexible strategy, but also the less savoury behaviours of aggressive competition, self-promotion, and a lack of empathy in social interactions online. Moreover, the social media sphere is enlarged in scope, reach, and perceived importance until ever more it becomes – to use Lieven de Cauter's (2004) term – encapsulated, or within the kind of fishbowl virtual world of an enormous network spectacle.

The conversion of actual capitalistic tendencies to the social capitalist structures of user-based accumulation has not somehow resolved the issues of inequality or resolved any of the deep-seated contradictions of capital. Instead, neoliberal capitalism has imprinted itself on the sociocultural dimension of social media, if not exercised a complete appropriation of culture and multiple publics. Other forms of inequality may simply be distributed differently, but the inequalities still exist, if not also some alarming upticks in the amount of sexist, racist and homophobic attacks on social media that give voice to fringe hate groups to amplify the historical use of power against marginalised groups.

Moreover, users seeking to increase their social capital are paying in real money and time to do so. Although it may be tempting to think that payment is toward access to a social marketplace, given the labour time involved on social media that colonises leisure time, it is more appropriate to understand it as a social factory. As Fuchs succinctly tells us, '[c]orporate social media prosumption is a form of continuous primitive accumulation of capital that turns non-commodified leisure time into productive labour time that generates value and profit for capital' (Fuchs 2014, 116).

In this chapter we encountered many instances where the social aspect of social media becomes effectively colonised by neoliberal and communicative capitalism as a form of work-time, and that an increasing sense of necessity has normalised the use of social media. We took on board the insights of Jodi Dean's communicative capitalism to track the fantasies that enshroud and mythologise a great deal of social media activity, while tentatively offering a fourth fantasy. We are also witnessing that those who seek to increase their 'share' of online social capital may either resort to gaming the system or be compelled by the demands of a workplace to adopt the risk and responsibility of becoming mobile and flexible sites of production and accumulation. Such acts may border on the mercenary and unscrupulous, and yet only serve to empower the circulation of capital by those powerful owners of social networking sites. Ultimately, we can pin blame on major network corporations for selling users on an ideology that seems to privilege the social, and yet uses this as a means to increase our participation and contribution activity on these networks for their own financial gain. This kind of commodification of the social is hardly a new observation; theorists such as Christian Fuchs and José van Dijck have amply demonstrated this. However, the accumulation of online social capital and all the gamesmanship that it may entail adds yet another layer of enticement for us to contribute according to principles that mimic market-centric capitalism with the veneer of the social as a way of rationalising the pursuit of these online 'high scores.' Does this pursuit of accumulation make us more empowered, socially whole, and happy, or does it simply route us back into the same or similar forms of alienation Marx speaks of with respect to the extraction of surplus value from labour?

It is my own view that the 'lure' of social media via the self-promotional and gamesmanship tactics to increase one's online 'score' exacerbates alienation, and particularly by substituting a more substantial social connection online with its mere appearance through accumulation efforts that valorise the individual over community. We become divided competitors in the social media 'factory' as opposed to united community collaborators. The solution is to create and maintain a social media platform that evades the capture of capitalism, rejects its alienating principles, and focuses primarily on community over competition or profit.

Main Points

- Communicative capitalism abstracts social power as something quantifiable, and imbued with the promise of exchange value. The user becomes the site of production for the social media site.

- The allure and convenience of measuring online social capital accumulation comes with the false promise of increasing personal validation and wealth through vigorously competitive social comparison. This presents a fantasy of equivalence and conversion through a mode of standardisation of comparative measurement.
- There are two interrelated circuits of capitalism operating here. At the user end, it is the pursuit of accumulating a higher score of social capital through strategic use of the platform, commodification of the self-as-brand, and the buying and selling of likes. The real value is situated in the enclosing capitalist circuit whereby the social media company monitors the inside (users) to sell users *experiences*, while marketing to an outside (advertisers) by selling *space*.
- The more users pursue online social capital via social media sites, the more social media sites profit through the exploitation of the user base and the collection of their data. Social media sites are the real beneficiaries of this simulated social marketplace economy that can primarily only promise a higher 'score' in a gamified environment designed and controlled by the social media site.

CHAPTER 4

From Accumulation to Alienation: Marx and Veblen

The previous chapter discussed some of the features of social capitalism and the nature of these flexible and mobile regimes to gain insight into the phenomenon of accumulation that occurs on social media, particularly with a view to online social capital's most readily apparent symbol: numeric counters that validate, valorise, and give some semblance of value to user production on social media. This is paired with the way social media sites accumulate and aggregate user data for its own purposes, not for the benefit of the user. Both of these forms of accumulation are not only circuits unto themselves, but are linked.

To what degree users on social media are alienated and exploited through their acts of online social capital accumulation must be answered in light of the specific affordances of social media, while also drawing from the works of Marx and Veblen. Given this chapter's focus on alienation and exploitation, appealing to the works of Marx would be an obvious choice; however, this will only represent part of the story, for there is also the institutional economic approach developed by Thorstein Veblen that may speak to social media users' conspicuous acts online. Combined, this will tell a more dynamic story about how alienation and exploitation manifest in the pursuit of online social capital. Both Marx and Veblen will agree that alienation is a major issue to be addressed and ameliorated, despite being in disagreement about its origins. For Marx, a raising of class consciousness is key to superseding alienation and exploitation, whereas for Veblen it is to wrest the power of invention and creation away from purely pecuniary interests, but also to raise consciousness in a different way: to get people to question their own conspicuous consumption and ritualistic behaviour. In the simplest of terms, the way out of alienation and exploitation leads, for Marx, to the classless society where workers own the means of production; for Veblen, to a society where education and technology will not be

---

How to cite this book chapter:
Faucher, K. X. 2018. *Social Capital Online: Alienation and Accumulation*. Pp. 61–86. London: University of Westminster Press. DOI: https://doi.org/10.16997/book16.e.

influenced or controlled by private sector interests, and instead be an available resource held in common.

There is still considerable debate as to whether social media use is increasing or decreasing exploitation, and the same for alienation. In the classic Marxist literature, exploitation exacerbates alienation, yet some authors such as Eran Fisher (2010, 2012), Boltanski and Chiapello (2005, 2006) make the compelling argument that the situation with social media today presents a very different case, whereby there is a split between exploitation and alienation, with social media increasing exploitation of its users while user alienation decreases. Whereas exploitation increases from data collection of users and user-generated labour on social media, users have more control over how they choose to express themselves and through the benefits of sharing and creativity, thus decreasing their alienation. Although the affordances of social media for creation, sharing and engagement exist, the instrumentalist logic underpinning capitalist social media pervades even these behaviours. When these benefits are geared toward, or measured by, accumulation of online social capital, this seems to bring alienation back into focus.

Subsequent to expanding upon the issues of exploitation and alienation as part of two interlinked circuits of accumulation, it can be argued that the pursuit of online social capital as expressed by the numeric counters reifies capitalist ideologies through a form of mimicry in an abstract or artificial economy within an actual economy of data collection and marketing. Furthermore, in the process of making use of social media to compete in the games of online social capital, users may in fact be producing themselves as branded digital objects, and thus can be said to be alienated from themselves as their own subjectivity is caught up in the circuit of capitalist production. As Lukács says of reification, 'a relation between people takes on the character of a thing and thus acquires "phantom objectivity," an autonomy that seems so strictly rational and all-embracing as to conceal every trace of its fundamental nature: the relation between people.' (Lukács 1972, 83). This phantom objectivity, core to Marx's arguments on commodity fetishism, is present whenever labour is appropriated by another. Thus in this exploitative situation of extracting surplus value, this precipitates alienation.

Alienation

Marx's core ideas on alienation function as an interrelated whole. There are four facets of alienation:

Alienation from One's Labour	Alienation from other Labourers
Alienation from the Product of One's Labour	Alienation from One's self

Each of these facets of alienation differs in degree and expression pending the qualities and conditions pertaining to each person, productive capacities, and labour arrangement. Marx's analysis points to how these may differ in terms of class, and he spends more of his time focusing on the proletariat as the class most negatively impacted by the conditions of alienation. It can be simplified to this: *what I do, what I make, who I relate with, who I am.*

With the division of labour, the creation of wage-labour, and the rise of the factory system, there would be a commensurate separation that would precipitate increased alienation, an end to the unity between human nature and labour through the inorganic and de-subjectifying aspects of capitalist production.

In the first of the four major separations, Marx points to a worker's separation from the work being performed, as the worker no longer has a say in what is produced, or how it is produced (Marx 1964, 13). In a traditional factory context, someone working on an assembly line is instructed to manufacture parts in a standardised fashion using techniques that are set in advance, thus enabling a kind of deskilling compared to the artisanal and craft labour more common to the pre-industrial era. This would also apply to a worker in the largely industrialised field of the fast food industry who has no choice but to prepare pre-set meals using pre-defined techniques to produce the standardised menu item. This form of alienation through routinised labour limits what the Autonomists will call the 'worker's affect' – the capacity for creation and to derive something transformative from the act of one's labour.

In the second aspect, we have the worker's separation from the product being produced. Not only does the product of the labour not belong to the worker, but the worker cannot choose to make alterations to the way the product is produced, nor can the worker decide how the product will be used (Marx 1964, 15). The product does not satisfy any need for the worker except that which is external to the productive activity: a wage. The worker's creative and cognitive potential is not permitted to develop under these conditions, and so is treated by the capitalist as something like a source of fuel for the capitalist production machine.

In the third aspect, the worker is separated from other workers by the capitalist tendency to divide and rule, pitting workers in competition against one another rather than to encourage collaboration (Marx 1964, 17). This is problematised further in our era by the advent of neoliberal economic-inspired forms of casualisation, telecommuting, zero-contract hours, and the sustained attack against unionisation – all of which are somehow touted in an optimistic fashion as providing benefits to the worker in terms of flexibility (casualisation and zero-contract hours), convenience (telecommuting) and rewarding individual merit while diminishing the value of workplace solidarity. This is exacerbated in the information economy: dividing workers spatially, temporally, and in encouraging individualist competition does not easily permit the kind of class consciousness Marx so strongly advocated, and it further seeks to increase profit upon practices that increase alienation and exploitation.

The fourth aspect binds all the other aspects together. The worker's separation and alienation from the self is the end result of this form of estranged labour in the capitalist system (Marx 1964, 16). A life dedicated to the production of things that not only must have an immediate utility in the profit system but is also the property of others, may serve as ingredients to the further immiseration and dehumanisation of the worker. Added to this that the activity of the worker, and the worker's relation to other workers, is afflicted by this pervasive alienation, reduces the human being to subsistence activity: live to work, work to live.

The concepts of alienation and exploitation are strongly correlated given that, in Marxist analysis, the result of exploitation is alienation. So, we must ask if (i) social media users are exploited and, (ii) if, as a result of exploitation, they are also alienated. Furthermore, we must ask if the pursuit of online social capital is a feature tied to this exploitation and alienation.

Fisher (2012) splits alienation from exploitation rather than conflating the two. It might otherwise be understood that the two are complementary or entwined functions of capitalism, but Fisher independently asserts that, in social media, the increase in exploitation operates by a tacit promise of reducing the alienation of social media participants:

> [T]he relations of production entailed by social media are based on an implicit social contract which allows media companies to commodify the communication produced by users (i.e. exploiting them) in return for giving them control over the process of producing communication, and expanding their opportunity for de-alienation. (180)

Social media on its own may not be alienating if we consider alienation to mean that users are somehow separated from fully realising themselves, others, their labour, or the product of their labour. In fact, there may be some reason to believe that social media may be a de-alienating force. The capacity for self-expression is limited only by the affordances of the network platform, as well as the means to connect and share information and values with others.

Fisher points to a dialectical relationship between social media exploitation and alienation; namely, that the communicative benefits of social media provide opportunities for self-expression and content sharing, etc., but this only occurs as exploitation of those users increases:

> [I]n order to be de-alienated, users must communicate and socialize: they must establish social networks, share information, talk to their friends and read their posts, follow and be followed. By thus doing they also exacerbate their exploitation. (Fisher 2012, 179)

The promise of de-alienation through social media entails authentic self-expression and the cultivating of online relations which, in turn, provide the means for further exploitation by the network platform as users provide more surplus value by communicating more frequently, sharing photos, etc. As alienation decreases, exploitation increases – even if a majority of users do not perceive themselves as being exploited. Users become 'reconceptualised in the digital discourse as atomized nodes of entrepreneurship in the network of social production' (Fisher 2010, 142). In this process of apparent emancipatory affordances for flexibility and creativity in this social production, Fisher makes the strong point that although this may be a 'dealienating' force, the turn to a form of entrepreneurial individualism and atomisation of users-as-nodes comes at the expense of more collaborative social structures as the work produced online becomes increasingly privatised. The increase in user productivity aligns with many of the touted virtues of neoliberal capitalism: workers who are adaptable, flexible, and atomised as opposed to fixed, secure and united by solidarity and collectivity. This, in turn, opens up more opportunities for the capitalist to engage in exploitative behaviour.

It would be too strong an assertion to say that social media de-alienates all its users, and particularly if we are unclear about what degree of alienation each of the users experiences prior to engaging in social media. At best, we might say that social media provides some or many with the means by which they can indulge in their positive aspects to be creative and engage in meaningful interpersonal relations not afforded them in their everyday work lives. The use of social media does not necessarily alleviate the alienation one might experience in the workplace or in offline life. Instead, social media's emancipatory benefits may function as a creative social outlet. However, this is not always the case. For those who work exclusively on social media as their profession, their opportunities are prescribed by the demands of their employment. One example is account ownership: litigation concerning cases where an employee who operates a company social media account (whether in their own name, that of the business – or both) is terminated is still without much precedent. The company may argue on the lines of trade secrets or that the acquisition of followers was due exclusively to the employee's connection to the company, and that those followers are the property of the company and not the employee.

Secondly, social media provides a *potential* for engaging in communicative exchanges and interpersonal relations that are meaningful and not alienating.

Thirdly, the increased integration of digital environments that augment even an offline world may also be indicative of an increase in alienation: the erosion of offline face-to-face social skills, a decrease in empathy, the unspoken demand to spend more time online to engage in instant communication feedback without being afforded the time for more meaningful reflection, an indifference to the outside world, the prospect that users become more like stimulus-response machines who react to online notifications as though thoroughly behaviourally conditioned, and the ways by which some online services augment reality by ideological means, so that a map of the landscape points almost solely to where one can consume products and services.

Lastly, there is both the structure and content of social media communication as potentially alienating. By structure, it is the network frames in which users are prompted to input their personal information, hobbies, interests and so forth for the ease of data mining; by content it is the proportion of online communication dedicated to discussing consumer products and services, endorsement of brands, etc.

None of these objections render Fisher's argument of de-alienation insufficient, but they point to circumstances where we cannot say for absolute certainty, in all cases, that alienation decreases with the use of social media. There are numerous examples of de-alienation with the emergence of social media, but there are also counter examples.

We see further how alienation is exacerbated by the embedded and largely unseen algorithms operative in our social software. As Dyer-Witheford (1999), Terranova (2000, 2004) and Pasquinelli (2011) point out, in different ways, that our human processes become encoded as machinic form, gradually reducing our capacity to act (our affect) in the name of speed and convenience. It is not just routinised labour that is gradually displaced by the algorithms, but creative choices. Instead, we may be presented with 'recommendations' for whom to connect with, digital reminders that we have not participated for some time, and served a selective list of items in our network newsfeed at the exclusion of others that limit our capacity to act in response to only those items in the newsfeed we are presented with. Even the process of expanding our networks – itself a product of the logic that more connections is intrinsically better as it may increase our social or professional opportunities – may be facilitated by social media. A good example might be in consenting in allowing the site to access a list of contacts via one's email account, offering to send on one's behalf a batch invitation email to subscribe or connect. Sites such as LinkedIn make use of this option, and will match existing users to one's existing email contacts for a mass invite to connect. Even in those cases where one takes the time to scrutinise each potential connection, LinkedIn provides a simple and editable boilerplate invitation message.

The following table may indicate a few of the still existing alienation 'flashpoints' associated with social media:

ALIENATION	SOCIAL MEDIA USERS
From One's Labour	1) The 'how' and 'what' partially prescribed by the framework of the social media site. 2) Automated processes that bypass creative choice. 3) Prescriptive terms of service that justify deletion of content deemed by that service to be in violation, including creative and political content.
From the Product of One's Labour	1) User content is the property of the social media site with its exclusive right to modify or distribute. 2) Data as the processed 'product' of labour is a commodity sold to third parties using a model reminiscent of factorage. 3) The content of the labour having no productive labour value, only that it has been performed and can be data mined for, say, keywords.

ALIENATION	SOCIAL MEDIA USERS
From Others	1) Privileging competition over collaboration and cooperation. 2) Connection for connection's sake. 3) Digital reputation management in construction of self-as-representation, and as digital object. 4) Algorithms that determine visible content.
From the Self	1) Representation of idealised self via the social media site's affordances. 2) Value migration so that offline experience is worth 'less' if not ported to the online milieu for validation by the social network. 3) Operating according to 'network time' as opposed to free time. 4) Selective exposure and self-selecting networks narrowing one's understanding of the self and world. 5) Expectations to react and respond rapidly as opposed to reflect and act at one's own pace. 6) Occupation of time spent away from personal reflection. 7) Vicarious living and social comparator activities. 8) Quantification of social activity as a measure of personal social value.

Alienation, Deskilling, and the Online Social Economy

There is yet another aspect of alienation that ought to be addressed given Marx's dire warnings over how capitalist technologies deskill workers and create the conditions for dead labour. Although not all social media users rely on social media in the classical sense of earning a wage for their labour, there is a haunting echo of work being performed and the gradual deskilling of that work transformed by convenient user experience. In tracking the rise of the world wide web, even the creation of websites may no longer require knowledge of HTML as there are several web hosting providers that make the building of a personal website possible with no coding knowledge whatsoever. In the world of social media, the freedom of design one had in such milieus as MySpace has been sacrificed for ease of use by constructing a rigid user-interface architecture where all elements share uniformity with every other social media user's account – a form of 'freedom' *from* design. This may actually serve to limit user action potentiality, prescribed by the network architecture (Papachrissi, 2009). On the one hand, the removal of barriers of specialisation required to build and maintain one's involvement in these sites has permitted more inclusive entry by the populace, whereby this specialisation is mostly undertaken 'in-house' by employees of the social media site.

If we take the accumulation of online social capital as a form of work, and one that relies on a huge social graph linked to competition, it is of some value to recall Marx's statement: 'All improvements in the means of communication, for example, facilitate the competition of workers in different localities and turn local competition into national' (1975 [1847], 423). However, we might update the statement to reflect the expansive shift to the global scale, following the associated reification of a global economy. Users are 'plugged into' the circuits of capital, especially on social media sites where production, consumption, marketing and circulation converge.

What links online social capital accumulation to social digital alienation? To take a strictly Marxist interpretation of capital as a social relation, what mediates this relation? In the case of social capital as something that is accumulated, what is accumulated is the image of social capital through its representation: namely the numeric indicators that confer a sense of value and currency related to the general economy of users on any social media site platform. These relations among users become objectified as counters and are linked to the apparent value of the user. Already, the user in this general economy is abstracted as a representation of the self, modified as a digital object through which the user produces content in an effort to accumulate social capital.

The larger the user base or general economy of a particular platform, the larger the potential volume of transactions in this space, as well as the potential to accumulate online social capital. The more active users a site hosts, the more chances one has to sell one's productions in exchange for the approbation cues that underpin social capital. However, if the global economy is any indication of a pattern that might be applied here, a larger economy can never guarantee any one individual's wealth accumulation. Worse, it creates greater disparity due to several factors. It may also create the conditions of 'many sellers, few buyers'. This has increasingly become the case for those who produce video content for such enormously popular sites such as YouTube, being the largest single 'buyer' of user video content. This was identified by Ulises Mejias when he correctly calls this relation a form of oligopsony as opposed to an oligopoly (2013).

This feature of oligopsony is directly in play when we consider that those who engage in online self-branding in order to acquire more online social capital effectively 'sell' their labour power to the social networking site. If the goal of a user is to accumulate the largest amount of online social capital, it may seem logical to create a visible profile on a social network with a huge social graph. A network with a billion users as opposed to a thousand presents a higher potentiality for accumulating a larger amount of online social capital resources. However, the oligopsonistic nature of social media has emerged as dominant players like Facebook have either outpaced or absorbed its competitors, leading to fewer providers of social media services. It is the enormous user base that sells their labour and personal brand to these major social media sites in exchange for the services provided.

There is still one way in which the dominant social media sites retain their oligopolistic nature: by being the sellers of data. So it is in this way that major sites such as Facebook, Twitter and YouTube can operate as oligopsonists to both users and those who seek to purchase advertising space on a site with one of the largest potential markets in the world.

Alienation and Veblen

The Marxist formulation of alienation is perpetuated by class division and capitalist exploitation, but it is far from the whole story when speaking of alienation in an online context. What Marx does not fully address is the cultural means by which institutions of power reproduce their status, and how individuals who seek advantage may emulate certain behaviours that are largely ritualistic in nature. Whereas Marx focuses on *class* struggle as part of the broader dialectic of chance and necessity, Veblen points to *status* and its forms of display as the human invariant.

Thorstein Veblen was among the first to recognise economics as thoroughly entangled or embedded in social institutions. In this age with the rise of democratised and digital forms of social institutions alongside traditional ones, it is feasible to apply the idea of an embedded economy in the social institutions of digital media, and particularly to extend the definition of social institution to such corporate entities as Facebook, Twitter and others. The very model from which all social media as private corporations follow is a distinctively market-based logic of accumulation. Veblen reminds us of the ritualistic nature of institutions, and warns against the depredations of pecuniary interest that impede true innovation.

Veblen identifies a fundamental dichotomy between an institution's more ceremonial function with its resistance to change, and the instrumental role technology can play in progress and change. Whilst he does argue to some degree about the manner in which technology can shape culture and society, his critics may be unfair to impute to him an outright technological determinist stance.

Traditional institutions in their most ceremonial aspects rely heavily on status-based hierarchies. The complexity of these institutions and the vested interests of those who occupy the power roles would characteristically be resistant to change, equating it with disruption and possibly jeopardising status. The threat of new technologies can precipitate change and disruption, be it crisis, resistance or adoption. Ideally, Veblen argues, adjustment is essential and technology should occupy a more instrumental role.

It may be argued that much of the activity on social networks has an instrumental basis, due to the nature of computerised networks operating by a network logic and epistemology. The instrumental use of social networks by the corporate hosts can be seen in the way it acquires user data for its pecuniary purposes, whereas the instrumental use for the network user may be indexed on the accumulation of online social capital that can later be leveraged for some extrinsic purpose. Both ends of the network – host and user – are caught up in a distinctly economic instrumentality, performing a cost-benefit analysis of time spent, connections made and reputation management as a means of increasing a return on investment.

The focus here on online social goods of conspicuous production and consumption is restricted to the social behaviours that are geared toward increasing online social capital and claiming stake in the attention economy. Moreover, it is important to question whether the terms of prosumer or produser are sufficient to replace the producer-consumer distinction, even when considering user-led collaborative processes for content creation. Contrary to Bruns (2009), production and consumption may still be useful and operative terms. If we were to turn to pre-internet media, a reader who submits a letter to the editor of a newspaper or a listener who participates in a radio call-in show, could theoretically be classed under prosumption. However, the functions of production and consumption are still clear and distinct. The fanfare associated with the benefits of prosumption (Ritzer and Jurgenson 2010) and produsage (Bruns 2009) are said to inform a radical shift in economic models (Benkler 2006), while possibly overlooking the predatory and exploitative aspects of freely created and distributed content (Fuchs 2010).

The alliance between the emergence and rapid proliferation of ICTs and neoliberal ideology has already been recognised by several authors (Castells 1996; Dyer-Witheford 1999; Harvey 2005; Bulut et al., 2009; Neubauer 2011). The specific context in which digital social environments may find themselves may have adopted in part some of the ideological shibboleths of informational capitalism insofar as that context represents:

> [a] dialectic between forces and relations of production and consumption (that) revolves around technologies specifically designed (and marketed) to enhance, capture, transmit, and store human capacities such as creativity, communication, co-operation, and cognition' (Manzerolle 2014, 206).

Under these conditions, production itself is transformed, and social prosumption in the online environment comes ever more to resemble competitive business.

There is a great deal of contention between the Marxist and Veblenian views regarding alienation. For Marx, alienation is contingent upon the legal legitimation of private property and capitalist accumulation which alienates workers from their labour, the object of their labour, each other, and their own sense of self. For Veblen, alienation has its source in the predatory and tribal economy whereby such things as raids and acquisition were less about satisfying basic needs and more indexed on status-raising. In this movement, the instinct for workmanship is impoverished as 'work is irksome' and extravagant displays of wealth are required in Veblen's view of conspicuous consumption to explain the drive to display wealth as a status marker in societies. According to Veblen's theory of conspicuous consumption, consumption patterns are less indexed on durability and utility and more about status display. A silver spoon may tarnish and is a softer metal than steel, but it conveys status. Mapped unto the pursuit of accumulating social capital in an online context, there may be quite limited durability (due to novelty-effect) and utility (as it may not lead to actual wealth accumulation on the basis of the labour theory of value and that surplus value is extracted by the social media site). To be a YouTube star may not result in financial riches, but one may earn (an arguably temporary) cultural cachet.

Considering Veblen's theory of conspicuous consumption is in itself incomplete without contemplating that, on social media, there is also conspicuous production. If the goal of online social capital in the like economy is to be seen and raise one's status in a digital community, what one consumes in terms of content becomes conspicuous as a form of status display. Following particular online celebrities becomes part of a user's status in that they are choosing to be seen as being associated with that celebrity and that celebrity's values. Certainly not in all cases, as one can follow a politician and be disposed against her or him. In conspicuous production, the means by which users will display their status by posting images of a luxury vacation, expensive car, or some other form of luxury accessory may be performed in order to gain more likes while being seen as having good consumer taste and wealth. Such examples are plentiful on social media, such as the Instagram accounts RichRussianKids – which displays the luxurious lifestyles of the children of oligarch families – Rich Kids of Instagram, and others who use highly staged and filtered photos to portray lives of extreme wealth and privilege.

Such efforts at status display are not consigned to just that small segment of society with a great deal of wealth seeking to gain likes, but can be found emulated across social media in a variety of forms, including glamorous selfies, travel and adventure photos, professional status posts and even the popular genre of taking photos of one's food.[16] Beyond conveying signs of professional status or wealth, some forms of conspicuous display can take the form of broadcasting social activist causes such as adding an awareness ribbon on an avatar or in associating one's profile with highly regarded public figures.

One may also point to some social media sites' use of specific filters for enhancing photographs that may alter the visual appearance of objects or persons in order to make them appear more glamorous than they actually are. For Veblen, such acts of reputation management and self-curation would be signs of conspicuous display in a competitive environment of seeking attention and positive status. This does not yet include other forms of conspicuous status displays such as those that clearly have a metric for easy communication of a user's 'value' in a network. A large number of friends, followers and likes attests to a display of popularity and importance to the network. Beyond what one buys, it is the conversion to what one produces in terms of content that points to conspicuous display with a goal of gaining more approbation and having a community legitimise the status of the individual.

Conspicuous forms of production that seek to enhance online social status is conspicuous when one's labour is specifically indexed on transforming the use value of a communication event into an exchange value in the 'like' economy. By optimising one's digital profile and content production with a view of increasing quantified social capital, such behaviour can be understood as opportunistic, instrumental, and conspicuous.

If large financial markets are too complex, if not chaotic, their oscillations privy to allegedly rational actors making rational choices, does the same apply to the social market and to the development of social capital? If human instrumentality as a motivation for behaviour in making choices to leverage social capital for individual gain can be viewed in Veblenian terms as infused with the broader sociological conditions of conspicuous consumption as an evolutionarily cultural invariant from the time of predatory cultures to the modern day, this in itself might serve as an indictment against the over-optimistic assumptions related to social capital.

In Veblen's technical terminology, features of the social media environment may attest to an evaluative apparatus of the invidious by which others may be compared according to quantifiable measure. How many 'likes,' or 'friends' online may be a function of reducing the subjective qualities of 'social' and 'attention' to numerical considerations alone as a measure of popularity. Mapping free market principles onto social activity has become the norm in many digital environments, and so the qualitative value is subordinate to the quantitative, more easily apprehended by a digital audience in the assigning of value. But it is the appropriation of the social by pecuniary interests that both Marx and Veblen would agree in finding deeply problematic. If social activity is more of a spontaneous one that speaks to one of the essential features of our social being, we might recall Marx: 'in degrading spontaneous activity, free activity, to a means, estranged labour makes man's species life a means to his physical existence' (Marx 1972 [1844], 73). However, in the case of our labour directed to the accumulation of social capital, this may be performed for reasons that do not have anything to do with survival. That is, making online connections and producing content on social media is not a pre-requisite for obtaining the means for our subsistence. Food, shelter, and clothing are not contingent upon n number of likes on Facebook.[17]

The search for status enhancement through a conspicuously economic means is portrayed as a route to self-actualisation. For Veblen, it is this desire for status that is the driving force in scaling production beyond that of simply satisfying basic needs. Just as Veblen argues, those who seek status must seek ways of providing a demonstration of their pecuniary strength, generally through acts of wasteful consumption and unproductive uses of time, the same might be said with respect to the online social venues whereby it is not explicitly material wealth that is being generated and displayed for status enhancement, but a particularly social variety that is also measured in much the same manner as material wealth.

Veblen and Competitive Accumulation

At the heart of egocentric or instrumentalist online social capital is the drive toward accumulation strategies. In search of virtual goods as a marker of social class, actions directed to accumulation and conversion lead steadily to becoming the 'accepted badge of efficiency' whereby the 'possession of goods, whether acquired aggressively by one's own exertion or passively by transmission through inheritance from others, becomes a conventional basis of reputability' (Veblen 2010, 19). Accumulation should not be thought in strictly material terms or the goods that are trafficked on social media. Instead, accumulation takes on an objectivising approach to the myriad subjects who are subscribers to social media in that they can be accumulated as a sum of connections that further enhance the perceived status of the central 'node' (in a social network, each node is central to itself as an egocentric access point). Moreover, social approbation markers on social media linked to a quantity constructs the appearance of value of the posted content of a user on the basis of a number, which in non-economic terms represent affinity and approbation, but function as a standardised measure of social wealth: The higher the number, the higher the perceived value of the user, and so, 'the end sought by accumulation is to rank high in comparison with the rest of the community in point of pecuniary strength' (Veblen 2010, 20). In this case, the competitive nature of said environments is not linked to money, but according to the premium attributed to quantifiable social wealth.

Although digital environments appear to conform to an economy of abundance due to the ease of duplication of immaterial goods trafficked online as endemic to the nature of digital information flows, both the acquisition of meaningful social capital and the attention economy are still indexed on an economy of scarcity, and hence the requirement for competition to acquire these resources. The comparative and competitive drive among users may be technically defined, with reference to Veblen, as invidious insofar as the grading or rating of others is based on relative worth or value (Veblen 2010, 22). This invidiousness pervades social media as part of the evaluative framework by which others may be said to be judged against a measure of peculiar markers that are quantitative in nature.

Social wealth, earned or inherited by association with reputable or popular persons, is not yet social capital. In the games of online social capital, social wealth must be first transferred to the digital milieu in some measurable way whereby said wealth can be leveraged for producing capital. In other words, the truly social and qualitative must be transubstantiated as something quantitative that reduces or effaces the subjectively social. As the socially rich offline may have a higher probability of being socially rich online according to Social Enhancement Theory (Merton 1968), this transfer or exchange may prove of some facility to those who already enjoy a large number of social connections in the offline world. These must be reiterated and formalised in the online milieu by way of invitations to connect, thus mapping offline social wealth online as evidence of social wealth. One of the unique aspects of social media is that social connections and interactions become, pending privacy settings, visible to a spectator audience, perhaps in a similar way as 'Society Pages' in the past detailed the lives and gossip circulating about members of the upper classes. Social wealth may be seen as intrinsic use value, whereas its mediatisation and commodification in online social networks gives it a new status as exchange value in the form of social capital. What is being traded and gained, generally at a perceived profit, is the commodity form of the digital self and its associated productions. Investment occurs through conspicuous production, and later management, of the personal profile. This 'property' of the user, which is in effect subject to the rent paid to the host in non-monetary forms, is a trading area where is housed all the 'goods' of the user. These goods may take the simple form of preferred tastes in music or film. Or, it may also be the images that associate the user with some popular product, or a marker of affluence and the means of disposable income in the form of travel pictures of Europe. One of the distinct advantages of social media environments is in the way these environments are structured: the media-rich qualities and specific arrangement of the site with a strongly visual bias encourages acts of visual display. Such displays are ideal for meeting the real purpose of conspicuous consumption: to be seen and judged as being of higher status and thus worthy of more attention. All the while, the tireless algorithm in the background harvests keywords for the express purpose of monetising social interaction.

Of Social Profits to Be Made Via Conspicuous Display

Social displays, particularly of social wealth in the online venue, do not escape the cycle of commodification, which

> reduces ourselves and those we encounter on the internet to glamorous and attractive personae. Commodification becomes self-commodification, but shorn of context, engagement and obligation, of our achievements and failures, of our friends and enemies, of all the features that time has engraved on our faces and bodies – without all that we lack gravity and density. (Borgmann 64).

Albert Borgmann identifies the dehumanising and marketising aspect of the internet in general, but it may also equally apply to the specific conditions of social media. The commodification of the self (and relations with others) has increased as capital has discovered new ways of inscribing market logic within these social relations, drilling down right to the level where conversations online are mined for their data value and in the behaviour of some users to pursue a quasi-capitalist agenda of accumulation. When it comes to the all-important context of our social relations and their supporting narrative, context itself may become victim to the over-privileging of the immediate, particularly when we consider that content usually appears in reverse chronological order on social media, thus placing the responsibility on a user to seek 'below the fold' to reconstruct the context of our conversations and interactions. This privileging of immediacy and novelty is an endemic feature that feeds into our desire for stimulus through microburst gratification, the depreciation of social capital as numeric value affixed to any particular content, and the pressures or expectations of informationism.

Friends and visitors who are alerted to a user's posted content can affect that user's social marginal utility value by clicking on the 'like' button or supplying a comment. Said friends and visitors may be said to be consumers of the image produced by the user, but are presented with a means for an instant polling. Jean Baudrillard tells us that contemporary media presents objects as a form of test that minimises our contemplative time in order to prompt us to respond with a 'yes' or 'no' (Baudrillard 1993, 63), so too is the user also participating in the selective test of producing just the right content that will gain the approval of the audience. Such a production may be judged a failure if it does not provoke a response that is made public. The production may be judged subpar if it fails to reach a certain numerical threshold such as number of likes or comments. If the user seeks to maximise on their return on investment for the production-event, a certain understanding of what is considered appealing to the social network audience is required. However, this is little more than the necessary but not sufficient condition for increasing social profit; other factors play a role in determining how the market responds to the posted content, such as number of connections the user has, and how well advertised the event happens to be according to the proprietary algorithm of the SNS. This suggests that despite what efforts are made by the user to generate and disseminate content that might appeal to an audience, there are a variety of factors outside of his or her control that may have an appreciable effect on social profit. From the standpoint of the user, labour is required that aligns with variables of relevance and regularity of posted content to avoid one's production falling below the proverbial fold.

Maximising social profit in an environment where one's everyday life is relatively unknown by the connected members of one's network requires developing strategies for making it known by attracting attention to it. Veblen remarks that social situations with a higher number of participants requires tactics for increasing the visibility of conspicuous consumption (2010, 49). Such social arrangements with larger numbers of participants who, ostensibly, are also vying for recognition of status among transitory observers increases the probability and intensity of competition.

One may argue that it costs little or nothing to join social media at the user end. Participation does require the purchase of devices and internet services. The devices themselves are caught up in a rapid cycle of production-consumption-disposal, at times themselves being conspicuous fashion items. As social media continues to increase rich media content affordances, this places more strain on hardware to keep up, and eventually necessitates the replacement of the devices themselves. The material costs of participation aside, the price to be paid in using social media may include a variety of less tangible costs such as giving the SNS permission to use one's data, as well as *time* computed as a cost in the use of social media. In some ways, using social media can be an extravagant use of personal time, and thus may be classed as a form of conspicuous consumption. Veblen makes the critical distinction that use and consumption differs from ownership, just as indolence is not a measure of leisure (Veblen 2010, 16).

The user's social media profile is the immaterial product of the user's labour. As such, it enters into an online social commodities market in a competition for attention and an increase in personal social capital. The new techno-social reality of social media emulates market logics and redefines users as micro-capitalists of the self. This occurs within a unified social economy that is global, out of which a new and virtualised form of wealth can be produced through strategic social partnerships online. Such labour, despite occurring in a space dedicated to entertainment and socialising, may be intensive when all factors that go into the production of the digital self and personal social capital are considered, such as posting new content on a regular basis, profile management, and engaging in offline activities that will have value when posted online. This emulation of marketising practices in social terms agrees with the neoliberal understanding of the citizen as consumer, and allows for the creation of a space wherein the prosumers of social media can enjoy freedoms not experienced in the offline world:

> Consumer freedom was originally a compensation for the loss of the freedom and autonomy of the producer. Having been evicted from production and communal self-rule, the individual drive to self-assertion found its outlet in the market game. One can suppose that at least in part the continuing popularity of the market game derives from its virtual monopoly as the vehicle of self-construction and individual autonomy. The less freedom exists in the other spheres of life, the stronger is the popular pressure on the further extension of consumer freedom – whatever its cost. (Bauman 1988, 95)

Ideology of Social Competition

The neoliberal ideology with its aims of globally deregulated trade, flexible accumulation strategies and promotion of the arch-individual becomes the new bedrock of online social relations. Economic concerns become the spectacular enclosure and teleological purpose of social relations in a rapid feedback-based environment governed by ruthless competition. The highest values of this environment become competition and connection, all of which can be quantified and conspicuously displayed on one's profile. Neoliberalism operates by adopting a 'strong' paternalistic discourse that attempts to naturalise economic Darwinism (Peck and Tickell, 2002). All labour – and social – relations succumb to a discourse of competition that is global in scale. Social media can prove a competitive battleground for those who seek to accumulate the most online social capital. As online social capital is visible for public display, and not only made visible to the user, this can be considered an expression of conspicuousness, for the display of such metrics play a role in proving one's status and value.

The means to access these networks may in themselves speak to the devolution of the cachet item of leisure to the range of affordability by the petty household economy. The devices themselves are also caught up in this economy that, marketed as aesthetic utility and are specifically designed to be objects that appeal to aesthetic taste, while still speaking to 'utility.' The production – and subsequent disposal at the end of the device's life cycle – is the fruit of poor working conditions in developing nations. Marx's patent truism holds that the more luxurious the product, the less likely it is that those who manufacture it will be able to afford it. What is to be retained here is the emulative process of consuming apparent luxury goods that also appeal to the conscience of the consumer as something useful and necessary, for a purely aestheticised gadgetry with no obvious utility might not result in popular adoption and thus brisk sales to justify the rapid and enormous requirements of the production and consumption cycle. Where the conspicuousness of the device is on its own not enough to convince consumers to adopt it, other means are invented by which certain features unique to the device come pre-loaded and embedded with proprietary software that cannot be ported to a competitor device.

In a time of increasing economic austerity with its knock-on effects for a steadily shrinking middle class, it might be reasonable to assume that conspicuous consumption must be seen in terms of scalar adjustments that take into consideration depressed or stagnant wages and available credit. As discretionary consumer purchasing power in North America has softened (despite a modest increase in the consumer price index since the 2008 downturn), thus having a deleterious impact on profit, consumption practices might be seen to shift or to migrate just slightly to a virtualised form, and this through consumption and production activities in the online social milieu.

Michael Hardt and Antonio Negri signal that, at the heart of network culture is the possibility for greater collaboration among a multitude that might subvert the aims of postmodern capital:

> Cooperation is completely immanent to the laboring activity itself. This fact calls into question the old notion (common to classical and Marxian political economics) by which labour power is conceived as 'variable capital', that is, a force that is activated and made coherent only by capital, because the cooperative powers of labor power (particularly

> immaterial labor power) afford labor the possibility of valorising itself. Brains and bodies still need others to produce value, but the others they need are not necessarily provided by capital and its capacities to orchestrate production. Today productivity, wealth, and the creation of social surpluses take the form of cooperative interactivity through linguistic, communicational, and affective networks. In the expression of its own creative energies, immaterial labor thus seems to provide the potential for a kind of spontaneous and elementary communism. (Hardt and Negri 2000, 294)

The competition to increase social capital in an attention economy is precisely what grants the online social self-servicing mechanisms their justification and coherence. It does not occur in a space or milieu outside of a corporately controlled environment, and even the notion of a 'gift economy' of social reciprocity online is effectively hijacked by a numerical system that assigns extrinsic value to the immaterial labour performed online. There is still a wage system in the form of likes and other approbation cues that digitally reify social value as something quantifiable. The very plain fact that these social relations which define capital occur on networks that have a material basis at least in terms of requiring cheap manufacturing labour to produce the hardware and precarious labour for the motley services that are created by these hardware may undercut part of Hardt and Negri's argument. But, just as importantly, the online social relations on SNSs are still patterned or defined according to accumulation and competitive strategies whereby each user attempting to secure their share of the attention economy must make personal calculations of temporal investment, and that any collaboration or sharing will somehow improve the individual user's online social capital, thus consigning acts of sharing to something entirely extrinsic. While a vast number of online users are engaged in a global competitive practice of accumulating social capital, the reality is that such 'accumulation requires commitment from many people, although few have any real chances of making a substantial profit' (Boltanski and Chiapello 2006, 163). The 'winners' in the games of social capital exist at the expense of a multitude of 'losers.'

Although many users may be engaged in the competitive games by which they can obtain a larger share of attention, this is not always necessarily linked to a concrete purpose. That is, setting aside those who have a specific promotional agenda to market a product or service they are selling, the question of what a user hopes to gain in achieving an arbitrary high number of likes, comments or connections remains somewhat mysterious. We might speculate that the higher the number of interactive events such as likes or comments, the more the satisfaction in terms of social validation. It is in a return to Veblen that we discover that the motivations are, in fact, deliberate, and although their purposes may vary in their particulars, the end goal is to be accorded by a community with a validated status. Veblen's analysis tells us that the drive or imperative for conspicuous consumption, either of goods or time and effort, is contingent upon the size of the audience to be impressed.

Conspicuous Prosumption

Conspicuous *prosumption* may differ only slightly from Veblen's notion of conspicuous *consumption*. In the latter, what one consumes becomes a sign of one's purchasing power. In terms of social media and the prosumption model, the signs of social approbation in high numbers become a sign of one's commodified social power. Social power, no matter how the SNS provides tools for its apparent measurement in terms of likes, does not lend itself to precise measurement at all. There is no formula by which n number of 'like-units' will produce a value that is anything but arbitrary and relative. One can measure power in terms of joules per second as watts, but social power cannot be reduced to standardised measurement. At best, the subjective notion of power – be this political, social, military, or economic – is a form of *potestas*, and can only be measured according to the relative values of more or less. With respect to social power on social media, there is no guarantee that a million likes on a post grants to the creator a special social power. Nor does having 5,000 connections necessarily mean that the user has more social capital at his or her disposal.

It might be said that there are implicit social norms on social media, and a gradual building of cultural capital that guides notions of taste, but also which guide to some degree what are the appropriate mechanisms by which to develop social capital specific to each social media environment. Software design restricts certain choices and behaviours. For example, rejected friend requests on Facebook do not result in the requester being notified of the rejection. These are intentionally designed elements to promote a positive social space that reduces the possibility of hostility and rejection, even if a determined user can find other ways of indulging in antisocial behaviour such as trolling.

The surplus production of goods beyond the necessities of life are absorbed by those who crave an increase in status, and thus can be considered the driver in the desire for economic growth, even if it may be considered derivative: 'The utility of consumption as an evidence of wealth is to be classed as a derivative growth' (Veblen 2010, 40). For Veblen, waste has a functional utility, albeit of a secondary value in the way it is leveraged to satisfy a human desire for status. Veblen, committed as he was to applying a Darwinist analogy to the field of institutional practices, largely saw acts of conspicuous consumption by a wealthy elite and leisure class – as well as those of the lower classes partaking of said behaviours as far as their means allowed, in emulation of the upper classes – as an evolutionary invariant; that is, the desire for status by material demonstration of wealth and its wasteful expenditure has only changed in its particulars while the general aspect has remained the same since the beginning of human civilisation. The reliance on some form of ceremonial and ritualistic component of wealth display and expenditure for status enhancement can still be seen in the practices of today's institutions.

Veblen's definition of waste is that which 'does not serve human life or human well-being on the whole' (Veblen 2010, 55). Although certain acts and expenditures may be viewed as having at least some value to the individual's well-being and satisfaction, when it solely based on the relative utility of the individual, then it might be deemed wasteful. If there is an apparent preponderance of adolescents and college students posting pictures of themselves in acts of intoxication and images of their food, this attests to the display of unproductive time and leisure that marks conspicuous prosumption.

Social media provides a platform for displays of conspicuous consumption that may possess wider audience reach, and therefore the increased opportunity for receiving validation for such activities. If a person purchases a yacht as a symbol of their wealth, the circle of admirers in the offline world may be small. However, should the same person then post pictures of said yacht, and a cruise in the Caribbean, on Facebook then this may increase personal social capital.

Online social capital indexed on the province of the self, or as a collaboration of groups, when conducted on SNSs such as Facebook, serves the interests of actual capital for Facebook and its affiliated advertisers that seek to marketise and profit from mediated social exchange. It is these entities that either play host to, or leverage social data for targeted advertising, that earns monetary profit. Self-service and self-branding activities provide the appearance of autonomy that underpin the fetishistic rhetoric surrounding the 'heroic' entrepreneur, if at the very least the individual user is 'liberated' from the managerial hierarchy in their own self-determination. And yet, the subordination remains as the user swaps out a 'boss' or a rigid hierarchical system that is plainly visible in an institutional and industrial logic to a fuzzier and more ubiquitous type now occupied by the owners of the networks. The unacknowledged labour involved in profile management and the temporal investment strategies involved in increasing online social capital may simply be a redistribution effect of free labour whereby these activities conducted by a large mass of users ultimately provides benefit for the SNSs that underwrite all attempts at social capital increase, be these successful or not. The parallel case, although more monetarily clear, might be the entrepreneurs who develop apps for Apple or Android platforms: no matter the success of the app, the only cost to these companies is hosting, while the developer provides free labour in the hopes of acquiring profit. Should there be a considerable profit, the host takes a significant cut of the revenue; the risk is assumed by the individual.

Users self-publish their content, but Facebook's model is mostly a modification on earlier forms of publication. The sale of advertising space that marked traditional print was to a readership: 'The profits of publication come from the sale of advertising space' (Veblen 2005, 182), but in this case, the producer and the publisher are very distinct, for Facebook is in effect the 'publisher' and the unpaid producers of content are not hired by Facebook. It is the users themselves that produce the content that further popularises social media sites like Facebook, while the network owner acts as a data broker in selling advertising space that is targeted to the prosumers of content. It was Veblen that acknowledged the priority of advertising space as a source of revenue, and that subscriptions were largely secondary.

For Veblen, the ideal for technical knowledge was that it would be held in common, apart from pecuniary interests. He envisioned a great Soviet of engineers (Veblen, 1921). When it comes to the productions and insights of social media users, however, this is not held in common, as the repository is entirely pecuniarily motivated, and to paraphrase Thiry-Cherques (2010), the price of inclusion in the network entails some form of subordination. In this case, Facebook extracts value from posts and profiles for the purposes of facilitating data matching between itself and paid advertisers for targeted advertising.

Social capital – that which is generated from resources held in common – would have to somehow develop a means of resisting the pecuniary interests of those who are not contributing their own capital to a specific community, and are simply profiting by what is generated. However, for as long as social relations are dominated by the predominantly neoliberal spectacle, and interactions on the social media platform are motivated with a view to enhancing status through conspicuous acts of prosumption in a competitive game, the advantages of social capital would only accrue in small part to the entrepreneurial individual, and in larger part to the social media platform.

Mestrovic acknowledges that Veblen 'would have pointed out that the Internet is most available in Western nations that exhibit the culture of narcissism he sought to unmask' (2003, p. 14). And, perhaps just as Veblen critiqued fashion and ostentation as status-based activity that aligns with a pronounced form of cultural narcissism, it is likely that he might have viewed certain ego-based behaviours of display on social media as narcissistic. The extensive use and reliance on platforms such as Facebook among a growing number of individuals exhibits the extent to which unproductive time is spent in virtual production, and that the competitive aspects reduce social interactions to the exchange value that can be generated from said interactions for personal gain.

Veblen was a caustic critic of capitalism, laden as it is with inefficiencies and irrational behaviour culturally inherited from previous phases of production and consumption. On the other hand, there is Veblen's view of technology, as something technical that could provide efficiency and progress, but would risk losing those qualities in being aligned with the profit motive. At the social and institutional level, Veblen's verdict on social media might be that it is just a part of the irrational and invariant human drive for status-aggrandisement.

Veblen and Capital Assets

Veblen never explicitly mentions social capital in any of the works in his oeuvre, although it may be argued that he held a view on knowledge, skills, and practices in a community (intangible assets) that speaks to a kind of social capital in all but name that might be a fit with that of Bourdieu's definition.

For Veblen, the predatory instinct of human beings is alive and well, whether it be through the explicit profit-oriented activities of successful capitalist industries, or at the level of individual workers who seek to improve their status appearance by conforming – via conspicuous consumption – to the tastes of the ruling classes. This aspirational emulation would seem to somewhat mute the power of labour to organise against exploitation, just so long as they are given the trappings of apparent wealth and may participate in the purchasing of digital objects, and access to the internet. If, for Marx, religion was the opiate of the masses by which an institution rationalised and attempted to justify continued exploitation of labour, it might not be too much of a stretch to say that Veblen might see the techno-optimism of the day as something similar. And, with the increased availability of credit, this may have had a slightly nullifying effect on a willingness by a majority of exploited labour to take up resistance against capitalist exploitation. The predatory instinct as emulated by the 'common weal' may now be expressed in truly intangible terms: the ruthless pursuit of online social capital by active participants in a 'like economy'.

For Veblen, institutions play a pivotal role in social life: '[h]abitual modes of activity and relations have grown up and have by convention settled into a fabric of institutions. These institutions [...] have a prescriptive, habitual force of their own' (Veblen 1909, 300). When this is compared to how digital networks have been empowered and lionised by various political and economic institutions in the information age, there is bound to be some degree of normalising efforts to promote a kind of habituation to social media usage. The extraction and sale of data, and the advancement of pecuniary goals by corporatised social networks, would not count for Veblen as a kind of social capital. Veblen instead would conceive of social capital as the accumulated technological/industrial experience of the community:

> As items in a process of cumulative change [...] these productive goods are facts of human knowledge, skill, and predilection [...] The physical properties of the material accessible to man are constants: it is the human agent that changes–his insight and his appreciation of what these things can be used for is what develops. [...] The changes that take place in the mechanical contrivances are an expression of changes in the human factor (Veblen 1898, 387–88).

This represents a considerable theoretical divergence between Veblen and Marx. As Dorfman notes,

> In Marx the productive agent in economic life is labour, in Veblen it is the accumulated expertise and initiative of the race, techniques created by man for human use. Veblen, like Marx, holds that capital goods cost nothing but labour, and that all gains to capital, aside from those going to the working community, are surplus gains, but Veblen maintained

that capital goods are instruments of production only by virtue of the technological knowledge possessed by the industrial community (Dorfman [1934] 1966, 285–6).

There may be sufficient similarities in Veblen's conceptual repertoire to at least point to operative terms that function as synonyms for social capital. As a means of preparing that ground, it is worthwhile to illustrate how Veblen conceives of capital in terms of tangible and intangible assets. For Veblen, tangible assets involve pecuniary capital goods that are owned and yield an income for said owner, and are assets insofar as they have a capitalisable value related to their serviceability as productive goods. Intangible assets are:

> immaterial items of wealth, immaterial facts owned, valued, and capitalized on an appraisement of the gain to be derived from their possession. These are also assets to the amount of their capitalisable value, which has commonly little, if any, relation to the industrial serviceability of these items of wealth considered as factors of production (Veblen 1908, 104–5).

Veblen saw the drive of businesses was to enhance their intangible assets. Examples of intangible assets today would include brand names, web domain names, customer lists, artistic products related to marketing, franchise agreements, leasing, databases, patents and proprietary formulae and processes (such as algorithms). Over time, Veblen noted that corporations focused more heavily in the pursuit and maintenance of their intangible asset classes.

So far we are only discussing the two main capital asset types of corporations, and yet it is not difficult to see how corporate social network sites continue this legacy of focusing more on their intangible assets. Tangible assets are still quite important and require the hire of technical experts such as engineers and computer scientists to develop the infrastructure. However, a recurring theme in Veblen's work is in wanting to make a critical distinction between industry and business; namely, the interests of technical or technological specialists and the pecuniary interests of corporations. Veblen saw true innovation stemming from skilled technical workers who shared their knowledge in common, while it was the role of corporations to seek profit as a primary motive even if it stifled innovation through the use of a patent system where such technical knowledge would be privatised as a possession to be carefully guarded and not shared.

Veblen saw the problem as being between profit-oriented corporations versus production-oriented industries that valued workmanship, the former type sacrificing the latter in pursuit of profit. For industry, the litmus is progress; for corporations it is property. For Veblen, human societies and the origin of private property is linked to the predatory instinct, first expressed historically through the possession of women and gradually extending to objects. Veblen says that this instinct has not been extinguished, and that it continues through a ruthless pursuit of profit. In industrial societies, this pursuit is at odds with the principles of workmanship (skills and practices held as knowledge), and precisely because the capitalist will be biased in favour of cheaper abundance of goods as opposed to focusing on quality and innovation.

On the basis of his analysis of tangible and intangible assets, it may be possible to speculate how Veblen might have understood online social capital. Social media users are the intangible assets of a social networking site insofar as they fulfil the labour function of marketing the site and producing a valuable asset (data) that can be capitalised as value through third-party sale. Even technical knowledge can be obtained as free labour in those cases when there is a need to beta test products, or members of a public are encouraged to produce content for a community for free (such as what occurs in the gaming industry in the development of mods).

For Veblen, the accumulation of online social capital may be expressible as a numeric value, but there is no true ownership by the social media user. This form of gain is not directly capitalisable by the user, but indirectly by the owner (in this case the corporate network). It may only be converted into a more social form, such as status. There are other more circuitous routes to convert online social capital into self-branding efforts to sell products and services, or in attracting the attention of companies to hire one on as an influencer. It is likely that Veblen would view the pursuit and accumulation of online social capital as serving the interests of the social network company, while the mechanisms for capitalising on the intangible assets of so many likes and new connections that may arise is limited in terms of who owns the data, and the affordances of the platform upon which this is obtained.

Marx versus Veblen?

It will prove beneficial here to summarise a few key points of agreement and disagreement in the approaches of Marx and Veblen in this chapter.

1. Veblen recognised profit emerges out of the unfair exchange process of capitalism, whereas for Marx it is located directly in the production process itself, which generates a surplus value as a result of a distinction between labour and labour power. In other words, Veblen points to market forces and the invariant of the predatory instinct embedded in the economic basis of institutions.

2. Veblen was far more pessimistic about the prospect of the rise of labour in the creation of a classless society; instead, his view of history was that the predatory processes would continue, and that any workers' movements would be dissolved into the broader institutional apparatus, usually through some form of small concessions and the promise of attaining higher class status through consumption practices.

3. Marx understood that the contradictions of capitalism could eventually contribute to capitalism's collapse, although his view is not deterministic, and would be contingent upon nothing preventing the law of the rate of profit to fall. Veblen does not dismiss this as a possibility, but views it as unlikely. He does hold out hope that, through the discipline of mechanical technologies, workmanship prevails over pecuniary interests.

4. For Marx, class *struggle* manifests itself in the crises inherent in capitalism, but for that to happen Veblen might object, there would have to be a widespread rejection of the trappings of *status*. During the time in which Veblen was writing, the expansion of consumer markets according to the Fordist model meant that another opiate of the masses had emerged via providing enough of a wage to workers so that they could consume more products, partially easing class conflict, and allowing them to participate more in consumer society and the pursuit of status.

5. For Marx, it is the worker in general that will precipitate the revolutionary change required, whereas for Veblen it is the skilled technical class of engineers who may be the real agents of change through their invention and sharing of knowledge. In other words, Veblen places his trust in technological progress as the only viable means to eliminate many of the harms capitalism inflicts on society. Such a view may, in fact, be a bit naive – at least insofar as capitalism has been incredibly adaptive in controlling and using modern technologies to maintain its dominance.

Despite these differences, which more or less are based on their respective understandings of history and human nature, there are also points of agreement. Veblen was not a full-throated critic of Marx, although he points up parts of Marx's analysis as being somewhat naive to the institutional aspects of economics and human nature. Veblen, however, is in agreement with Marx that the plight of workers in terms of continued exploitation and alienation are very real phenomena. Veblen blames capitalism for the continued immiseration of labour, if not also actively reinforcing institutional processes that perpetuate the allure of class status attainment. For Marx, we might say that religion is the opiate of the masses that keeps labour complicit with their exploitation, whereas for Veblen it is consumption practices that are dangled as the promise of achieving higher status: an aspirational desire that can never be truly fulfilled no matter how much one consumes.

Main Points

- Marx's four aspects of alienation still apply to the mechanisms of social media, despite the absence of the wage relation.
- Although claims that social media's affordances may appear to decrease alienation is supported by the freedom of users to create, share and express

themselves, countervailing aspects also speak to an increase in alienation given that the content is not owned by the user, what is made visible is controlled by the social media site, a feeling of obligation makes participation on social media seem more like work, and the emphasis on accumulating online social capital inevitably leads to dissatisfaction as more user production is geared towards accumulation of a resource at the expense of self-reflection.

- Adopting Veblen's analysis of conspicuous consumption and considering the production side, production becomes linked to a goal of enhancing online social status by performing labour specifically indexed on transforming the use value of a communication event into an exchange value. As users are caught up in a cycle of production and consumption of class or status-based imagery, these conspicuous forms are 'rewarded' in part by a visible metric by which to display online social wealth.

- As users compete to participate in status-chasing activities, such acts are tied to Veblen's understanding of the predatory instinct in competing for power, which is expressed in possessions; in this case, the possessions to be displayed are transmuted into images for display and social approval. Competition in this artificial economy is what drives this invariant form of behaviour.

- As social media provides the means for conspicuous display, it also conceals inequalities so that those with less economic means can be enticed to participate in status-chasing pursuits rather than critique the institutional status quo apparatus of which social media is a part.

CHAPTER 5

Alienation 2.0 – Symptoms of Narcissism and Aggression

A *Washington Post* article from May 2016 followed a then 13-year-old girl, Katherine Pommerening, who was an avid user of the popular image-sharing site Instagram. Apart from detailing the life of a 'typical US teen' growing up immersed in online social media, what may be considered very intriguing about the story was a description of her habits when using Instagram:

> She has 604 followers. There are only 25 photos on her page because she deletes most of what she posts. The ones that don't get enough likes, don't have good enough lighting or don't show the coolest moments in her life must be deleted (Contrera 2016, n.p.).

What is of interest with such behaviour is how this form of self-curation is indexed on the value given by other users, expressed as likes. The seeking of larger numbers of likes appears to function as a strong motivator for what content is produced for public consumption. Like rolling out a new product, if it does not achieve high enough sales, it may be withdrawn from production and another product released. For younger social media users, there appear to be high stakes in achieving a sizeable number of followers and likes as proof of social value. Some may go to extremes in order to achieve this, as well as making use of various tools for photo enhancement or engaging in overt sexualisation and risk-taking behaviours in an effort to appease an audience.

This normalisation of social competition in online spaces is linked to accumulation and the ease by which popularity becomes measured. Marx understood that, for as long as human beings and their production were governed by individualism and cutthroat competition under the profit motive, alienation and exploitation would continue where sociality is subsumed by reification. Being

How to cite this book chapter:
Faucher, K. X. 2018. *Social Capital Online: Alienation and Accumulation.* Pp. 87–108.
London: University of Westminster Press. DOI: https://doi.org/10.16997/book16.f.
License: CC-BY-NC-ND 4.0

cost-effective, competitive, flexible, and adaptable become economic virtues while also exacerbating alienation from one another and our own sense of self.

We are afforded more opportunities for social activity online, with greater convenience, speed, reach, and access. That being said, these ICTs emerged out of a distinct ideological worldview that glorifies capitalist individualism. In order to achieve and preserve this form of capitalist individual autonomy, the social relations of production are reified and partially determined by the 'natural law' of competition. This concern for the inward, narcissistic turn and its consequences has been shared not only by some members of the Frankfurt School (such as Adorno and Horkheimer) but also the fields of psychoanalysis (emerging from Freud and extending to the Object Relations School) and cultural studies. In this chapter, we will explore some of the implications of these more broad-based online behavioural trends in social media, and how these connect to online social capital. The main connection to be made here is how the nature of competitiveness on social media not only empowers self-aggrandisement in the form of narcissism, but also leads in some cases to aggression.

From Digital Narcissism to Online Id

Social media may appear to be heavily dominated by narcissistic behaviour from a proliferation of selfies, the diligent archiving of the details of everyday life, the dogged pursuit of online social capital, and conspicuous acts of digital display — a digital form of narcissistic behaviour watched over by the corporately owned networks of loving grace.

In a broader context, there has been the unprecedented rise of populist demagoguery, the shocking re-normalisation of racism as an attack on politically correct or civil discourse, the sweeping return of old nationalisms throughout the US, the UK and some European nations, and a living political discourse that starts to resemble Sinclair Lewis' *It Can't Happen Here* (1993 [1935]) and Philip Roth's *The Plot Against America* (2004). With Brexit and the election of Donald Trump, we are seeing ever more digital examples of public aggression and evidence of various forms of narcissistic entitlement that may have surprised even Christopher Lasch, who wrote the arguably sensationalist *The Culture of Narcissism* in the 1970s.[18]

Any observable increase in narcissism and aggression cannot be said to be definitively *caused* by social media and any preoccupations with increasing various forms of social capital since it may simply just *facilitate* such behaviours. The affordances of social media and the broader ideological context may serve to understand how, for example, someone like Donald Trump was able to build his own political capital using Twitter, tapping into widespread discontent and using it to his political advantage, under-spending his opponent in terms of media buys while relying more on social media to disseminate his message. Many of Trump's tweets can be seen as apparent manifestations of the aggression and narcissism being witnessed on, and possibly facilitated by, social media.

Aided in part by the customisation options that 'personalise' the experience and make the user a central node in their social interactive digital space, we might subject the data-flood of selfies and self-promotional utterances to keener analysis through several lenses such as political economy, psychoanalysis and subdomains of identity construction.

Digital Narcissism

The term 'narcissism' is subject to a broad definitional latitude, and the conceptual particulars of the term can be expressed and applied in a variety of ways and approaches. A clear distinction needs to be made between ordinary or healthy narcissism, and more extreme forms. A healthy sense of self-regard and self-interest is not problematic, but there are behaviours that can be deemed harmful for the self and others. In the foregoing discussion, I will keep loaded terms such as 'pathological,' 'unhealthy,' and 'abnormal' in suspension, and consign their usage only to when speaking of the clinical literature on the subject.

At issue would be the prospect of a specifically *digital* narcissism. Melding the term 'digital' with the standard definition of narcissism might at once open up questions of the possibly enabling, amplifying, or ambient effects social media may have on the construct of the narcissistic personality, *or* invite exploration of how the integration of ICTs in everyday life play a major role in identity construction and development. The digital narcissism 'tent' is large enough to include a full spectrum of approaches that range from technological determinism to instrumentalism. At issue would be what central pole holds up this tent.

A neoliberal ideological apparatus appears to enable such behaviours as simply a benign manifestation of self-branding entrepreneurialism, the crucible of American exceptionalism from which much of our ICTs originate; the 'ecstasy' of immediacy in communication facilitated by these technologies in an effort to anneal digital presence, and many of the optimistic assumptions buried in the seemingly value-neutral terms of 'information society,' 'economic growth,' and 'freedom' may in fact be little more than glittering generalities. A constructivist viewpoint may direct us to understand digital narcissism as simply an outgrowth of the broader sociopolitical forces that shape both the digital technology and the formation of the individual, perhaps having its narrative extended into the digital domain from the insights provided by Christopher Lasch (1979). In his work we locate the scathing indictments of CEO worship, enabling sociopathic tendencies, of breeding disloyalty as a form of valorising arch-individualism, of a decanted Ayn Rand gospel of selfishness as a moral virtue, and the self-centred practices of everyday life. Lasch's work may be dated, but there are eerily prescient features in his work that resonate with effects of the integration of social media and portable digital devices. What is unique about digital narcissism is not the mechanism of narcissism itself, but a kind of megaphone effect with increased opportunities for pursuing narcissistic goals, if not also a competitive pressure to be seen and heard in a vast ocean of social media noise.

The emergence of the ability to manage one's own personal profile on social media is descended from previous digital forms of self-representation online, such as personal websites and blogs. Much of social media today has been able to absorb many of these functions of the earlier web with the incentive of having access to a much larger potential audience. Expressing one's personal views or posting one's pictures can now be done in a much larger social marketplace, but with potentially more competition.

The representation of self and its behaviours migrate to the digital realm, with more recent scholars and commentators such as Jean Twenge and W. Keith Campbell (2003, 2009), Soraya Mehdizadeh (2010); Christine Rosen (2007); and Sherry Turkle (2012) considering how the digital social domain may have an either causative or correlative effect on alienation from the self. Case studies on the subject of online narcissistic behaviour become more plentiful despite the challenges of employing an objective measure for analysis of a constantly shifting and highly personalised digital landscape. There may be some strong correlations between digital expressions of narcissism and the enabling features of social media. It may appear that there is 'more' narcissism, but this may simply be an appearance: with more people having the means to express themselves openly on social media, and the traces of those expressions housed in an ever-expanding digital archive; this may only suggest that we now have more readily available evidence of narcissism that has been with us long before the rise of social media.

Whatever the approach to the subject, what remains somewhat ambiguous is the ultimate aim of digital narcissistic behaviours without risking generalisation. To that end it is useful to consider a variety of strategic objectives that the online narcissist aims to achieve, be this to increase self-validation, online social capital, cornering the market in the 'attention economy,' and online influence, whether these can be treated separately or combined.

Digital Objects and Objectification

Narcissistic traits are more readily recognisable on social media due to the software platform that facilitates more options for self-display. In such venues, narcissistic traits in users were associated with a higher volume of social networking site usage, and particularly through self-description and strategic use of profile photos (Buffardi and Campbell 2008). There may also be a patterning effect whereby new users to social media may engage in behaviour that seeks to adapt and emulate the more successful and established social media users.

When thinking about social media behaviours, one example that may spring to mind as something patently narcissistic would be the proliferation of selfies. Social critics in popular media are quick to raise the alarm that such behaviours are unhealthy, but this fails to appreciate that selfies are hardly anything new. As Jill Walker Retteberg (2014) reminds us, selfies, as a form of self-representation, are descendants of previous means to represent the self, including cave paintings, self-portraits, pre-digital photography, diaries and autobiographies. It is important to understand what a selfie is in the digital context before too quickly leaping to the assumption that all selfies are to be pathologised as dangerously narcissistic given that there are a wide range of other self-display behaviours that are not explicitly a form of posting a selfie.

The traits of extreme or pathological narcissism involve a fragile ego-construct, a punitive and sadistic superego, and poor object relations. In terms of relations with objects, the pathological narcissist will 'identify with an object and love an object standing for their (present or past) self' (Kernberg 1975). This stands in contrast with the ordinary narcissist object relation that attaches to an object as representing the parental image. The online representation of self operates as a far more cognitively comprehensible object that the narcissist can identify with in terms of a relation patterned on narcissistic disturbance. 'Both adult and infantile narcissism include "self-centredness," but the self-investment of normal adult narcissism is in terms of mature goals, ideals and expectations, whereas the normal infantile self-investment is in terms of infantile, exhibitionistic, demanding, and power-oriented strivings' (Kernberg 1975). These two modes of narcissism are not yet pathological. The pathology becomes manifest through a series of steps or phases which include a regression from the adult to the infantile, the investment of love toward an object that represents the self, and finally in dispensing with the object-status entirely to allow the full deterioration of object relations so that the grandiose self cleaves to a grandiose projected image of self (1975, 323–4).

The flashpoint for the pathological narcissist emerges when the economic flow is disrupted; i.e., narcissistic supplies decrease or are removed entirely. In the case of the tributary relations the narcissist relies on for validation, such as the constant praise and attention from others. It may be at this point that the tributary relationships conflict with the narcissist's punitive idea of self-reliance and the reality of dependence upon those very relationships. With the assistance of online representation, the pathological narcissist can have an externalised object of grandiose self that can be manipulated (or otherwise transformed into a punitive superego that will reflect back at the self with unrealistic expectations). The paradox emerges between the self's belief in extreme self-reliance, and that of depending on others for constant praise and attention. One can imagine the frustration or rage the extreme narcissist would experience in not receiving a steady supply of likes for her or his online contributions. In less extreme cases, there may be a sense of disappointment, or even a questioning of self-worth: a scenario that seems to be more prevalent among adolescent users of social media.

Tracking and Striving For the Perfect Representation

This management of online representation is a perpetual process. Christine Rosen (2007) states that the creation of one's self-portrait used to involve canvas and paint, but that our online self-portraits are composed of pixels. Extending the analogy further, the online self-portrait is always a work in progress, and 'self-portrait' is more than just the visual image, as it includes everything that is said to represent the self such as textual posts that convey personal beliefs and affiliations which contribute to a multimedia-based narrative of the self.

Tracking the impact of our online presence carries over from previous modes of self-tracking behaviours. Using the term 'quantified self-representation,' Retteberg uses the historical example of Benjamin Franklin, who charted how well he was observing thirteen moral virtues in his life, placing each of the virtues in rows, and each day in columns, placing a single black mark on the day he did not live up to the virtue (2014, 10). Retteberg also uses other examples, such as a prisoner marking days served on a cell wall, and the more recent example of people using activity-tracking devices such as FitBit to record number of steps walked, the results of which can be integrated with social media. These kinds of self-accounting behaviours are not an uncommon human trait, and are usually goal-oriented. For instance, Ernest Hemingway would record his weight on a daily basis, just as other people may track their caloric intake, monitor their consumption of alcohol, plot fertility calendars, blood pressure, or bodybuilders who measure the consumption of macro-nutrients and the number of maximum repetitions and sets they can perform. Social media has provided a large number of affordances for people to track and display their progress with the aid of apps, spreadsheets and wearable devices, while also broadcasting that information to an audience that may or may not be attempting to achieve similar goals.

Such tracking and self-accounting behaviours can usually be clustered as self-improvement initiatives, and the sharing of that data might serve a variety of purposes, from seeking encouragement and support from others, motivation, health benefits, to simply boasting. Retteberg, drawing on van Dijck's term of dataism, is interested in how we use quantitative measures to interpret data in a better understanding of ourselves, and to assert control (2014, 68; 73).

Tracking takes on a more pernicious form when it is focused solely on one's online representation and the number of likes one has acquired. It is of some value to consider Baudrillard's discussion of the body as the 'finest' consumer object and object of salvation that constantly needs to be managed with deliberate narcissistic investment (1998, 129). By extending the analogy of this objectification of the body to that of the online self as an object for display and narcissistic concern, it may suggest a false form of 'liberation' and accomplishment since the online self is a form of reappropriation for capitalist objectives: 'where it is invested, it is invested in order to produce a yield' (1998, 131). Whereas bodies in consumer culture come to stand in as a representation of identity that we 'inhabit' and manage with a view to some degree of narcissistic investment for some form of yield, our online profiles with their proliferation of selfies and statements may be the successor: a kind of digital 'body' we inhabit, manage, fetishise and capitalise upon.

Posting selfies can present a means for self-expression and the potential for experimentation. The more problematic issue arises when those who post selfies feel they must comply with standard beauty myths in order to compete for attention and approbation, particularly when perceived societal expectations are highly gendered. Those who do not garner the attention they hope for may suffer a blow to self-esteem, and it may exacerbate body image anxieties through a kind of digital dysmorphia; namely, rather than looking in a mirror seeing only 'flaws,' a lack of attention and approbation on social media can result in magnifying feelings of inadequacy.

It may become ever more expected among certain demographics to post selfies and engage in competition for attention, and although on the surface this may seem to some as self-aggrandising and narcissistic behaviour, one should not discount the social context in which these users are posting this content. By contrast, the committed narcissist is seeking attention for different reasons. What unites the two is the seeking of online social capital, measured in terms of likes as proof of value.

Not everyone who has a committed interest in tracking their likes on social media is a pathological narcissist, but may be caught up in the curious artifice of the like economy as a way of measuring their social impact. What is unfortunate is when this results in negative outcomes such as body image issues, dangerous risk-taking behaviours, and – in the case of the narcissist – a willingness to adopt extreme or aggressive behaviours when public attention falls below expectations.

This shift in social attitudes that makes the self a digital object of constant improvement, an idealised projection, or a constant work in progress may not necessarily indicate that there is a pathological dimension to a majority of users. What it will indicate, however, is that the need for exhibitionism and validation is exacerbated by a variety of anxiety-inducing phenomena precipitated by broader social expectations with regard to the growth and popularity of digital social communication that may be numerically based. This splits int the twin concerns around self-as-brand management for increasing online social capital, and 'FOMO' (fear of missing out). The perceived need to have presence, to participate on social media with more content and more often, and the perception that the institution of celebrity has been democratised as something achievable through the exclusive use of social media, may alter expectations of how interactions occur on these platforms.

Online social interaction is diverse and difficult to evaluate with any definitive accuracy. The rate at which social bonds are formed or dissolve, the number of nodes involved and the rapid nature of today's instant-communication networks makes it impossible to diagnose – an analogous scenario to Heisenberg's uncertainty principle in physics where we cannot know both the speed and location of any particle. And yet there is reasoned suspicion that online social networks cater to a growing desire for unstable, superficial social arrangements. Whether or not these depend on high or low commitment varies from user to user, and what is meant by 'commitment.' For example, a social bond can be high commitment in terms of expectations to be online and to respond regularly, while also being low commitment because of low quality cultivation of interpersonal sharing. For several users, the quantity of social connections they are involved may be too high to cultivate high commitment connections that possess qualitative depth, and for those who have an unmanageable amount of connections even high commitment at the level of regular superficial responses are not possible. It might be reasonable to assume that the higher the density of one's online connections, the lower the individual commitment to maintenance or cultivation when taken as a whole since the analogue nature of time prevents us from doing more than allocating the limited time we have available. However, this may suit the pathological narcissist who is not particularly interested in forming high commitment relationships and may seek a return on investment by maximising the quantity of connections. This strategy was once employed by advertisers who sought to bet on marketing to everyone, but since advertising budgets are not infinite, it made sense to realign a marketing campaign to target niche groups where the statistical odds of getting a return on marketing investment dollar was higher.

Social media is potentially ideal for adopting a narcissistic strategy given the large potential supply of users. Inasmuch as access to a large audience in one-to-many or many-to-many communication opportunities can be developed for noble purposes, there is also the enabling feature of such communication opportunities for providing narcissistic supplies that further exacerbate a pathology. Coupled with the heightened expectations of regular and near immediate communication, this may generate an enormous supply of exploitable human resources for self-validation, yet may also exacerbate the dependency/self-reliance paradox of narcissism.

Intensity and Attention

The intensity of constant communication and the desire to make intensive use of commercial signifiers speaks to how embedded and integrated capitalist values are in many online exchanges. Users who cater to their own narcissistic impulses may feel it is their obligation to engineer intense presence and make intense speech acts. Intensity of this kind is also measured by duration: short burst salvo through aphoristic utterance (we can include photos here as part of intensive speech acts) with the hope or expectation of a long lasting effect (through cross-syndication of content). In this way, the narcissistic user is chained to a belief that s/he is the locus of attention – a position more easily held given the nature of social media networks to be egocentric in structure. When the narcissistic project of maximising virtual territory and the garnering of public attention is geared toward this project, constructive development of the ego may be waylaid or deferred in favour of a dedicated model of developing one's online character as part of the regime of social capital. The enjoyment of reward is to be had only after the labour is complete, and even then (despite a frequent return to brief adulatory feedback as a sustaining inspiration for further labour) full satisfaction is never achieved. The desire for self-aggrandisement and larger doses of measurable validation far outpaces any short-term and ephemeral sense of self-satisfaction. If there is a source for this kind of communication anxiety, it may be a deficit of satisfaction, the perceived widening gap between effort and reward. The desire itself may become monstrous in magnitude and scope, making it virtually impossible to satisfy. For every temporary satisfaction achieved, full satisfaction is out of the narcissist's reach (bringing the story of Narcissus in line with that of Tantalus). The cluster of particular anxieties experienced with regard to online connection and communication may have their root in a perceived obstruction or failure to make use of one's time. This urge to labour on one's online representation for the purposes of achieving a higher online social capital 'score' only further entrench the narcissist's dependence on others, but also amplifies the anxiety associated with online ego management, not least of which may be exacerbated further if one's online persona – spread out over a variety of venues – requires frequent modification or alteration. The more social network profiles one maintains, the more exhausting the labour might be in maintaining these profiles.

Online Ego Management

The behavioural tendency of the online narcissist to engage in acts of accumulation can be explained by the unacknowledged motivation that collecting a high quantity of online social connections is a means of recollecting the primary narcissistic self to achieve the impossible unity when there was no distinction and differentiation between self and world. This recollection of the (undeveloped) self is not interested in cultivating quality relationships online since that would take considerable investment and self-awareness the narcissist lacks. In the narcissist's failure to understand or acknowledge that others exist autonomously, quality connections are not desired or cannot be cultivated.

Much of the social communication on social media has an ephemerality to it. Despite the ephemerality of so much social information made public on social media, much of it is archived permanently. The inundation of constant information has the effect of diminishing the value quickly. This rapid devaluation of information presents a difficulty for the committed online narcissist who seeks to make a lasting impression with his or her online efforts, so inasmuch as social media provides a seemingly ideal platform to indulge narcissistic behaviour, there are a variety of structural elements that make this task difficult or even impossible to satisfactorily achieve. Firstly, individual reach must contend with the high volume of others who are also locked in competition for their share of the attention economy. Secondly, a high volume of new social information tends to diminish the returns for online ego investment. Thirdly, although reach may not extend as far as the narcissist desires, it may extend to such a size that invariably a narcissist will be in direct or indirect competition with another narcissist. When so much of the narcissist's energy is already devoted to defensive measures (the barrier known as the 'narcissistic defence'), direct competition may pose an even higher degree of threat than the usual reserve of envy the narcissist might feel in the presence of indirect competition. Lastly, the efforts to maintain enough presence to satisfy the need for narcissistic supplies can be very labour intensive, involving a great deal of management of both online persona and cultivating a large supply of social connections. Studies continue to indicate higher engagement with SNSs correlated with narcissism (Mehdizadeh 2010, Wang and Stefanone 2013).

Digital Narcissism and Aggression: This is My Sandbox!

Although there may be no reliably conclusive empirical proof to claim that narcissism has increased, or that the web has enabled the traits of narcissism to such a degree as to suggest (as some authors have) an 'epidemic,'[19] one can point to the connection between narcissism and aggression.

The link between narcissism and incidents of aggression generally arise from threatened egotism where there is a perception by the narcissist that there is an attempt to undermine or devalue said person (Baumeister et al. 2000, Konrath et al. 2006), or as a result of social rejection (Twenge and Campbell 2003). The ease by which the classical narcissist can treat other users online as mere objects, thus objectifying them, can result in aggressive behaviour when the perceived objects either do not provide tributary supplies or seek to frustrate the narcissist's control. In addition, the narcissist may be imbued with particular ego-attachments that are linked to an infantile sense of territory (Noshpitz 1984). Thus, if the narcissist is presented with a challenge in any self-defined territory such as beliefs involving politics, religion, health etc., this may result in narcissistic rage where a cathartic discharge results in a hostile and aggressive attack on the perceived threat to that territory. One of the first linkages made between narcissism and aggression is attributed to Heinz Kohut who viewed it as separate from the drives, and thus a behavioural reaction, especially when the narcissist's sense of self is perceived to be under attack (Kohut 1984, 138). By contrast, Otto Kernberg adopts the more classical understanding that aggression belongs with the drives, and that its manifestation involves defence and resistance. If we take Kohut and Noshpitz's view of infantilisation and arrested development, and transpose these to digital territory, one may question whether social media enable these behaviours in being constructed as infantilising spaces linked to the competitive nature of online social capital. Although there may not be a sufficient causal link between the gamification of social media and competitive 'social' gaming as leading to aggression, there may be a correlation with respect to how the pathological narcissist may understand the competitive nature of these digital milieus, and responds aggressively depending on the social context. In terms of a connection between the digital and aggression, one might recall Marcuse who says that destructive 'energy becomes socially useful aggressive energy, and the aggressive behaviour impels growth – growth of economic, political, and technical power,' and that 'the more powerful and "technological" aggression becomes, the less is it apt to satisfy and pacify the primary impulse, and the more it tends toward repetition and escalation' (Marcuse 1969, 257, 264).

Many online news comment areas provide both the benefits and deleterious effects for the narcissist through the software architecture of social comparison information such as counters. The quantification or metrification of online social capital presents the narcissist with a real-time feedback system for where s/he stands in a digital community. On one hand, any praise given to the narcissist in an open comment will provide a higher degree of gratification to them because the comment may be read by others. On the other hand, if a user provides a criticism, this same effect of public reach may cause narcissistic injury. The extremes of gratification and injury may be much higher in the online venue due to ego attachment to one's online persona as an object extension of the self, and so there is an element of risk between an increase in the narcissistic reward or the devastation to the narcissist's fragile self-esteem.

The Triumph of the Id

What we seem to be left with is a life indexed on the pursuit of a false happiness where the best result is simply adjustment to the social media environment's competitive nature, and the pathway to this spectacular happiness is littered with signs that tell us to amass virtual objects, to consume our way to self-actualisation. By posting updates as content in an act of conspicuous production to enhance our status as happy beings engaged in happy acts of play, all while chasing after this digitised dream, alienation may be further exacerbated. Accumulating more likes or connections or retweets may only provide fleeting satisfaction – a pattern well worn in how desire functions in consumer society with its range of new objects that promise a happiness that is temporary and tied almost exclusively to an image of true happiness.

The proprietary demands placed upon personal electronic devices to facilitate internet access are an attempt to translate analogue time (the time of the external environment) into one of digital time which may be compressed or fragmented. It is in internet behaviour where the Id flourishes, pursuing a program of pleasure seeking and pain-avoidance with no conception of consequence. The idea of consequence can only function if there is a corresponding adoption of continuous time in the triadic register of past, present and future. Instead, the enabling function of social media seems to facilitate and cultivate Id-based behaviour (or else brings about a closer communication between the demands of the Id and the ego, translated into a reconfiguration of the ego-ideal that the superego will punitively enforce). The time of the Id is the eternal present, the epideictic function of self-display, self-disclosure or self-masking. The participatory nature of social media facilitates the expression of the ego-ideal, as well as providing a milieu in which to gratify Id-based impulses. What is particularly of interest would be how digital interaction has splintered the psychological subject by externalising in materialised form the various levels of the conscious and unconscious. Although many of these online social networks provide a playground for the robust Id, the superego's presence is also felt in the way these network platforms are constructed, announcing the rules and controlling how discourse can appear in these milieus.

Online social relations may be governed by the determinist function of capitalist ideology in the form of the spectacle so that most communication seems to orbit around commodities. Since capitalism operates best according to a series of crises (*Kairos*), these are experienced as minor panics or agitation to further retrench one's self in the act of consumption activities, even if no product is being purchased and only referenced. Since commodities take on the transcendental ideal, promising an end to alienation from each other and ourselves, only the trace or residue remains with the particular object rather than the abstract image of self-completion. Since many commodities are indexed on pleasure seeking or the illusion of leisure, these are generally packaged in such a way as to appeal to the Id. The violence endemic to this spectacle is expressed through acts of consumption and aggrandised self-display that operate as a means of achieving the ego-ideal of celebrity status. Since the very term celebrity is tautologous and can only be defined in reference to itself, the ego-ideal transfers the demands of the Id to the online representation of the self. The quiet merger of the Id and superego complete the process of auto-celebration, and yet requires tributary relationships in order to attain external validation. Achieved celebrity status on social media requires a constant reinvestment and staying in the social media game.

In *The Ecstasy of Communication*, Baudrillard writes: 'Today the scene and the mirror have given way to a screen and network. There is no longer any transcendence or depth, but only the immanent surface of operations unfolding, the smooth and functional surface of communication' (1988, 12). If taken to mean that the staged scenario of representation has come to an end because there is no longer any interplay of subject and object in the currency of meaning, then the value of signification has also changed.

Our online consumption is based on images and signs which ensure the illusion of our proximity and access to information while also producing a distance that operates according to a different spatiotemporal order. In a world governed by objects that are imbued with exchange-value as their primary meaning, the next step was to transform human subjects into objectified and manipulable signs. There is both narcissism and solipsism in this attitude toward other users where among the main goals of online social interaction is self-confirmation, ego validation, control and carrying out the continued commodification of all social relations amidst the promiscuity of digital networks. The nomadic user is in constant pursuit of recollecting him or herself in the maternal, oceanic milieu of the online world and its promises of unity and completion. In reality, much of the internet can be an abyss of screened dis- and misinformation, stock opinions, and venues for self-display.

Online social networks provide for growth for its own sake, be this the accumulation of one's own images, the images of others, the collection of connections, and the overall expansion of these networks in general. For those who can be classified as addicted to these online platforms, the offline world presents itself as a nuisance, as a series of irritations and interruptions that distract the gaze from the screen. Yet, online presence alone can become a redundant marker of one's actual presence as though a deficit in online presence conjures up the fear of ego-scarcity. Online presence may be understood as a territorial marking. For those who are dedicated to increasing their online presence, the aim may be to expand that presence so that it occupies maximum space – an aim that frustrates itself given that the spatial dimension of the internet itself is constantly growing. In this way, users with this view to maximise space may operate under an analogue understanding of space. This analogue way of understanding the internet does not correspond to a digital order of organisation where spatial restrictions are no longer a factor. The real limitations are not in spatial terms, but speed; that is, the speed by which information can travel, and the speed by which one has the energy to expand within digital space. Digital time and digital space are ecstatic in nature in so far as they operate largely outside of analogue space and time. They are not governed by, nor do they keep pace with, the natural environment.

It is not the classical psychoanalytic assumption that we are fundamentally irrational creatures governed by the destructive subconscious drives of the Id which needs to be contained by state and social structures, Freud's later work notwithstanding in *Civilization and its Discontents*. It would be Freud's nephew, Edward Bernays, who would attempt to apply some of the principles of psychoanalysis in the development of public relations and in channelling the unconscious drives to the benefit of marketing products and services. In this way, the attempt was made to redirect the destructive drives toward more economically beneficial activities such as shopping. However, despite this safety valve on the Id, it was not the individual's Id that was ever at issue – that would erupt in anarchic destruction of the state – nor was it simply a matter of controlling individuals in isolation to induce aggressive consumption. Instead, it was the control and perfection of the collective Id. Early crowd studies (Le Bon 1895,

Canetti 1962) point to the abdication of the ego in large mobs, and to how crowds function as a kind of Id-driven dynamo. It is not just the mobs that erupt in violence against the state, but a spectacular society's ability to marshal the Id collectively toward mass consumption.

Online identities, divested of depth and placed within their hyper-individualised content in a pre-made online social network form, have already made the transition to being commodities that others can collect and treat as on-demand objects. This occurs alongside the natural disjunction between the traffic of actual goods and information about them where the latter can be mobilised at an accelerated rate according to the compression of digital space-time (Harvey 2011, 190). These online representations are reduced to their exchange value (their surplus value pegged on an infinite potentiality that is never truly actualised), and as well reifications of the communication economy. Baudrillard (1988) argues that each lives within his or her own bubble, a self as satellised from the natural world as the natural world becomes satellised from the self – and the revised version of this claim can found in the highly customised and tailored experience social media users are subject to. This distance is entirely abstract, as opposed to the closing (or pollution) of that distance through the instantaneity of global communication. This bewitching sovereignty where each is a master at his or her own controls operating their online puppet, ventriloquising their identity, is a continuation of a game of personal aggrandisement and narcissism which, in the end, only succeeds via the commodification of all online interaction and social relations, into a further retrenchment of ego by alienation. No longer is it simply the alienation of the labourer from his or her labour since consumption and production become identical rather than symmetrical processes. What was once circumstantial consumption in the early public sphere, such as the gathering at coffee houses to discuss politics, has become the driving force by which these social relations can exist at all. At the point which any popular online social utility like Facebook or Twitter make the transition to becoming verbs, these replace the terms associated with social acts as speaking or writing with a new kind of mouth and hand, the prosthesis of communication colonised by a commercial brand and its economic interests.

Online Aggression

Hardly anyone needs to be reminded that the online world can be a hostile 'give no quarter' environment. Potentially divisive and incendiary topics including politics, climate change, religion, gender, and ethnicity can erupt into vitriolic polemics, hate speech, threats,[20] and a general rancour where civil discourse is eliminated in the process. The drive to compete with other users to be heard can involve ever more extreme utterances, and such competition may aggravate already aggressive attitudes lurking beneath the surface. Although one may witness such behaviours on the uncensored 4Chan site or in various subreddit, examples abound on more popular social media sites. Moreover, these utterances and acts of aggression are not consigned to the stereotype of the basement-dwelling troll feverishly tapping away on a keyboard to incite a reaction: even public figures such as celebrities and politicians have been known to engage in impulsive speech acts on social media that may be little more than bullying, insensitive, hostile invectives, indicative of malice or deficit of empathy. In addition, even seemingly well-composed individuals can be baited into an online dispute that escalates to the point of making direct attacks and issuing threats. Even when such events disrupt more civil discourse and are met with condemnation, it has become ever more the case that the instigators of the aggression may castigate the straw-person of 'political correctness' as standing opposed to freedom of expression.

The traits of narcissism and aggression are combined in trollish or bullying behaviour as there may be little regard or reflection by the individual on the consequences for one's online speech acts, and apparent low empathy. Shielded behind a screen, and with the unspoken demand to respond with the immediacy with which social information arrives, childlike eruptions can certainly be more easily triggered.

These forms of online aggression, tied to competition in an attention economy and the perceived demands of instant communication, might be traced in some cases to a form of impulsiveness emerging out of a heated exchange. They may be further facilitated by signs of support for making such utterances; namely, in interpreting a large number of retweets or likes as condoning the act, akin to receiving applause.[21] Such rabble-rousing is certainly not new, but social media presents a new platform with a much larger audience where such an audience can more easily be measured for proof of support. Pundits and propagandists have long understood the value of making use of the media of the day to incite crowds using hyperbole, polemic and other forms of eliciting pathos to exacerbate divisions with simplistic slogans while demonising the Other. And, as lines are drawn on various issues, pitched battles between users may rage as each side will have a vested personal interest, and these fights may quickly escalate – particularly as more users get involved as spectators or participants who thrive on conflict, using provocation and encouragement to keep the flame wars hot.

Studies in online aggression point to a variety of types that define its dimension, including variables that can be measured on the Message Invective Scale including hostility, aggression, intimidation, offensiveness, unfriendliness, uninhibitedness, sarcasm and flaming (Turnage 2007). A good working definition for online aggression would judge such incidents as fundamentally conflictual in nature. In terms of manifestations, online aggression 'can result from personal dislike, ideological or political disagreement, racial or religious prejudice or bias against a certain group. Aggression can also occur in response to a violation of accepted social rules and etiquette or *for no apparent reason*' (Di Segna Garbasz 1997; emphasis mine).

The domain of online aggression and hostility involves a cluster of related studies that include, but are not limited to, current research on cyberbullying, interpersonal studies, computer-mediated communication (CMC), participatory journalism and the digital public sphere. The vast majority of news sites that allow for user-generated commentary are considered generally asynchronous communication environments which can be classified as having lower human-to-human interactivity due to a lack of contingency and mutuality (Burgoon et al 2000). Asynchronous environments differ from synchronous ones on the basis of the latter's capacity for communicative immediacy (such as in live chat). In addition, the rates of interpersonal interactivity may show differences pending the moderation used by the news sites' comment section. User-generated commentary on news sites generally falls within the interaction model of reactive communication (Rafaeli 1988). Interaction can be assumed to be more direct where comment sections are threaded, thus allowing for the nesting of reaction and reply to a 'lead' comment.

The motivations for engaging in online aggression and hostility are multitude and specific to a variety of behavioural traits tied to the user. Combativeness in the online venue can be said to have some basis in ego defence, which can also include indirect ego defence by rising to the occasion in defending another person or group for either reasons of personal validation or on account of identifying oneself with the person or group perceivably under attack.

What generally characterises aggressive online commentary is some form of antagonistic statement that will either make direct attack against another person, or indirectly by associating a point of view with the other person to demonstrate that the position and the people who hold it are equally maligned. Another trend, particularly found in political discussion, is the repetition of talking points and slogans as represented as inviolable truth, thus a rhetorical attempt to shut down further discussion. The person who ritually engages in these behaviours to belittle others, to perform malicious personal attacks, and intimidate – beyond relying on fallacy, crudity, and sensationalism as their weapons – could be defined as possessing lower self-esteem. What functions as ego-insulating behaviour is also indicative of a popular online trend that emerges alongside the rise in punditry and the media by which punditry may be spread.

Aggression and Approbation Cues

Many news sites have implemented a means of approving or disapproving of a user's comment with the aid of the social buttons that permit rating comments up or down. Some news sites have removed the comment feature due to excessive forms of hostility, flaming and spamming. The costs associated with pre-moderated structures whereby comments have to be approved prior to being made visible can be cost-prohibitive whether it is done in-house or outsourced to a separate company.[22] Post-moderated structures rely on users and volunteer moderators to flag content that may violate the rules of the comment area. Unmoderated structures cost virtually little, but open up the space for all the problems moderation seeks to avoid.

Whether comments appear on news stories or on social media that makes use of social buttons in showing approbation or disapproval, users can make decisions without having to justify them. With the deployment of sophisticated botnets or paid trolls, it is not difficult to aggregate a larger number of apparent supporters or objectors to any comment, tweet or post. This may lead to a misleading bandwagon effect akin to social proof as opposed to deeper critical engagement. On those sites that bury user contributions if their aggregate score for approval is too low, such as Reddit, this may lead one to trust the apparent democracy of the majority in deselecting the contribution from the visible feed. This may be construed as social proof of the value of the contributions.

Social proof generally will direct approbation so that the higher the number of thumbs up (or down), the higher the likelihood that other users will contribute as a gesture of social belonging. In a broadly numerical contest of obtaining a large ratio of approval to disapproval, this sets up a competitive aspect where the 'prize' is the community approval of the user as being credible, witty, truthful or informative. Pending the disposition of the user who does not win this 'contest,' ego injury may result which may further elicit an aggressive response.

Aggressive online behaviour might be amplified by over-investment of ego as a result of priority distortion. The perception that the 'stakes' in online comment contests is disproportionately higher than the reward might be. Aggression might result from either the prospect of threat (another user criticising or attacking the user) or as an act of confirmation. Both threat and confirmation denote passionate involvement, sometimes to the extent that it might impair judgement. Catering to an aggrandised sense of opinion entitlement has proven to be prosperous for many news sites given that providing a platform that directly engages self-interest is an effective web traffic driver for getting more eyeballs on ads. By directly or indirectly playing into the narrative of fierce competition, and in providing 'rewards' for 'victory' such as earning a high number of thumbs-up may not only infantilise the space, diminish rational-critical engagement, but also enable aggressive competitive behaviours among those predisposed to such conflict. What makes the 'give no quarter, win the internet' game via user-supplied comments a worthwhile pursuit? The prize or victory only occurs as a form of temporary self-validation, possible intimidation of others, and in potentially gaining an equally fleeting validation from the user community.

When taking online news sites as an example, is difficult to assess if reader-generated opinions today have increased in hostility compared to the past, since traditional news media used editors as gatekeepers, thus rejecting letters to the editor that were harmful, defamatory or libellous, given the legal responsibility of the publication. What problematises effective analysis of hostility levels in opinion is precisely the lack of access to rejected materials. Just as it is unlikely for any researcher to acquire the rejected letters to the editor of a newspaper from 1918, it is equally unlikely to do so for news sites that may simply delete offending comments in 2018. Problematising analysis further, every editor will most likely have a different threshold of tolerance for comments that will determine what is and is not posted online, partially harmonised to the news site's acceptable standards. This, apart from standardised rules that automatically reject user-comments that contravene hate speech or libel laws, presents a variable, relative and flexible number of outcomes depending on the threshold of each moderator and how s/he responds to any given user-generated comment situation. One disturbing question emerges: if the assumption that online hostility proves true according to a measuring of current trends, how much more hostile might it actually be had not the moderator weeded out the worst comments?

Contributing Factors

Although there exist several diagnostic tools for measuring aggression such as the Buss-Durkee Hostility Inventory (BDHI devised in 1957 and more recently modified as the Aggression Questionnaire, or AQ) or Anderson and Bushman's General Aggression Model, none is perfectly suited to obtaining a reliable measure of online hostility and aggression given the very nature of interactive media itself which is constantly replenishing its textual stock or possibly customised to each user to only display relevant content according to the presets of an algorithm. In addition, the effect of online comments on readers as a means by which it might provoke an incident of conflict may be influenced by the 'digital water line'; namely, the probabilities associated with a user being confronted with a provocative comment among currently visible comments as opposed to those that have been 'buried' or relegated to subsequent pages which would involve navigation to said pages not immediately visible.

The optimistic view that online forums bring together like-minded people for the purposes of group sociability has been challenged on the basis that such online activities might in fact tend toward individualisation in particular cases (Hodgkinson 2007). Although broader and more ambient effects constitute peripheral considerations, they no less may play a role in exacerbating and escalating conflict in the online milieu.

Social comparison information may also prompt extreme disinhibition behaviours due to the magnitude of available real-time content. Any gain in online social capital may have a brief shelf life, which requires constant renewal or escalation to be heard in the clamour of online social competition for attention.

Social media, for some, is a hostile battlefield governed by retaliation and initiating either strategies for revenge or instigating conflict, while also a means of building the negative aspects of social capital. Although such behaviours may be seen as simply a natural migration of human tendencies from the offline world, arguably the number of conflict events online might prove much higher than in the offline world on account of virtual distance and the ability to conduct attacks anonymously. Virtual distance provides a buffer for the attacker or vengeance-seeker, but also reduces confronting any of the in-person consequences of such behaviour, thus making it a far more preferred mechanism for the rise in what is now recognised as cyberbullying. Despite a considerable and long overdue increase in focal studies on the issue of cyberbullying,[23] there is a conspicuous dearth of studies that deal directly with online hostility in comment culture apart from a few notable exceptions that deal specifically with what is ambiguously called flaming. Given the lack of access to users' nonverbal communication cues, the primary means of evaluating online conflict had been through textual analysis. With the rise of rich media, photo and video examples of hostility can now also form part of the aggressor's arsenal.

Understanding online conflict relies heavily on psychological distal and proximal causes for aggressive or hostile events. Assessing the users' textual production may provide further evidence and insight by the study of these utterances and how they may conform to existing models in understanding aggression such as the general aggression, cognitive-social or the cognitive neo-associative models. Such methods for understanding online hostility may prove highly beneficial in understanding the issue on a case-by-case basis, and assist in developing a strategy for conflict assessment, analysis and resolution. By adopting a broader socio-cultural and psychoanalytic view of the phenomenon as a whole, larger environmental and ambient influences facilitating aggressive behaviour can be more effectively considered.

Social media does provide a space for its more hostile users to engage in bad behaviour. These behaviours may provide validation and satisfaction to those who seek negative attention, or are paid to provoke such incidents. Cynically, conflict sells if only because it may result in more participation on the platform where, ostensibly, more users will be subject to ads for longer. To a certain extent, online aggression in the form of flame wars and acrimonious, glib exchanges provides a form of entertainment for spectators. When the 'combatants' are high-profile figures, it does not fail to make the news, whether it be the feuding tit-for-tat between actor Mark Hamill and US Senator Ted Cruz over net neutrality, or Donald Trump versus his many targets.

A curious kind of tribalism may be emerging from a social milieu that was so frequently touted as an inclusive, democratising space by optimistic network theorists. The spread of fake news, a rise in cyberbullying, trolling, and the use of 'doxxing' by ideological extremists, points to a new kind of emphasis on both virtual territory and using social media to shout down constructive criticism and reason, if not also the use of hostile threats against the lives of those such individuals and groups target.

'Always Be Closing'

For a number of users, the need to be popular and to always be seen 'winning' in one form or another speaks to some of the unspoken expectations of the social media environment. Users may engage in a variety of online persona management tactics such as staging and curation in order to present an ideal self-stripped of any perceived imperfections or dull moments. Focusing on only the glamorous times and the enhanced image does present a warped world scenario on social media where, for some, the environment is heavily populated by individuals living fantastic lives of leisure, luxury and adventure. This may set up an impossible bar for others to aspire to, and particularly because such representations may deviate from reality. Heavy investment of time and labour in the curation and representation of the digital self in order to obtain the benefits of online social capital is caught up in the games of an attention economy, and its most visible sign is the accumulation of likes, friends and followers as a comparative measure. Winning also becomes the object of some online aggression where the aggressor wishes to be seen as the victor.

In the highly competitive environment of social media where attention is critical to increasing one's stake in the like economy, it should not surprise us that aggressive and hostile tactics may also result. Despite the hundreds of millions of users operating on social media on any given day, attention can be considered something of a scarce commodity, and if it is not those who choose to game the system, others may be choosing to let disinhibition govern behaviour in ways that increase risk-taking, adopting a warped world view of the self and engaging in hostile acts.

It may not prove difficult at this point to see the implications of a more self-involved and competitively driven social media space for the pursuit of online social capital. If, in fact, there is a significant number of social media users following a kind of pleasure principle enabled by the affordances of platforms that can deliver regular notification and potential instant gratification through multi-casting (and cross-syndicating) content, there will be moments of frustration, disappointment, questioning of self-worth and even anger when things do not meet expectations. The fact that we can measure and rank users according to web counters sets up the potential for creating hierarchies and engaging in value judgement on the basis of these counters.

Marx's four aspects of alienation, in scenarios where the pursuit of online social capital fuses with instances of correlative narcissism and aggression, leads to a kind of 'alienation 2.0'. Consider an extreme case of a social media user whose primary goal is to bump up her or his 'score'. Does the pleasure gained by seeing a change in numbers justify all the effort of production, presence, connectivity and deliberate reputation management? Is there a moment of awareness of the futility of such efforts, and that said efforts only truly serve the interests of corporate social media? In the ruthless pursuit of online social capital gain, would said user one day acknowledge that these numbers do not represent actual, intimate bonds? In the end, the social media user does not own the product of their labour, and the numbers associated with likes and retweets and followers may, in fact, be trivial tokens of so much labour time spent in building up these metrics.

Narcissism and aggression are arguably more extreme symptoms of the dogged pursuit of online social capital. However, it does call up the existential question of what these counters actually mean. What real value do they represent as they may be little more than a quasi-social version of making one's bank account public, a form of displaying a social media version of class status.

An obsession with analytics – click-throughs, impressions, site visitors, etc. – is facilitated by the affordances of our digital technology, and used by corporations to track and predict, modify and improve operations for the purposes of maximising profit. This migration of analytics to online social spaces allows users to have a visible output of their presence and efforts on social networks, but the danger arises when this also becomes a motivator for engaging in what would otherwise be deemed capitalist traits of branding and vigorous competition, creating what can be more appropriately called a social *marketplace*. This form of transactional model for social interaction that awards or seeks to gain 'points' appears heavily market-centric.

When the social is subject to being measured, and to sometimes viciously competitive aspects of seeking attention, those who have stronger narcissistic and aggressive tendencies may indulge their worst behaviours. Social media may, in fact, bring this out in many users – even those who are otherwise less competitive. The ubiquity of social media's presence, the apparent broader ideological message of its necessity, and the presence of counters to measure popularity, all work as a confluence of factors to enable and facilitate these behaviours.

Just as it is said of lotteries that one must play to win, the same might be said of social media and its highly competitive environment. For those who see so much at stake, what happens to those who lose? What of those who, for one reason or another, just refuse to play? And for those who 'win,' it is largely on the basis of accumulation, which is its own form of alienation in the end – or at the very least leads to those uncomfortable existential questions of what 'winning' means when such victories are fleeting, and one's production is not owned, serving the ends of the social media corporation.

There is some hope that the continued de-stigmatising of mental wellness issues in public discourse can provide some measure of support in understanding the impact social media in its current competition-centred form has on self-esteem, and perhaps lead to a call for corrective changes. Moreover, there may also be pressure to at least make the devices that are used to access social media less 'addictive.' For example, a group of shareholders of Apple have petitioned the corporation to do just that. A number of apps have been developed that track the amount of time one spends on social media, or in silencing the constant and tempting ping of notifications. If the social media environment cannot be made less competitive in the short term, perhaps opting for means to limit time spent on it may prove of some benefit.

Main Points

- The egocentric nature of social media sites that cater to the individual also facilitates and actively enables more narcissistic investment in the digital self.
- The prevailing ideological discourse that privileges individualism and competition provides an ideal ground for narcissistic behaviours on social media, as well as a focus on accumulating a quantity rather than quality of social connections. This may lead to the view of other users as mere objects to be manipulated and to provide narcissistic fodder for the user.
- As social media facilitates self-display and competition for online social capital, there may be ambient pressure for other users to integrate narcissistic behaviours in a competition to be noticed and be considered relevant. Moreover, narcissistic behaviour may be a dominant social norm on social media, and so new users may adopt certain behaviours in an effort to 'fit in.'
- Narcissism's reliance on the Id may result in a larger profusion of grandiose claims, and actions that are performed on social media with little empathy or regard for consequences. This is further facilitated by the nature of computer-mediated communication environments where there is an apparent buffer against consequences due to distance and the ability to conduct oneself under screen aliases.
- Competition for online social capital in conjunction with more impulsive Id-based behaviour can also result in more online aggression as a means to intimidate, attract attention through provocation, or as a reactive narcissistic defence mechanism.

CHAPTER 6

The Network Spectacle

Networks of promotion/control slide imperceptibly into networks of surveillance/disinformation.

Guy Debord (1988, 74).

This chapter takes up the issue of whether more of us are being caught up in a kind of network spectacle whereby all that is digitally networked must, by definition, be good – including social life. Moreover, online social capital becomes a kind of lure to entice more participation, where obtaining signs of approbation through social buttons and incremental increases is built into the platform as a means of perpetuating this spectacle. To carry this out, it will be important to explore the nature of the spectacle as theorised by Guy Debord, applying this to the digitally networked world that he might not have foreseen. In having focused on the theories of Marx and Veblen regarding alienation, it is time to complete this book's 'triad' by including Debord's often prescient – and sometimes gnomic or oracular – statements on technology and alienation as it pertains to online social capital. The goal will be to discuss the movement from the notion of the spectacle and simulacrum to that of the social algorithm, and in this way provide more of a 'meta' understanding of the implications of online social capital as it operates on platforms powered by networks and the 'digital sublime.'

Neoliberal capitalism, having made technological innovation its exclusive instrument, develops more effective ways of perfecting social separation. This, combined with the perversion of cybernetics and the compression of both time and space in digital environments, gives the illusion of connective immediacy and proximity. However, despite the collapse of spatial distances and the ease by which connections can be made speedily in larger quantities, the social ties may be weak and contingent upon mediating through the devices sold by capital. More than simply neutral devices, the devices themselves exist in a

How to cite this book chapter:
Faucher, K. X. 2018. *Social Capital Online: Alienation and Accumulation*. Pp. 109–133. London: University of Westminster Press. DOI: https://doi.org/10.16997/book16.g. License: CC-BY-NC-ND 4.0

spectacular commodification network that promotes their adoption and use as the prerequisite for many forms of our social connection.

The network *as* spectacle conceals the rate of exploitation, or surplus value generated by a large prosumer audience, behind a veil of optimism, novelty and stimulus. It extols the values of speed, efficiency, convenience, and connectivity. Dissolving the nature of labour in digital walled gardens that appear to privilege play and creativity. The network spectacle presents itself as sublime, and within its apparatus all who are participants within it are enjoined to support and reinforce the spectacle as good, for which there are no other viable alternatives. With the lionisation and fanfare associated with the information age and the network society, overly optimistic pronouncements about how digital technology would revolutionise everyday life have been heavily oversold. There is no denying that there have been significant changes in the speed of transactions, connecting more people over larger distances, and even disruptive technologies in the form of ride-sharing services such as Uber or finding places to stay via Airbnb, but ecological, sociopolitical, and economic problems remain. Only when these new technologies lose their mythic lustre and become normalised do they present options for real change:

> the real power of new technologies does not appear during their mythic period, when they are hailed for their ability to bring world peace, renew communities, or end scarcity, history, geography, or politics; rather, their social impact is greatest when technologies become banal—when they literally (as in the case of electricity) or figuratively withdraw into the woodwork (Mosco 2004, 19).

Digital representation becomes the active process and product of this milieu, a hyperreal environment that subordinates the now impoverished value of the non-digital to the production of images that are destined for digital re-production. The network spectacle is presented as unassailably good, perfect, and the primary source of the positively represented values decanted from neoliberalism such as efficiency, speed and connectivity. However, it is those very values that not only speak directly to issues of exchange value and commodity fetishism, but also physically impoverishes those who labour to support the spectacle. In that sense, there are those who labour to produce the content via their own digital representations who now may have an impoverished sense of the non-digital world, which is now subordinate to the aims of the network spectacle (as a kind of raw material of experience that must be refined and processed into digital content representation); and there are those who labour in the extraction of actual raw materials, sweatshop manufacture, and precarious work in the service industry to provide the network spectacle with a steady supply of labour time.

Just as the rise of large corporate social media was able to plug in the social function into its network, today the network has succeeded in being plugged into daily life where sophisticated algorithms monitor online behaviour are then used to serve up more of what users want in terms of what will make them happy and comfortable, creating islands or bubbles where competing or alternative perspectives never intrude. This kind of walled garden functions to channel online behaviours and clandestinely restrict social interactive opportunities. Such 'matching and pairing' mechanisms of the algorithm on these networks is hardly new, as they are largely based on principles of homophily and powered by cybernetic thinking. Such thinking assumes sameness or similarity is socially generative and desirable. Today, that principle of group conformity is still active, be it in recommender services for products, or in what appears in one's news feed that the network deems 'relevant' to the user.

It is the unceasing monologue of the network spectacle in presenting what is good that contributes to generalised separation. As Debord states (2000, 28), the technology 'is based on isolation, and the technical process isolates in turn.' More than simply being 'alone together,' this isolation and separation operates at the heart of production – in this case the production of the digital 'worker' who is, in effect, reproducing his or her own experience as an image to be exchanged on the social market to increase online social capital.

In the very first aphorism of *Society of the Spectacle*, Debord provocatively modifies the first sentence of Marx's *Capital* by claiming that life is the accumulation of spectacles as opposed to commodities. This proceeds from a telling quote from Feuerbach where illusion's increasing power over truth inverts the relationship between the sacred and profane. This inversion of truth and illusion threads through much of Debord's sustained critique of the spectacle. One might immediately point to some of the symptoms of the power and allure of illusion in the ways by which social media users may compete for attention and online social capital in creating artificial representative images of themselves online in visual and textual forms, the rise of fake news that unapologetically appeals to belief over facts, or that the incremental increase in various forms of counting using social buttons has a direct correlation with perceived human value.

In the place of capital, the spectacle is the social relation between people – not mediated by commodities or money, but by images. The images are autonomous insofar as they exist separately from the commodities they refer to. It is to the extent that one purchases the image of the product as an experience, and only receives in exchange the product: the vehicle and not the breathtaking winding road, the clothing or technology item and not the fun the image seems to promise. The images are perpetuated in a society with all the assumptions that they are true aspects of reality, but they are but mere representations of the dominant language of spectacular society. The language of the spectacle promises unification (we can all traffic in the same imagistic references to brands and standardised experiences) and delivers separation: from ourselves, each other and the world. All of these relations have been inverted, and so our alienation emerges from this kind of detachment from the real. That which resides on the outside of the spectacle may be seen as a threat, obscured from view, or filtered as yet another image. A kind of availability heuristic is empowered by the language of the spectacle, and operationalised by the algorithm's tendency to create filter bubbles.

Examples of the availability heuristic on social media can operate in more automated or clandestine ways given the depth to which the social aspect is integrated into the platform as part of a high-trust culture that lumps more user content according to what is likely to conform to set beliefs, values and customs. If we take the example of adolescents in particular who are arguably at a very formative stage in social and cultural development in terms of their identity, they may be treated to online status updates and stories depicting users who live a life of constant leisure, glamour, excitement and whose carefully curated self-images appeals to unrealistic beauty standards.

The spectacle is positioned in Debord's work as the social relation between people hijacked by capitalism. The accumulation of commodities has been demoted by an accumulation of images that refer to these commodities. Owning the object being sold, or having and experience is secondary to being seen doing so, and documenting it for public display. However, when social media users dedicate so much of their time trying to gain online social capital by posting images of their possessions or experiences, in some cases the main goal of this form of conspicuous display is simply to increase online social capital in the like economy. Even the most sacred or personal moments may not be directly lived as such, and one only needs to think of that person who will say that their wedding is not official until it is posted on Facebook, or those who rush from one historical monument to the next snapping pictures without taking the time to appreciate them. Until these are posted online, they seem to have little value.

Debord's claim is that the world of the spectacle is ideology materialised: the correspondence between dominant ideology and individual worldviews is enshrouded in a mythology of optimism. The ubiquity of the spectacle and the practices that arise in the construction of social software architecture are manifest in unseen algorithms that facilitate connection and use as products of this ideology materialised as 'datapolitik.' This is supported by the way in which economic activity and communications technology are frequently touted as neutral, thus insulating both from critique. This effectively naturalises both economic and technological discourse as neutral and objective, and the ideological intent of these is obfuscated by instrumental reason. Debord pushes the Marxist line further by claiming that it is not just the producer or labourer that is alienated from his or her labour, from other members of their class, and from life which has been inverted by a capitalist model to appear as though it were the only viable option, but that this also holds true for the consumer. The consumer is caught in this inverted life of the spectacle, capable only of unilateral communication by doing the work of the spectacle through constant reification of its aims. 'Behind' this spectacle is economic determinism and algorithmic control that has only its own power and growth as its goal, and thus requires that the economy be in a constant state of crisis in order to properly function.

This kairotic dimension is facilitated in part by the blurring of the traditional binaries of producer and consumer (the 'prosumer'), the discrete aspects of the digital and the continuous field of the analogue, and the subordination of the problematic under highly standardised social media software regimes that control the flow of social economies online. The social in this way becomes a representation by information where power is articulated, reticulated, distributed and mobilised as packets and segments in multiple bitstreams. Social meaning itself becomes vulgarised by the apostate defenders of a technical information-theoretic perspective that is focused on developing multiple channels at the expense of meaning production, which is always secondary.

Baudrillard as Postmodern Interruption?

There are some apparent similarities between Debord's concept of the spectacle and Jean Baudrillard's concept of the hyperreal. In the hyperreal, the real has been condemned to a proliferation of signs and their exchange that seem to operate in a world governed by illusion. For Baudrillard, this disconnection from the real – due to the way we mediate our experiences– creates a simulacrum that precedes the real. Our own self-representations of experience already point to this simulacrum. In taking a picture of a trip to Paris to see the Eiffel Tower and posting it on Facebook, this is a representation of the event of being there and seeing the object, but the form-copy relationship is disturbed as that 'event' bears no relation to that distinction, but instead is something other – a simulacrum. One might have an idea of Paris, the Eiffel Tower, leisure, travel and so forth as depicted through media. This representation has already broken an alliance with the real, and as a result we may have a highly mediated image of the reality of place and objects that we may seek to recreate and represent by placing ourselves in the frame. One might go a step further to say that social media itself becomes an environment of simulacra where social relations have broken their alliance with what is real about being social, and that others behave in ways where social relations become co-opted by the expectations of being in these environments that are indexed heavily on increasing online social capital through its dominant signs of social buttons. Online social capital itself is a kind of simulacrum of capitalist accumulation where the increase in the like economy is only an apparent resemblance to actual capitalist accumulation (which occurs in the background between the social media site and its partners).

Baudrillard's view of capitalism and consumption practices does not restrict itself to speaking only of alienation, since that is to court an unacknowledged moralism which speaks more to the alienated moralist. Yet, it is clearly identified in Debord what the spectacle and economic determinism has made of social relations: they are entirely dominated by commodity exchange where alienation becomes a central commodity for the society of the spectacle. This idea continues to be restated in several forms, or rendered in a manner that suggests that our communication is dominated by a pervasive economic mysticism that both quantises and etherealises social relations. This shares a zone of overlap with Debord's notion that we never acquire the object itself, but only its particular manifestation that we hope will bring our desire in contact with unity and transcendental reward. Whether we call this failure to achieve the oceanic bliss ideal where goods answer all needs, a progression of alienation or the slippage of signs in the Lacanian register, we are faced with a deficit on the order of meaning, fulfilment and contentment. This deficit is transformed into its own meaning, and perpetual lack of fulfilment operates as a principal driver in consumer behaviour.

In a system that has co-opted the methods of religious awe and reconstructed the real according to its own inverted, self-styled image, both Debord and Baudrillard demonstrate that the pursuit of happiness or contentment is itself misguided, and this for reasons endemic to a system with its own functional logic that is also rife with contradictions and tautologies (such as 'individual' and 'celebrity' that do not have definitional criteria with a stable reference). The rampant hyper-capitalism of today continues its progress to achieve its exclusive aim: growth for growth's sake, and this is also reflected in the dogged pursuit of online social capital where one can never have enough friends, followers, likes, retweets and up-votes. This growth is achieved through orchestrated crises, the increase in wealth that is also an increase in wealth disparity, the further disequilibrium of a system that seeks to dominate with no other purpose or final design than to expand itself.

One of the principal concerns of hyper-capitalism is the continued erosion or even wide-scale eradication of community-mindedness. The failure to conduct social relations without the intermediary of commodity images makes social relations dependent upon an economic determinist model that permits all that may be possible in our social relations as customisable preconditions. It is not the objects themselves that function as the conduits of social expression, but their signs, the broader commodity culture meanings they are burdened with. Our social relations become thoroughly infused by commodity culture's semio-capitalist code.

The spectacle, powered by capitalist economy, is able to produce the very objects that promise connection but actually continue to exacerbate isolation and alienation. In autocratic societies such as Germany under Nazism and Soviet communism, the one unifying yet alienating product produced to gratify desires was ideology. All productive forces were committed to the production of ideology reified in images of the dictator, symbols, and the ideological message. In order to make that effective, it required constant reinforcement by vertical integration by authority figures and the strategic surveillance and detention practices of police. In our spectacular society, we do not need a secret police or army to reinforce our obedience: commodities possess an ambient regulatory effect that function as proxy conditioners. It is the economy whose major productive means and ends is alienation.

Debord holds to the view that the commodity system will only develop, and along with it, alienation. One cannot expect to stage a revolution against it from within. This strikes off one of two of Marx's possible solutions: liberation from the economy and liberation from within the economy. '*Separation* is the alpha and omega of the spectacle' (Debord 2000, 25). Although referring to exacerbating class divisions, there are other cleavages by which this separation unites segmented groups across racial, gender and political lines, thus feeding a kind of tribalism that is partially supported by self-selective network connections and selective exposure. 'From the automobile to television, all the goods selected by the spectacular system are also its weapons for constant reinforcement of the conditions of isolation of 'lonely crowds' (Debord 2000, 28).

If, as Debord tells us, life is presented as an accumulation of spectacles, and that everything 'that was directly lived has moved away into representation' (Debord 2000, aph 1), with respect to time scales, we are barred from the past since what is presented is merely representational, and these representations are convened, manufactured or designed by the spectacle itself. However, one wonders if even the present moment can attain to any significant value if it is simply a remediation of a representational past that is disseminated by way of images that carry the cultural messages via its visual channels. In a telling interview, when then-presidential candidate Donald Trump was confronted with an error in the statistics he presented about race-based violent crimes, he replied, 'all I know is what is on the internet.' This kind of chamber or echo-effect of selective exposure is highly problematic for a variety of reasons, not least of which being that confirmation bias has an impact on decision-making and the possibly narrow or distorted worldview one may embrace. When it comes to what people choose to believe, this may also be on account of the narrow selective process of hidden algorithms. The tautological nature of the spectacle's 'truth' forecloses the possibility of seeking beyond it to mount a significant or resonant challenge:

> The spectacle proves its arguments simply by going round in circles: by coming back to the start, by repetition, by constant reaffirmation in the only space left where anything can be publicly affirmed, and believed, precisely because that is the only thing to which everyone is a witness. (Debord 2000, 19)

Given the emergence of the prosumer, the work of the spectacle is increased, as well as its ability to permeate and colonise all social relations as now the 'spectator' can be a more active worker in the proliferation of the spectacle. The images by which so many live by, conform to and subordinate their subjectivity, are capable of being transmitted much faster and with less need for direct intervention by the state, mass media and advertising. This horizontal form of social reinforcement of the spectacle decreases costs for capitalists, and crowdsources the reinforcement of these imagistic messages. It further retrenches Debord's claim of a true proletarianisation of the world.

Baudrillard's concepts provide some useful connections to understanding social media as a simulacrum, but they may fall short of understanding the broader mechanics at play in the way the spectacular society operates.

The Integrated Spectacle

Debord had identified two forms of the spectacle, each pertaining to geopolitical divide during the cold war. The *concentrated* spectacle was the domain of the Soviet Union where the entire social and political reality concentrated power and belief in the celebrated, almost religious figure of the dictatorial autocrat. The *diffuse* spectacle was the domain of Western values, and primarily with 'Americanisation' in the lead whereby American values pegged onto consumerism, the image of democracy, an image of freedom and the sacred value bestowed upon private property and were aggressively exported around the globe. In effect, the two forms of the spectacle correspond to two functions: the one inbound in its communications, and the other outbound. With the collapse of the Soviet Union, to these two forms Debord adds a third: the *integrated* spectacle, which adopts certain features of the previous two in dialectical fashion. The nature of the integrated spectacle is still to concentrate power, but to do so in an ambiguous fashion where it remains unclear what the reigning ideology might be, who heads up the transnational corporation, and so forth, as a kind of apparent decentring of power. Yet, power and wealth continue its concentration into fewer hands – even if it may not be as obvious to whom those hands belong. In terms of the diffuse spectacle, we still see the aggressive attempt to export particular values and ideas, but these are not the outputs of production on a global scale, but carried in products themselves. In its diffusion, the integrated spectacle undersigns all social products in such a way that what it describes as reality is merely itself.

This integration is total and ubiquitous, making it nearly impossible to assess the spectacle as something foreign to reality, as if some external object that can be critically analysed; instead, all the tools of analysis that make up the discourse are provided by the spectacle. Anything we can say about this spectacle is already prefigured by the spectacle's constraints on our social vocabulary.

There are two examples of the integrated spectacle worthy of mention here: one that is concrete and cloaked by the abstract, and the other that is abstract and concealed by apparent materiality. The first concerns the economic order, the stage of neoliberal capitalism that far more resembles transcendent forces united with a distorted Darwinism. Economics appears as a science if only because it makes use of models to predict market behaviour (as though a market is a hybrid living organism and computer program), supported by a roughshod application of mathematics, and spurred on in its enterprise by specious and unscientific axioms that point to the unquestionable rationality of human beings as calculating agents of self-interest. Tied up with this are hyperbolic values that speak of 'freedom' as the greatest of all possible goals, even if the economic system does more to control and limit the freedoms of others, and justifies growing inequalities in the name of this freedom. Another example might be the more abstract notion of the network as a form of social integration of activity, and the network epistemologies that become integrated within the new so-called 'digital reality' of our information age. The materiality of the network can be found in the popularisation of the network architecture, websites, and the devices required to access them.

The integrated spectacle would not have prevailed as it has without the steady rise of ICTs. It is precisely the entanglement of the integrated spectacle with the highly regimented network technologies and their valorisation as the greatest public good that leads to the network spectacle. It is useful here to provide Debord's five cardinal aspects of the integrated spectacle to infer how this progression has since materialised: constant technological innovation, the entwining functions of the state and economy, generalised secrecy, unanswerable lies and an eternal present.

The Integrated Spectacle: Spectacular Innovation

Debord makes only a brief comment on how technological innovation is part of the capitalist repertoire and dominated by specialists. There is, of course, much more to the story, and one that can be traced to Veblen's warnings on not confusing the interests of technologists and finance. But it can also be seen to address how such technology facilitates the increasing power of neoliberalism's gospel of borderless trade, efforts at deregulation, labour-displacement through self-service models, microsecond market trading, increased state potential for mass surveillance, the extraction of surplus labour through crowdsourcing initiatives under the guise of 'community participation', the discursive framing of the spectacle as being the only permitted answer for which there are no alternatives, the obligation to purchase the newest devices at regular intervals, the obligation to be connected to the networks and the proliferation of proprietary hardware and software as opposed to open source and modifiable forms.

The entwining functions of the state and economy become more readily apparent when we consider the current state of neoliberal governments with their view that borderless trade, deregulation and creating laws that favour private enterprise are all part of a strategy to downshift risk and responsibility to citizens (who become ever more viewed as consumers). In terms of social media, and its enormous impact on both social relations and economic development, there may be very little oversight on how these major online social networks operate. Although there are moments of friction, such as in getting sites like Facebook to comply with government requests for user information, the relationship is far from being a complicated one. Given the benefits social media provides for corporations, and as a valuable tool for governments to conduct surveillance, there would appear little appetite for more stringent regulation. Both the state and economy have the goal of domination through power and wealth as the means of perpetuating more of the same. Markets have much to gain in this close relationship with government. As Debord tells us, it is 'the autocratic reign of the market economy which had acceded to an irresponsible sovereignty, and the totality of new techniques of government which accompanied this reign' (2000, 2).

The Integrated Spectacle: Generalised Secrecy, Lies, and the Eternal Present

Generalised secrecy points to the fact that such secrecy is less about secret services attempting to silence dissent and remove 'inconveniences' from spectacular discourse, but that more agents of the spectacle emerge to perform this function. For example, there are a considerable number of grassroots movements that optimise their use of social media to carry out their agenda in support of the spectacular status quo. In addition, celebrities and specialists can become the conduits of these agendas, more powerfully facilitated by the size and reach of social media.

The fourth aspect of the integrated spectacle points to unanswerable lies, which 'have succeeded in eliminating public opinion, which first lost the ability to make itself heard and then very quickly dissolved altogether. This evidently has significant consequences for politics, the applied sciences, the legal system and the arts' (Debord 1998, 13). We might question if this has come to pass given social media's affordances for providing the public with a forum to provide their opinions. Yet, the mixture of the availability heuristic via algorithmic sorting and the coordinated efforts of the vocal few to dominate the online conversation may have altered the impact of public opinion in ways that 'dialogue' continues to be one of spectacular domination. By adding the use of astroturfing clandestinely operated by government agencies and corporate entities to promote various agendas such as climate-change denial or the protection of brand reputation in the face of scandal, this fosters an environment that only *appears* to reflect the majority public opinion by sheer numbers of users alone. As Jodi Dean (2005) has argued, the mass profusion of opinion symbolises the fantasies of abundance and participation very well and thus devalues the *content* of political discourse, as well as working against unity.

In the final aspect of the integrated spectacle reside the notion of an eternal present and the negation of history. Debord's statement is worthy of being quoted in full:

> The manufacture of a present where fashion itself, from clothes to music, has come to a halt, which wants to forget the past and no longer seems to believe in a future, is achieved by the ceaseless circularity of information,

always returning to the same short list of trivialities, passionately proclaimed as major discoveries. Meanwhile news of what is genuinely important, of what is actually changing, comes rarely, and then in fits and starts. It always concerns this world's apparent condemnation of its own existence, the stages in its programmed self-destruction (1998, 13).

Debord refers specifically to how the May 1968 movement in France was conveniently revised. Taken in other contexts, the control or negation of historical facts grants power to those who seek spectacular domination. Politicians, for instance, who run on platforms that campaign on nostalgic images and sentiments are among numerous examples. Debord points to an almost Orwellian historical revisionism where the 'truth' of any past event is contingent upon the present needs of those in power, even if it contradicts a past statement.[24] Even politicians who are called to task over statements made in campaigns can readily dismiss or deny those statements and change the conversation by attacking the media for engaging in 'gotcha' journalism and discrediting the source.[25] It is also Debord's somewhat prescient warning that seems to speak to social media's fixation on novelty as dangerous:

> When social significance is attributed only to what is immediate, and to what will be immediate immediately afterwards, always replacing another, identical, immediacy, it can be seen that the uses of the media guarantee a kind of eternity of noisy insignificance. (1998, 15).

The negation or revision of history is hardly new, be it the destruction of libraries by various rulers, or the rampant revisionism in the Stalinist Soviet Union and Maoist China, or even in the attempts by the previous Harper administration in Canada to privilege the country's military history with a view to create a vision of glory to be associated with the ruling government's values. The one chief difference with the emergence of social media is its emphasis on novelty, and the ability to reconstruct the past – even one's own. 'With the destruction of history, contemporary events themselves retreat into a remote and fabulous realm of unverifiable stories, uncheckable statistics, unlikely explanations and untenable reasoning' (Debord 1998, 16). Perhaps no better proof exists than the proliferation of fake news stories.

In this process of revisionism and an eternal present may stand the individual who may abdicate personality as 'the price the individual pays for the tiniest bit of social status' and that it leads the individual to 'a succession of continually disappointing commitments to false products. It is a matter of running hard to keep up with the inflation of devalued signs of life' (Debord 1998, 32). In the pursuit of online social capital, the sale of the self is what authenticates value, measured in part by incremental social buttons. Engaged in such pursuits, and valorised by any number of services that promise for a fee to increase number of hits, likes, etc., this in turn transforms the social component into a kind of network of falsification where these numerical 'values' hold sway, and online users adopt the strategies provided by online social networks to falsify themselves in order to compete.

One has only to think here of the ubiquitous presence of digital devices that facilitate the recording of events to be consumed as images later. This accumulation of representations of a lived event, leveraged as a status object to be trafficked on social networking sites as 'proof of presence' is ensconced in the practice of self-alienation. These images detach from life and join a 'common stream in which the unity of this life can no longer be re-established' (Debord 2000, 2). These images merge into an autonomous image of the world which is an inversion of the real. However, in our current informational and communicational predicament of nonlinear processing and self-organising algorithmic pressures that determine the representation of online behaviours, the quasi-dynamical aspect of self-selecting and customisable software has produced a closed system where the images and the objects are united and displace life: first as a supplement, and then as a 'master token' that replicates the very conditions of existence as a productive mode of constant mediations.

Debord tells us that the spectacle postures as all society, part of society and the instrument of unification. As part of society it is the sector responsible for concentrating gazing and consciousness. This sector traffics in the 'official language of generalized separation' (Debord 2000, 3). The spectacle is not derived from propaganda or advertising or mass media. It is the objectified *Weltanshauung*. This is to say that the spectacle is the driving force behind propaganda, advertising and mass media. Debord relegates mass media as a form of equipment by which society can be administrated: 'if the administration of this society and all contact among men can no longer take place except through the intermediary of this power of instantaneous communication, it is because this "communication" is essentially *unilateral* [and the] concentration of "communication" is thus an accumulation' (Debord 2000, 24).

The spectacle is the end product as well as the very purpose of the current system of production. The 'spectacle is the present *model* of socially dominant life.' It is affirmed even after the choice was already made on behalf of others. What might seem like active choice is passive consent. The spectacle presents itself as its own justification, the alpha and omega of life. The unity of the world was already based on a fundamental separation of reality and image. The spectacle inherent in social life has convinced us that the spectacle is the only goal. 'The language of the spectacle consists of *signs* of the ruling production' which produces signs, while the spectacle produces this negation of life as part of its monopoly on appearance: 'In a world which *really is topsy-turvy*, the true is a moment of the false' (Debord 2000, 8). What is taken now as being the real is only the real as generated by the totalising force of the spectacle. Furthermore, the spectacle is the affirmation of appearance and human social life as mere appearance. This negates human life, and what truly appears is this negation. Social relations become little more than flattened signs in a vicious commodity exchange. The spectacle is the main production as seen in its objects, the alleged rationality of the system, and the economic sector that develops image-objects. This perspective aligns in part with Baudrillard (1998) in *The Consumer Society:*

> The usage of signs is always ambivalent. Its function is always a conjuring – both a conjuring up and a conjuring away: causing something to emerge in order to capture it in signs (forces, reality, happiness, etc.) and evoking something in order to deny and repress it … the generalized consumption of images, of facts, of information aims also *to conjure away the real with the signs of the real.'* (33)

This is a slight deviation from Debord's idea of accumulated images to that of a semiotic system. Debord's images may imply this semiotic system, one that operates in a tautological loop where signs or images function as the basis and output of signs and images. For Baudrillard, 'Affluence' is, in effect, merely the accumulation of the *signs* of happiness' (1998, 31). These signs of happiness are the mirror image of the signs of ruling production. Affluence takes on the role of signifying the bliss to be achieved through hyper-production and hyper-consumption, both practices tied to a form of labour. This promise of affluence bequeathed by the spectacle or the simulacrum, is nothing more than an image or sign, and much of it is propagated by the equipment of media. As Baudrillard reminds us, '[w]hat mass communications gives us is not reality, but the *dizzying whirl of reality.* […] So we live, sheltered by signs, in the denial of the real... The image, the sign, the message–all these things we "consume"–represent our tranquillity consecrated by distance from the world' (2008, 34).

Between Debord and Baudrillard, there is a similarity on how they view alienation and the inversion of truth. For Debord, the spectacle is powered by the false taken as the true, whereas for Baudrillard the simulacrum becomes a disconnected and specialised play of an excess or overabundance of signs constructing a new context that plays the role of the real. That is, the simulacrum divests itself of all referentials, purging any stable connection between one sign and another. Signs become, in the postmodern fatalism of Baudrillard, aleatory. However, what Baudrillard may neglect to consider in this excessive production of signs is that new non-linear dynamical systems colonise this excess sign production and arrange them within a metastable system that allows for flexible production. Moreover, the step beyond is to simply unmask the simulacrum (which is neither real nor its opposite) to find the true relation, which is alienation itself. Alienation exists as a 'bond' insofar as it can function as a relation between an individual and the world, an individual and the self, and between individuals. The economic system, which is based on isolation, exacerbates isolation. Even our technology and the technological processes are isolating, alienating, serving to reinforce that alienation. The unity is indeed built on separation, and can be pithily expressed: 'the spectacle is nothing more than an image of happy unification surrounded by desolation and fear at the tranquil centre of misery' (Debord 2000, 63).

The optimism and novelty surrounding the opportunities of social media do not cease. The dominant language of the spectacle includes the use of social media as the means to participating in good faith in the market economy. With an emphasis on a false sense of sovereignty, self-expression and novelty, there are any number of authors who will proselytise somewhat uncritically on the many virtues of social media. Under this effect of the network spectacle that dominates online social life, banishing the past, implicitly encouraging disinhibition that might lead to more Id-like behaviour, there may be a process of infantilisation occurring where the promise of play conceals the reality of social media work, and social media is portrayed as something always liberating. As an example of such a view, Paul Levinson focuses strictly on the positive:

> Adults become children–usually in the best sense of the word–when we encounter and adopt a new mode of communication, especially one such as Twitter, which with a few keystrokes can open new vistas for our personal and professional lives. (Levinson 2009, 139)

Thus in contrast with the more pessimistic views of Lewis Mumford who was writing at the very beginning of the era of electronic communications, whose statement may very much apply today:

> [M]ore commonplace thoughts, events, and scenes, transmitted only to keep the deprived senses from starvation, by giving the illusion of life, do not deserve such enlargement […] To be aware only of immediate stimuli and immediate sensations is a medical indication of brain injury. (1970, 298)

The spectacle's domination over social life appears to demand and privilege novelty, the eternal present, and constant chatter – with a bulk of that chatter being indexed on commodities. Equally disturbing is how quickly the transition moves from non-alienated subjectivity to alienation in full force as part of representation. Debord points to this historical progress as moving from being (I am), to having (property as defining identity) to mere appearing (I am the image of myself, represented in a series of objects, which are also imagistic). What the spectacle demands is compliance and passive acceptance, while it also offers a false unity through its techniques of separation, as well as an inverted world stripped of complexity, composed of static images of happiness through consumption. In a way somewhat reminiscent of Nietzsche's notion of passive nihilism, the 'spectacle is the guardian of sleep' (Debord 2000, 21). The relation between self and world is reconfigured through the reduction of the self to mere image whereby the 'acceptance and consumption of commodities are at the heart of this pseudo-response to a communication without a response.' (Debord 2000, 219).

Online appearance is one of the most important games of strategy as the shift in emphasis from offline significance to online increases. Much is said about maintaining an online presence almost as though the failure to achieve this will result in failure as an individual or a business, conjuring a totalising opposition: online presence or irrelevance. Capitalising on this zeitgeist are thousands of firms dedicated to increasing web presence using many of the strategies of the public relations field. Effective web presence is very much part of the spectacular process of promising a personal transcendence through the unity provided by participation. One must be in 'good faith' and thus show fidelity through online communicative acts that attempt to occupy the digital space with one's representative marks of presence. Behind this is the strategy, itself built on a principle of competition—an online pursuit to gain attention at the expense of attention being invested elsewhere.

This applied online narcissism requires strict discipline to produce and sustain. Given that such presencing mirrors the principles and strategies of the economic market under the spectacle, it has a duty to optimise its exchange value in a regime of signs. The strategy involves minimum investment with an expectation of maximum return. Investing the sign of one's self online does entail risk, but also comes with this expectation that the digital realm's social feedback mechanism will increase the value of the initially invested sign. The result is that the digital version of the ego takes on an accumulated value much higher than that of the initial ego that invested the sign, thus increasing the disparity of value between off- and online self, which incidentally increases self-alienation. Much of the same logic applies to celebrity culture with regard to the PR mechanisms that facilitate the production and inflation of value. The individual can no longer live up to the online representation of web presence, and thus finds his or herself a slave to it. The intrinsic value of ego is crushed by the spectacular value of the representative image. The cult of celebrity and the belief in the easy acquisition of prestige has increased in the last century, creating the conditions of transforming ideals into live-in illusions. Some have become their own most fiery promoters attempting to market the product of a self that may have not been marketable. Devoid of substantive, profound, or significant content (such as developing and manifesting talent in some industry like the arts or knowledge or craft, etc.), it is simply the act of selling for selling's sake. This is not particularly unheard of given the raft of objects that are devoid of any significant use value.

Much of digital-social relations are modelled on economic transaction. We do not enter into human relations without sharing commodities, and thus some may be alienated from each another by trading in representative images of life. But all of this is over-coded by an economic determinism that is antagonistic to life. We are left with desire as lack, as the fantasy, which brings together the two streams of psychoanalysis' study of desire and Debord's spectacle. The spectacle fulfils the need for the fantasy, even if that satisfaction is temporary. Individuals become locked into a common cultural alphabet of celebrity gossip and commodities in a loop since the spectacle monopolises communication.

The spectacle has two major aims: constant technological renewal and the integration of the state and economy. In Debord's assessment, the state and economy are dominating forces in the spectacle, and there is no public sphere. Rational debate would involve access to the past and orientation to the future, but as we see in mass media, the past is reduced to the spectacle of retro-philia and nostalgia (and so therefore transformed into an image that becomes real because all of reality becomes simply an image) and the future simply deferred. So, in this way, we live in an eternal present, a kind of *epideictic* moment. What this means is that the only 'power' – which is no power at all – is to like or dislike the images put before us. There is a lack of critical engagement and no shades of grey in the eternal present. The spectacle serves up a constant series of images that, like a Facebook post, can be 'liked' or ignored. In this movement of the commodity to render its own version of the world visible, it is also the movement of further estrangement of people 'among themselves and in relation to their global product' (Debord 2000, 37).

It is the trick of the spectacle, to reinvest in reality by providing its inversion, its reconfigured conception of it, in order to change our entire social relationship to the world so that all our actions are performed under the direction of serving the economy and believing with an almost religious faith in the salvation the end that is production will provide. The crisis model is wedded to that of capitalist economy since it operates best by alternation between market highs and lows. It is a machine of unstable excesses, a system that can only work by means of overstimulation since the real has long ago become inert and unresponsive. Baudrillard tells us 'if it was capital which fostered reality, the reality principle, it was also the first to liquidate it in the extermination of every use value'(1983, 43). Use value is effaced and only exchange value remains, even in social relations where the transactional model online is conducted by way of signs. The commodities become intangible, as they are simply images in the accelerated play of perpetual simulation. Further, Baudrillard says, '[w]hat society seeks through production, and overproduction, is the restoration of the real which escapes it' (1983, 44). So, salvation and reunion with the real is conditional on participating as much as possible in the acts of production. Reward can only be gained through this production, but this reward is impossible to achieve since it exists only as a transcendental image outside of the ability to grasp it. All that is obtained from the image of the real (which is inverted in the spectacle) is its impressions, a bit of the glitter and dust from the shaking of the angel's wings. This alienation from ourselves and reality occurs through the prism of production's demands, and so the new opiate of the masses is the myth of achieving transcendence at the end of overproduction.

Although Baudrillard also tells us that '[w]e become obsessed with the game of power, its death, its survival. A holy union forms "around the disappearance of [true] power... in fear of the collapse of the political"' (1983, 45). But what has really happened is that the traditional form of the political sphere has already collapsed and is replaced by the phantom image of political power. It is now economic power, embodied by transnational corporations and the demands of overproduction, that prevails.

Simulacrum? Spectacle? Both or Neither?

Best and Kellner (1999) point to a new stage of the Debordian spectacle as the *interactive spectacle*. Rather than be complicit with Baudrillard's critique that simulation in a postmodern age renders Debord's concept of spectacle moot, Best and Kellner indicate where both terms retain their relevance as interconnected.

The relationship between Baudrillard and the Situationists is a complicated one. Although both Debord and Baudrillard were concerned with the effects of rampant consumerism and the use of media and communications through technological mediation to further the interests of those in power, Baudrillard began to break away from the Situationist and neo-Marxist viewpoint considering these outmoded. For Baudrillard, the concept of the spectacle no longer applied to a world where the real had been replaced by the virtual in a regime of simulacra, and the failure to understand the new postmodern nature of signs:

> Baudrillard sometimes spoke of the 'spectacle,' but only provisionally. He rejected the term for two reasons: because it implies a subject-object distinction which he feels implodes in a hyperreality, and because the Situationists theorize the spectacle as an extension of the commodity form, rather than an instantiation of a much more radical and abstract order, the political economy of the sign, or as the semiological proliferation of signs and simulation models (Best and Kellner 1999).

For Debord, the issue can be traced in the inversion of appearance and reality where the true is a moment of the false, and vice versa, governed by the spectacle. Baudrillard instead advanced the idea that a world of objects becomes replaced by a world of signs that no longer refer to the real; all we are left with are self-referential signs, serial copies mediated by technology.

And yet the spectacle endures, and social media is a prime example where the spectacular nature of consumer society is embedded and integrated into what are ostensibly social spaces. Sidebars and promoted content on social network sites reflect back a personally customised series of advertisements based on algorithmic prediction and selection. Topical news stories become bite-sized headline feeds, and these too are preselected and customised according to the data collected from each user. Niche social media audiences seek to spectacularise their own lives by depicting a life of glamour and decadence, carefully curating personal images using filters and other software enhancements. Distinctions between labour and leisure, social and commercial space, marketing and speaking, and identity construction and self-branding become ever more blurred. Moreover, social media is seen by ever so many as not only a necessity and inevitable, but as inherently good.

It appears in the society of the spectacle that a life of luxury and happiness is open to all, that anyone can buy the sparkling objects on display and consume the spectacles of entertainment and information. But in reality only those with sufficient wealth can fully enjoy the benefits of this society, whose opulence is extracted out of the lives and dreams of the exploited (Best and Kellner, 1999).

The *interactive* spectacle reflects a change in the audience. No longer the passive viewer that consumes content in the old hypodermic model of mass media, the audience become active producers of content while still remaining consumers. In this way, Best and Kellner signal that the distinction between passive object who consumes and the active subject who produces media content is effaced, and thus shows fidelity to Baudrillard's claim that the subject-object dichotomy is at an end. Yet, at the same time, this interactive activity online is still structured, coded and dominated by the network owners. If, say, Facebook still controls what content is visible and engineers its user interface to skew discourse in favour of producing more usable data that can be commodified, we are still operating within a society of spectacle. Social media's use of automated prompts, recommendations, reminders and suggestions effectively guide or manipulate social behaviour with a goal to making it productive and thus profitable to the network owner. The interactive spectacle differs from the traditional spectacle by way of one of Baudrillard's key insights of a thoroughly cyberneticised communication platform of command and control, albeit cloaked in the spectacular discourse of social play, positivity, the sale of experiences, and the enticement to compete for personal gain and instant celebrity status by leveraging potential popularity.

The Social Algorithm as the Successor to the Simulacrum and the Spectacle

Key to understanding the social trend toward online self-disclosure would be the refinement of the interactive media environment (IME) that facilitates real-time exchanges which increase the possibility of online feedback with respect to possible immediate gratification for utterances made. Feedback is essential to mechanical devices that rely on external or internal processes to supply corrective information. The cybernetic aspect of feedback, coupled with Shannon's mathematical theory of communication, is an important factor in preventing entropy. However, when the same feedback mechanism model is applied to the social domain of online interaction, what is presented is a crude mechanistic analogy that presupposes an inherent mechanistic process to social interaction by virtue of the fact that it is being conducted digitally. This is evidenced by the reliance on the conduit metaphor embedded in the mathematical theories of communication that suffuse all machine-mediated language (Day 2001). And yet, at the same time, the architecture of social media software underwrites this mechanistic process through its largely invisible methods of organising information. For example, Facebook's algorithm determines on the basis of 'relevance' and quantitative inputs what information is presented to each user (thus 'personalising' each user's experience) according to estimated relevance. 'Top stories' in one's news feed speaks to a concealed sifting and organising process that is algorithmically determined. Users are encouraged to fine tune this feedback mechanism by providing added inputs; i.e., to click on a tab that gives the user an option to remove posts by certain users from appearing in the 'top stories' in the news feed, but also through the more quiet collection of data in tracking each user's navigation, browser cookies and what buttons they interact with. Left on its own, the algorithm will continue presenting stories on the basis of its most current calculation of user inputs. In the same way, ratings, rankings and likings are additional inputs that function as feedback mechanisms to 'personalise' the user experience. What is not seen, however, are the stories that have been selectively omitted from the news feed. The choice function with respect to information in such cases becomes largely hidden from the user who provides indirect feedback to the site by clicking on particular users, postings, links and images. In essence, the user is not making direct choices about what content is visible, nor are these choices being made on the user's behalf transparent.

Algorithms for information sifting and content display decisions might have 'resolved' the problem of a user being presented with too much social media information, and assist in focusing on what the user would find more relevant on, say, a Twitter feed. The personalisation of the user's experience that is furnished by input-determined activity is part of the algorithm's ability to record, process, and produce a particular output commensurate with specific inputs.

Despite the highly personalised appearance of a user's news feed, we are not dealing with a simple correspondence of one-to-one user communication. Instead, the social relations would best be visually depicted as a complex array of Venn diagrams (the overlap zones representing shared information content). One user's input does result in a feedback response in the form of the news feed (organised according to relevance in its sequence). However, user input does not stop at simply providing the user with organised content: the social software itself prospers from these inputs to better construct a large data-portrait of usage trends which can be applied as a corrective model to refine the algorithm. These inputs will have value if they are taken over a longer period of time to show trend-based changes for each user, and for large groups of users according to how the demographic pie is cut up (for example, the sum of all inputs among 15–17 year olds in urban areas may suggest that these users favour stories about kittens rather than puppies).

At bottom, the algorithm mechanistically determines online social activity by taking on the choice or selection function for all displayed information. Users are then more likely to engage with the information selected, thus reinforcing the idea that the algorithm is a useful predictive tool for online social activity. The sequence of events that emerge from algorithmic selection to user interaction, at first simply a sequence, transforms into a causal relationship on the basis of ad hoc inputs that are designed to appear as though anterior to selection. This is aided further by user inputs that confirm the selection. In a way, this is a game of forced choice within a restricted number of options. Or, just like a video game where the options are limited by the programming: one can shoot, run or hide, but there is no option for negotiation or any other action.

Since social media infrastructures are predominantly owned, designed and operated by corporate entities, it should come as no surprise that said digital environments will reflect capitalist biases either explicitly through the commodification of data or implicitly through the sift-sort-separate algorithm that treats social relations as an economic problem. Debord's claim that the spectacle controls all that we see, and how we can see it, is reflected physically in architecture – a point which Debord himself initially expounded but seemed to abandon in his later works. Transpose the idea of physical architecture in urban planning to the social software architectures of the web in the move from the analogue to digital conceptions of space, and we may come to view this new social space as effectively deterministic in much the same, ostensibly neutral or obscured, way. However, the one trick the spectacle must perform is that it must both be totalising as well as supplying the myth of freedom; that is, it must be totalising without alerting the public that it is.

Network Spectacle and the Alienation from Self

What is troubling in this age of social software is how social connectivity may actually function as a barrier to self-reflection. When so much emphasis is placed on self-promotional activities, chasing after numerical benchmarks for social approbation, and the steady increase in screen time spent in this digital environments, one may pose the question: what time is left for critical self-evaluation? Ultimately, we may need to question if beneath all this ostensible social activity there is not a further entrenchment of alienation from the self. The interactive image of the social may prove to be anti-social or non-social in character.

The neoliberal ideology has been successful in decanting itself in everyday discourse so that its objectives have been naturalised. This in itself lionises the individual who can attain wealth and celebrity effortlessly, to become a hero by means of the ideals of self-reliance and a surreptitious war of the one against all. The individual in this climate, mediatised by the ubiquitous devices of the web and their carnivals of frivolity and banality, pandered to by means of excessive perks of 'customisation' and 'personalisation' to render all uniform features with the appearance of individualism, has had to embrace a mercenary or ruthless character of self-promotion and selfishness. There is little to no self-reflection involved in this behaviour: only an urge to succeed at all costs and to envy the entitlements of others by voting for populists who preach an end to welfarism and unionism. The Id is well catered by a steady flow of violent sport spectacles, convenient consumerism abetted by wireless technologies, and the transformation of the political process into a game of aggression and hostility where campaign debates increasingly take on the form of a wrestling match with repetitive slogans where the object is to be perceived as wittier, more polemic than the opponent.

The spectacle enchants as it enchains. It dominates and dictates while doling out tiny, inconsequential pleasures. Social activity operates as a mimicry of economic activity. Production of the online self functions as an agent of separation in a field thoroughly disposed to processes of segmentation. Socio-technological activity is already an embodiment and reflection of spectacular ideology. The misery and fear of the digital social order is camouflaged by the fabric of rapid, giddy communication and the pursuit of readily available novelties. This flash-migration of alienated discontents moves from one digital milieu to another, their time subtracted from self-reflection in the need to personalise or customise new network profiles. Before them is a diffuse catalogue of icon-identities little different from a catalogue of consumer items on display. The network analyst, topographically viewing these migrations, measures the symptoms and activity migrations.

It is the image of the social that governs social relations on social media, a newly organised territory by which the dictatorship of the mobile device reveals its authority in a network of flows that make social relations possible. Just as physical architecture can be said to be inherently ideological, so too can software architecture that has as its goal the compression of space: 'The society which eliminates geographical distance reproduces distance internally as spectacular separation' (Debord 2000, 167). In Debord's analysis, the more space and time become compressed into commodity-space and commodity-time, the more the individual is alienated from space and time itself, those becoming foreign. One has only to note how space and time are reconfigured by Facebook in terms of 'timelines' where one can record the moment of one's birth (now underwritten by Facebook as a colonisation of individual history, its absorption of the individual into its own spectacular enclosure) or in the use of geolocation software that converts space into places, a map of commodity sites where particular products and services can be purchased.

A new abundance arises in the form of social labour, itself a disguised version of commodity time, whereby 'the concentrated result of social labour becomes visible and subjugates all reality to appearance, which is now its product' (Debord 2000, 50). In the spectacle's total occupation of social life, it is the spectacle that reconstitutes itself at every interval of social interaction. The earth, now stitched together in the most abstract form of social relations as mere images in network flows, becomes a global market. Every action or production has its goal in the growth of the spectacle, which is the image of the dominant economy and its motivation to grow for growth's sake.

By representing themselves as leisurely individuals, social media users engage in an emulative exercise of reproducing situations that may not accord with offline reality. As the spectacle serves a purpose of maintaining a program of perfecting separation, it does so through an illusory reunification: in this case, all being 'equal' in the happy banality of social media that speaks in a single voice, that being the univocal expression that justifies the current economic society. It is the spectacle itself that grants meaning to every individual user's ideas, feelings and experiences. This can be observed in the collection fetishism that motivates the taking of pictures of travel and social events that are taken solely for posterity and in service of display as a form of conspicuous prosumption. This type of alienation may replace the motivation for achieving recognition in an offline world. For some users, an experience may be considered a non-event unless it is uploaded to social media. The intrinsic use-value of the experience is demoted to the exchange-value that can be generated for the purposes of social capital. However, it is the false use-value of posting the content online for gaining validation and approval by others that appears to satisfy a social need. In reality, the representations of experience and the self, now digitised, take on a kind of autonomous reality.

We might characterise such autonomous images of the self as posted online with an appeal to Goffman's (1969) distinction between expression and communication. For Goffman, expression occurs in simply being present, whereas communication is tied to a message that is made with intention, such as a writing or a vocal message. Although social media users are not perpetually present, their representations are in the form of the accessible profile page that will continue to express on their behalf. The initial act was one of communication; that is, a user constructed a profile and posted content such as a personal photo and an 'about' section, expressing the individual on the individual's behalf.

The false and spectacular unity afforded by social media allows for the trafficking of social value as homogenised units, while at the same time inscribing the users' new relationship to space and time as an abstract image of the spectacular society where commodities reign. These homogenised units of approbation, such as the thumb-icon, effectively represent a sign or token of social worth. Or, to quote Veblen (1919):

> to sustain one's dignity – and to sustain one's self-respect – under the eyes of people who are not socially one's immediate neighbours, it is necessary to display the token of economic worth, which practically coincides pretty closely with economic success. (67)

Spectacular Digital Labour

If social capital, however construed, is a formal cause, its final cause is desire, the material cause is nature in the form of the devices and networks, and the efficient cause that realises the telos of the capital is labour. Desire, on the other hand, is the 'goal' of social capital insofar as the individual or group seeks gratification according to the demands of desire as a motivational force; that desire may be satisfied by achieving a certain level of status.

Social labour is measured by the objective value of time just as economic capital can be measured as accumulated labour time. As Veblen recognised, the upper classes found labour irksome, and thus preferred unproductive uses of their time as a mark of their status. If social media is cast as a leisure activity, it would then fall under the domain of unproductive time; however, the actual labour being performed does benefit the network and its affiliated advertisers, and the quantity of time expended checking in, posting new content, and managing one's profile does suggest it is not exactly leisure. As Debord tells us: 'All the consumable time of modern society comes to be treated as a raw material for varied new products which impose themselves on the market as uses of socially organized time' (Debord 2000, 151).

The alienated labour of social capital occurs in the unwaged space of self-development writ digitally, much of it contrived for a market audience of other entrepreneurs of the digital self. The user, in conducting labour under the auspices of social entertainment, never truly owns the manicured profile or the digital self-portrait as much as 'rents' a workspace. Nor does the user own the representation directly for it is the alienated product of the projected ego ideal that can never be fully integrated in the actual self. Neoliberalism's devolution of risk in the form of extreme responsibilisation of subjects assigns all the *duties* of ownership without the *benefits*. The user performs his or her labour only ostensibly for the self, but the online self is little more than an accessory and an access point for the advertising narrative and the appearance of enjoyment that is essential for the network to promote itself. Social media has true ownership of the tools and the space in which social interactivity occurs, and it is contingent upon its subscribers to supply their own content and generate the appearance of enjoyment that indirectly performs the function of advertising the network to others whilst also maintaining the belief in its social value in the form of constructed communities.

Just as industrial capitalist production fragmented the life-world of the worker, informational-capitalism abetted by neoliberalism fragments the social-world of the prosumer in a new regime of compressed and discrete time as actual fragments in the form of the tweet, the status update, and social buttons. Social time becomes commodified as discrete intervals of quantised social value. The production is no longer indexed on goods, but on the capitalised subject whose digital representative must maximise positive attention as expressed through quantifiable measures.

The stated advantages of a decentralised entrepreneurial model of content production and consumption via sharing and collaboration does not result in a return to the pre-industrial practices of craft production. Instead, the system of desire in economic expansion as a quantitative one simply fragments labour which is still under the domination of the network. Whereas the shift 'transformed human labour into commodity-labour into wage-labour' (Debord 2000, 40), the labour of the entrepreneurial subject is effectively pittance or unwaged labour. This continues to be in the service of the more general economy: 'The economy transforms the world, but transforms it only into a world of economy' (Debord 2000, 40), to which the now unwaged, entrepreneurial social capitalist continues to serve under the illusion of self-direction, and without institutional supports. This allows Facebook to substantially profit from users seeking to increase their status through production in a hyperactive environment governed by competition: 'surplus labor is transformed by relentless technological activity, and the means of virtual production produce abuse value' (Armitage 1999, 3).

If the network spectacle is certainly an instance of the 'world of vision' triumphant, inverting the relationship of truth and illusion, what else can numeric social capital be but yet another symptom of the positive assumptions tied to a drive to accumulation that follows a similar logic to capital? Would it not also be the spectacular production and proliferation of images by which social relations are mediated that the promise of 'social riches' by accumulation is what partially drives increasing social media participation as a kind of reward? By giving it a standard measure, the social quantified can better align itself with other markers of wealth such as money.

All that appears on social media is good, and all that is good appears on social media. Even those offline experiences might seem to require validation by their conversion into photos, blog posts, status updates so that they may be conferred with a value by other social media users engaged in similar acts of conversion from analogue experience to digital representation.

Main Points

- The artificial economy of online social capital, which resides within the very real economy of social media sites, is a product of the network spectacle where the network discourse and epistemology dominates.
- The network spectacle inverts the relationship between truth and illusion, moving from being to having to mere appearing. Much of social media's production is caught up in a relay circuit of images that come to replace the real.
- The network spectacle controls the space in which the discourse occurs, as well as the discourse itself. The networks themselves are seen as positive or value-neutral. Discourse that is critical of the networks still uses the language of the network, and is generally subsumed within its logic.
- Online social capital becomes but an image of the economy, while the network itself converts the all that is social into economic terms. This creates the conditions of a totalising economic determinism with its 'virtues' of

growth for growth's sake, competition, and the endless pursuit of the signs or images of happiness.

- The network spectacle via social media promises unity, but only provides separation. It is a unification of all users as being alienated from each other and themselves as they pursue mere images that are largely devoid of meaning.
- Ideological domination of space can now be automated, courtesy of sophisticated algorithms that sustain the spectacle's ceaseless monologue of itself. What is made visible or relevant is pre-selected on behalf of the algorithms that deliver the spectacular discourse.

Conclusion

The accumulation of online social capital is largely economic in nature, and this results in the exacerbation of exploitation, alienation, conspicuous prosumption, online narcissism and aggression linked to capitalist circuits of the platforms of social media. The end result has been the solidifying of a spectacular society under the power and control of networks. By bringing together historical and contemporary theories, and drawing from a few salient examples on social media, it may appear that we are left with a bleak conclusion. The use of critique to explore and reflect upon phenomena represents only half its purpose; the other half is to indicate what can be done to ameliorate the situation. At this point it will be helpful to put all the components together to provide the full picture:

1. Social media sites monitor and convert our social interactions into the commodity of data, which is then sold to advertisers in the form of space. Both the social media site and the advertisers sell back the commodity to the users in the form of 'experience.' The raw data is processed or refined into curated data by a sorting algorithm where content visibility is controlled internally. The data itself has a use value, which is then converted into an exchange value when it becomes part of the marketplace for advertisers to purchase.

2. Users on social media commodify themselves while slotting their data into the convenient compartments of a social media profile, while also doing the work of the social media site through the production and consumption of content. In their social exchanges, this produces more data.

3. The rate of production and consumption by which to extract more surplus value from users is increased by increasing the incentives to participate and compete for online social capital. The integration of social buttons to share and measure online social capital, in conjunction with notification alerts, has resulted in both the increase of data collected and more

---

How to cite this book chapter:
Faucher, K. X. 2018. *Social Capital Online: Alienation and Accumulation*. Pp. 135–145. London: University of Westminster Press. DOI: https://doi.org/10.16997/book16.h. License: CC-BY-NC-ND 4.0

eyeballs on adverts, which then justifies the social media site charging more for advertising opportunities. As the network continues to grow, the sum total of data can also increase or be better optimised through refinement of demographics or segmentation.

4. By dangling the promise of social validation and online display of social 'wealth,' users can get caught up in pursuing a growth for growth's sake mandate to increase their visible scores. A social marketplace emerges that aligns with the ideological values of competition and entrepreneurialism. Social interaction becomes more of an exchange value unified by the 'price' as reflected by the number of likes, followers, retweets, etc. These values have no standard basis as a unit of currency, and cannot be directly converted into other forms. In the competitive pursuit of increasing the 'score,' some may opt to purchase illicit services, or otherwise adopt strategies for optimising accumulation.

5. This accumulation for its own sake is based on predatory and primitive capitalist market logic and principles, and may require a significant amount of temporal and labour investment. Ever more surplus value is extracted by the social media site in this process whereas users pursue accumulation of a resource that is based in a simulated economy.

6. Apart from exploitation, users become subject to alienation as social interaction becomes more of a competitive game rather than having intrinsic value unto itself. Acquiring more likes takes precedence over the more traditional forms of social capital, such as skills sharing or community building. Social interaction online becomes subsumed as exchange value in this simulated economy, as social relations become ever more colonised by capitalist values. Users become commodities in these exchanges; apart from providing the data and content, users give proxy support for consumer products and services via conspicuous acts of display.

7. While users are engaged in acts of accumulation through their labour, alienation results from their spending more time working to develop and manage their online selves as opposed to collaborating with others or reflecting on the self. Self-reflection is short-circuited by the constant pressure to produce and consume social media content, while the filter bubble provides a carefully curated vision of the world that is not complete, thus contributing to alienation from the world itself. As market-based competition is rife, acts of narcissistic investment and aggression become growing symptoms in this environment.

8. Demand for online social capital outstrips supply in the attention economy. Despite growing number of users and more time spent by users, the increase in competition to accumulate more online social capital speaks more toward scarcity or to possible inflationary pressures where the value of one's measurable online social capital becomes devalued as expectations for higher scores increase.

9. As the network spectacle maintains this social capitalist enclosure, it fortifies and accelerates all aspects of alienation by controlling the discourse

of what people can see, say, or do as prescribed by the affordances of the network. Real inequalities become concealed, while more time and effort is put into 'winning' the social capital game through conspicuous acts of prosumption. Not only does the network spectacle aid and abet this, but the popular excitement in the prevailing discourse enables this market-based logic, with a wide range of products and services designed to increase one's accumulation potential. This is further embroidered by the entrepreneurial narrative, where success stories are disseminated about those users who leverage their online social capital to become wealthy influencers who market products and services on social media.

10. The acceleration of the symptoms of alienation are produced by the very features of the social media platform (notification services and social buttons that include counters), in conjunction with an overarching ideology that encourages and enables online social behaviours to be indexed primarily on the act of accumulation.

11. User production and consumption is rationalised by the appeal of a standard measurement to compare the apparent value of each user in order to make judgements on social value, which is code for marketable value and potential. There is no way to win the game as the purpose is growth for its own sake, but one can easily lose by simply not playing. The enormous pressure to compete is tied up with the obligations to maintain a presence online and be perceived as relevant. Given the privilege on immediacy, novelty, stimulus and an eternal present, this labour is perpetual.

12. Capitalism prospers by these games of online social capital as it has succeeded in concealing an increase in social labour time behind the appearance of games, play, and social interaction. While within the users' world of the social marketplace, the outer walls are that of a social factory where users continue to consume and produce more, giving freely of their time and labour while being paid in 'experience,' access, and the potential to win at a largely inconsequential game patterned on capitalist accumulation. The users have no ownership of their own content, and are further alienated in being offered limited choices in how they perform their labour. The end product is more data, more commodification of social life, and more advertising.

13. The user's pursuit of online social capital is a circuit nested within the larger capitalist circuit. The use of sophisticated algorithms automates this process…

A Model of Online 'Social Capitalism'

The clearest winners in the highly competitive games for accumulating online social capital are not the users, but the social media sites, and secondarily the advertisers who are sold the data commodity in colonising online social space. There is something shrewd about the integration of social buttons that provide incentive for users to get caught up in increasing scores that are, by and large, of only nominal value as opposed to the very real value of capital produced by these competitive activities and accumulated by the social media site. If it were just a kind of video game, then perhaps it could be argued that the users participate for the pleasure of playing; however, there is so much more at stake when more substantial human values of social validation, relevance, or even one's employment are in play. For many users, these are not just numbers attached to their profiles and posts, but measures of their worth socially and economically.

There is something patently alienating about converting the human need to be social and reducing it to a viciously competitive game that emulates market-based logic and instrumental rationality. Furthermore, making it the basis of commodification for profit is exploitative. By enjoining users to voluntarily commodify their experiences and compete for social value through these kinds of numerical rankings not only results in alienation from self, world and others, but can exacerbate social and economic inequalities, provide incentive to narcissistic and aggressive behaviours, and have an appreciable impact on self-esteem. Some users may attempt to accumulate more of this resource through outright commodification of themselves in portraying on social media lives that are not in line with reality, focusing on moments of leisure, luxury and other forms of consumption through conspicuous display. In emulating capitalism, and valorising consumption as a form of high social value, users empower the real capitalism that exploits and alienates them in these online social venues.

Beginning with the internal capitalist circuit from within the social media site, the user's labour, which includes both production and consumption of content (as consumption does require labour to click or interact with the content which then cross-syndicates it across the network while also providing data), is surplus value. By creating incentives to for users to compete, this potentially increases time spent on the platform while also increasing data capture. This raw commodity of data is further processed into the commodity form. The user also contributes to self-commodification through the conversion of experience into content, which is then caught up in the cycle of online social capital accumulation. While in that cycle, it is part of a broader social marketplace where the content vies for attention and the accumulation of 'likes.' These likes or other forms of numerical markers of accumulation may then be leveraged for the accumulation of more of the same, or for potentially for other purposes linked to social standing or employment. The social reproduction of labour occurs in this circuit as more social interactions are multiplied in the production and consumption of content, which is further data mined by the social media site, but also leveraged by the users for more online social capital. As more labour *time* is consumed in this process, the more production of content leads to the production of data.

The larger enclosing capitalist circuit involves the conversion of user data into a processed commodity that is sold as *space* to advertisers, and thus becomes the main revenue point for the social media site. The social media site then acts as a broker between the advertisers and the social media users in selling back the product of the commodity as experience.

In this relation between the circuits, the user is a commodity point, as is the content the user generates. Online social capital becomes real capital in this dual process of commodification. The user's labour time functions to serve the interests of the site's advertising space under the pretext of further 'experience.' So, the user pays in time and labour, and is paid in 'experience' while being given the incentive to participate in the competition to increase the in-platform 'currency' of online social capital.

Remedies

Although it is beyond the scope of a single book to provide a remedy, we can gesture to a few possibilities for resistance, but it is important firstly to rule out those solutions that are overly simplistic or untenable.

Perhaps the most simplistic solution of all is to simply unplug from social media, to abstain from its use. Inasmuch as this may appeal to a kind of common sense view, it fails to acknowledge a position of privilege from which such a view derives. Those who are established academics, celebrities or hold significant positions of institutional power can afford to abstain from the use of social media entirely if they so choose. Many others who are not in such positions do not have the luxury to simply unplug, and particularly those who are attempting to establish themselves in a given field, or for those whose opportunities and employment depend on making use of social media. Moreover, those who lack in social opportunities due to distance, ability, or degree of marginalisation can ill-afford to simply dismiss social media. The position of privilege that has the choice to unplug is akin to the same kind of class divisions we see in offline life, such as in the ability to choose not to endure long hours at the work place, an arduous daily commute, or having to shop at a discount grocery store out of financial necessity. Being able to unplug from social media is more the privilege of those who belong to what Veblen would call the leisure class, but also for those who occupy positions of institutional power.

It can be tempting for some who embrace the unplugged view to consider social media entirely frivolous, and certainly they may draw some inferences in this book to confirm their own views given the largely negative social and economic effects covered in this book. Such a view seems to cultivate a kind of naive romanticism of a 'better time' before the rise of social media. This nostalgia neglects the fact that there is no empirical evidence to suggest that societies are more narcissistic, aggressive or frivolous – the only difference is that there is more opportunity to express such behaviours to a larger audience, and that we now have a digital archive that records what once went little recorded. To assume otherwise is to make a causal argument that social media has a strongly deterministic impact on human behaviour, and would qualify as a fallacy. We can say that social media has had an appreciable effect on behaviours, as any new medium does in reshaping social and cultural contexts, but having an effect is quite different from declaring an absolute determinism. Although we have covered mostly the negative social consequences of social media in this book, social media has also provided a number of benefits *despite and sometimes in resistance to* capitalist control of major social media. As a tool, it has united otherwise disparate groups and been effective in mobilising for social justice. Social media has been instrumental in raising awareness of an emergency situation, such as in times of a natural disaster or in locating abducted children. Its real-time affordances have also been useful for users to detect and intervene when another user is expressing suicidal ideation. Social media has been a tool for organising progressive resistance, such as the massively attended Women's March in response to the inauguration of Donald Trump.

Resistance is not futile, but simply unplugging is not a satisfactory answer. If we take the Institute of Network Cultures, founded by Geert Lovink, and their release of the *Unlike Us Reader*, they do not advocate for simply walking away from social media, but in creating alternatives that are not corporately controlled. Their solution is to bring together artists, theorists and other practitioners to engage in the critique of new social media in working towards a truly open, democratised, and people-centric form of social media. This is but one of numerous examples where groups have united to move from critique to action.

This solution is but a half-measure. What is needed is to resolve a great number of issues pertaining to exploited social media labour and a reconfiguration of what online social capital could be, returning to the forms of open community exchange and sharing that granted the concept more lustre before the emergence of the like economy. In the end, our task remains to confront those entities that perpetuate exploitation and alienation, remaining critical of social media and demanding fairness and transparency. We must accept that social media is not going away anytime soon, nor are its plethora of problems.

Devising solutions can only be based on what we know matched against a current state of affairs, and any efforts to be anticipatory would be speculative at best. As we know, social media is in constant flux. A corporation such as Facebook is highly flexible and adaptive, and they have the money and the human resources to find new ways of integrating itself into our social lives in order to turn a profit and keep its users appeased.[26] I am choosing to close this book by offering a few general potential solutions, possibly idealistic, as a point for further discussion as we continue to engage in robust critique of social media phenomena. Some of these are far from new, but bear reiterating.

1. Education: Critical Digital Media Literacy

Given the ubiquity and significance of social media in everyday life for a significant portion of the world's population, critical digital media literacy ought to be introduced earlier in public education curricula. It is hoped that this will cultivate more critical consumers and producers of social media content, some of whom may one day be in a position to help shape the social media of the future.

There are several entwined issues in our usage of social media that deserve our attention and should become part of a broader discourse, be it the psychological implications of how social media is used, critical issues pertaining to labour and exploitation as we enter into a 'new collar' disruptive economy, how we understand community and extralocal issues, how the democratic process itself may be endangered by filter bubbles, astroturfing efforts – just to name a few. Social media has a presence in every aspect of many people's lives, politically, legally, psychologically, socially, economically and even at the level of our physical health. One of the many benefits of increasing our critical digital awareness is that it may lead to a groundswell effort to ensure some principles of fairness, accountability and transparency.

2. Legislative Change in Terms of Data–Ownership and Control

The extraction of data from social media users, app-adopters, and site visitors has become normalised in everyday web usage, and is a significant business practice. From the use of cookies in browsers to the use of location services for better understanding our behaviour, data collection feeds big data in terms of improving predictive software and the delivering advertising to 'enhance' our online experience. In most cases, there are laws whereby social media and other sites have a legal duty to inform us that our data is being collected, either by a notice on our first time visit to a site, or as part of a user agreement such as a terms of service. At bottom, however, the general idea is that we 'pay' for these services by trading our data, from which site owners may profit in selling that data or engage in data-pairing with targeted ads based on the data profile that has been created using algorithms. The notion that we could receive a 'cut' for the sale of our personal data is simply not on the table.

Seemingly progressive attempts to gain control over our own data have had mixed results. The European Union's 'right to be forgotten' law would seem to empower individuals to make requests to have certain sites naming them not appear in search engine results. Although this may seem a good idea, it has also been used by public figures seeking to revise their own public image to remove scandalous events from the public record. In this way, the right to be forgotten may conflict with a right to know. Moreover, we might argue that this only obfuscates data, not permanently deletes it. In addition, it does nothing for how data is used by social media to target users with advertisements, nor how the algorithm will use this data to control what is made visible in a newsfeed or Twitter stream.

One possible solution would be legislative changes that allow for better disclosure on precisely how one's data is used. Social media users, for example, ought to have access to how the data provided has led to algorithmic decisions beyond vague statements of 'according to your interests, location, and demographic information, these ads and content were chosen specifically for you.' This disclosure should also make clear to whom this data is being sold, and even provide a choice for users to conceal portions of their personal data from algorithmic sorting.

3. Legislative Change in Terms of Digital Labour

Given the expansive growth in, and reliance upon, digital labour in of terms non-routinised cognitive labour, labour crowdsourced from the general intellect, and routinised digital support labour (online tech support, for example), better protections may be required. Recognising all digital labour *as labour* should be considered under all laws pertaining to the labour laws of the land, including provisions for overtime pay, leaves, right to form unions, minimum wage, eligibility for state-run retirement and unemployment benefits, and workplace safety.

With respect to social media-based digital labour performed by those hired as employees on salary or on contract to manage a social media account, fair labour laws should apply. Moreover, there ought to be an acknowledgement of the precarity of such positions, and a further recognition of the intellectual, cognitive labour that is employed to perform these tasks to deliver persuasive experiences on behalf of the company that hires such people. It goes without saying that companies should not be permitted to rely on unpaid internships to occupy these key public-facing roles.

When we consider social media users who are not employed by any companies to perform marketing or support duties, there needs to be an acknowledgment of the general labour being performed by users. As they continue to contribute to the circulation of data in communicative capitalism, we may need a new accord with social networking sites to dispel the old canard that our labour is compensated by access to the service.

4. Cracking Down on Botnets and Click Farms

We have since seen what can happen when social media and comment boards become flooded with a well-orchestrated botnet, or when 'political action groups' attempt to astroturf the web to persuade a populace that there is more support for something than there actually is. Such efforts qualify as propaganda, and more stringent efforts are required to prevent the gaming of social media. In order to achieve this, there has to be international consensus in recognising the problem and in taking steps to put a stop to it. This, of course, is a major hurdle. With ongoing allegations of covert state-sponsored social media botnet and astroturfing campaigns emerging out of Russia, the US and Turkey, both domestic and foreign-directed, this will prove a very daunting task.

We have also to consider those who have little option but to work on click farms under wretched working conditions. These are not industries any person of conscience ought to support. Better detection software with full cooperation by major social media companies is required to put a stop to troll farms such as those operated by the Internet Research Company (IRA), and to develop a mechanism for the proper sourcing of information provided online, such as making clear that particular messages are arising from coordinated political action committees, etc.

5. Social Media as Public Utility

Social media sites will claim that displaying advertisements to users is the price paid by users to have access to the features of the social media site. And, certainly, the costs of running a major social media site are not trivial. Less convincing may be the justification for the ownership and control of user content.

The creation of a publicly-run, non-profit online social media network to be promoted as an alternative can be considered, but would have to be done carefully to avoid legal wrangles of anti-competition laws. In such a case, existing laws governing the provision of national broadcasters could be repurposed for this initiative. The question of where funds would be acquired to launch and maintain such an initiative remains an open one. It would in essence be funded by taxes and either operated by a government or – possibly more ideally – by an arm's length body that would receive funding as a subsidy, and fall under a nation's telecommunications laws. The one downside of such an idea would be that it would tie users to a site that might only admit citizens of that state. Opening up such a site for global access might present conflict between different nations' respective laws and would raise serious questions from taxpayers who might feel as though they are subsidising free access to citizens of other nations.

There are a few examples of social media that are non-profit. The example of The Fossil Forum is but one of many online forums that runs on donations to keep the proverbial lights on. Not every forum has to run ads in a sidebar, nor allow corporate sponsors to occupy the space by posting adverts.

6. Third-Party Algorithmic Sorting

Algorithmic sorting for what content becomes visible to users ought to be under a trusted, third-party regulatory framework. The objection might be that making the 'recipe' public would result in unscrupulous people being better able to game the system. In the earliest days of search engines, what appeared in search results on the first page was determined by a very simple algorithm, compared to the ones that function on search engine giants like Google and Bing today. In those early days, the artful manipulation of back-linking could artificially inflate the visibility of a website, and thus give it a higher priority in returned search results. These would be cautionary tales in whatever algorithmic 'recipe' is adopted in this case.

Although this solution may go some length to make social media companies more accountable in how they deliver visible content, as well as how much of the content is linked to advertising, the one major legal hurdle would be patent protection: social media companies carefully guard their algorithms as proprietary, and might argue any attempt to open the proverbial black box and permit a third-party regulated service to manage the algorithm might have detrimental effects in terms of data security, site functionality and logistics, and potentially making the social media sites less competitive or capable of attracting corporate ad buys.

A compromise, however, is possible as there already is an existing model used by some sidebar advertising services. As algorithms are only as good as the data that feeds and refines their processes to deliver more relevant output, providing options to social media users to choose with a click if they wish to see more or less of particular kinds of content may help better customise and tailor a user's environment by granting the user more control.

7. Ending 'Metrification'

Urging existing social media companies to remove the numeric counters from social buttons is another possible solution. Although this may not resolve the issue of competition in the attention economy, a stronger emphasis on engagement and sharing without counters, and not using these to inform the algorithm that may be indexed on what is popular, may reduce social herding and the evaluation of other users simply based on numbers.

What would happen if there were concerted pressure to dismantle the 'like economy' by removing all these counters? It would not prevent corporately controlled social media companies from continuing to extract surplus value from its users, nor the use of other forms of social buttons, but it might remove the emphasis on accumulating likes and engaging in numeric comparison with other users. Quantification would still run in the background, within the social media algorithms that will still deliver content on the basis of numeric popularity, but it might help in getting more users to use a more quality-based criteria for evaluating user-generated content and reduce a capitalist-inflected kind of competition on social media. And, perhaps, the incentives to participate would take on a whole new direction. The likelihood of major social media companies to even consider removing that feature is virtually nil as it is so thoroughly integrated as a strategy for higher user participation and in their business models.

With that being said, assuming social media companies might see good reason in discontinuing visible counters, this would potentially render the business model of exploitative click farms irrelevant. This would not, however, undermine the use of botnets to carpet social media with bulk content designed to alter the behaviours and opinions of potentially susceptible users who might mistake a very high proportion of one-sided content as representative of a majority view. In that case, the quantity aspect is embedded rather than visible as a metric.

The removal of visible social counters may, however, reduce overall demand on the black market for those services that provide clicks, even if it would not put an end to those services entirely as long as there is some residual demand.

Admittedly, this is not an exhaustive list, and some of these suggestions may be naive and idealistic. However, as I have argued in this book, there is a very real need to continue critically addressing these issues and to question if there are other ways by which we can enjoy online social capital in a different way without being caught up in the games of capitalist-inspired accumulation, which only seem to result in alienation in one form or another, and which only serves to increase competitive rather than collaborative social activity, while it is the social media sites that continue to profit.

If the promise of social media is to unite us, to provide for equal communicative exchange free from creating a system of winners and losers, we know that the use of visible metrics implies hierarchy, and invites comparative valuation based on those numbers. Social media perhaps ought not to be a space where 'winning' is the goal, but actual socialising. The alternative where we 'metrify' our social relations is far too reminiscent of capitalism's values, and reinforces the network spectacle by playing into a strange fantasy game based on accumulation, but a game that has very real human costs.

Can we reimagine social media as truly communicative without capitalism? Can social media users reclaim the space as one that encourages conversation without becoming a kind of competition for popularity and artificial gain in a like economy? I, for one, would like to hope so.

Notes

[1] For the purposes of clarity, the use of 'metrification' in this book is used in a more general sense to denote the conversion of non-numeric qualities to numeric quantities, and not in its more specific sense of the metric system of measurement.

[2] Also concealed in this process is the very real costs of these networks, generally borne by exploited labour in the extraction of rare earth minerals or the expanding (and exploitative) service economy in the developing world, the reliance on employed labour to perform coding and network maintenance, the use of unpaid interns, etc. For a more in depth focus on how information technologies contribute to ecological crises, see Maxwell and Miller's *Greening the Media* (2012).

[3] Despite several attempts, from psychometric data to social network analysis, there has yet to be any definitive validation for consistent measurement, which is yet again impeded by a lack of consensus over the term and its scope.

[4] Small town networks have their benefits and disadvantages. Despite the potential for stronger ties, it can also result in stagnation if there are so few new social, material and knowledge inputs that are usually imported with new members. The strong ties and inward-looking aspects can also present barriers to newcomers. In this author's practice in local government consulting, one community stakeholder put it very pithily: 'you aren't really from here until you have at least one grandmother in the local cemetery.'

5   For the duration of one week in January 2012, Facebook conducted an experiment on nearly 700,000 users, without their informed consent, to observe and measure how altering the content available to users on the basis of mood or sentiment might affect the mood or sentiment of the users. The authors of the study (Kramer et al 2014) claim that informed consent was already established by the users' agreement with Facebook's Data Use Policy. However, as James Grimmelman (2014) points out, apart from the low threshold of what is considered legal consent in this instance, there are lingering questions about funding, harm, and research-based ethics clearance. In essence, the 'study' was far from merely observational, but was an experiment that relied on manipulating the emotions of users without their knowledge. If Facebook's image relies on providing a high-trust culture network, this experiment would seem to contradict any such claim.

6   In particular, the work of danah boyd appears to focus primarily on youth cultures and the benefits of social media for this demographic.

7   As of 27 June 2017, Facebook's number of users has more than doubled to 2 billion users since 2012. Despite Facebook's attempt to use more sophisticated methods for purging fake accounts, botnets, and click farming, it would be reasonable to assume that it remains a challenge.

8   And, indeed, some examples of social media production do gain a new and different value for posterity, such as the Library of Congress' move to archive select tweets.

9   Other sites, such as klout.com, give a rank value on one's social presence, although it is unclear on what they base their methodology on to arrive at these values.

10   There are some notable exceptions, but they are *exceptions*. Offline activity spurred by online interaction will more generally lead to the consumption of products and services through online recommendations.

11   In a 1990 interview with Antonio Negri in *Futur Anterieur,* Deleuze muses that 'speech and communication have been corrupted. They're thoroughly permeated by money.'

12   On this point of our energy footprint, Mark P. Mills, CEO of the Digital Power Group, says that an average iPhone consumes about 361 kilowatts a year, whereas a regular fridge consumes about 322 kWh (Mills, 2013). In the US alone, over 70 billion kWh were consumed annually as of 2014, representing about 2 per cent of the total energy consumption of the country. This is spread out over 3 million data centres and 'cloud farms.' What we might keep in mind here is that the energy being supplied is not all coming from renewable sources, but also heavily drawing upon oil, gas, and coal – all finite resources.

13   Whether intentional or not, the invocation of 'empowerment' is imbricated in the neoliberal-informationist discourse alongside 'mobility' and 'choice.' Fogg touts the optimistic benefit of MIP, but may not have considered some of the assumptions in how empowerment is actually deployed, under what

conditions of more etherealised command and control, the disempowerment of cognitive labour in the development of apps, vendor-based devices that restrict choice and the ways in which data harvesting more empowers corporations for targeted advertising and predictive marketing.

[14] It should be noted, however, that the veracity of the list of named politicians and celebrities could not be confirmed, and that it would not prove difficult for someone to engage in the mischief of setting up a profile account for another person.

[15] Initially, the experiment was designed to run for seven days, but was in future iterations cut down to five, and now down to three due to the increasing expression of anxiety over the exercise from one cohort to the next. Certain exceptions were made, such as if the use of social media was for emergency, family, school, or work-related reasons.

[16] A Google search for Instagram food photography delivers numerous results of tips on how to take better photos of food, with sources ranging from BBC to the *New York Times* and numerous blogs.

[17] One can imagine such a scenario. An episode of *Black Mirror* portrayed a speculative future where one's online social score determined one's opportunities (or lack thereof).

[18] It is important to sound a note of caution about the mobilisation of the term narcissism and how quickly it becomes pathologised and gendered. As Elizabeth Lunbeck's book, *The Americanization of Narcissism* argues, Christopher Lasch had performed an unbalanced and selective reading of the psychoanalytic literature, focusing only on the negative aspects while dismissing the form of 'healthy narcissism' explored by Heinz Kohut. Moreover, Lasch generalises narcissism to society at large, and does not acknowledge that Otto Kernberg's more negative portrayal of narcissism was markedly gendered and seemingly opposed to feminist approaches.

[19] Work by Jean Twenge, J.D. Foster, S. Konrath et al. have employed meta-analytical approaches to determining that there has been an increase, at least with respect to sampling among college students. However, we must exercise caution here when we migrate such observation to a digital milieu: to make overarching claims that suggest that people are more mundane, narcissistic, exhibitionist or any other quality must take into consideration that the participatory nature of SNSs and microblogging now facilitates a means by which people can digitally document their lives with more ease. That is, the underlying attitudes and behaviours of people may not have changed, but we now have the digital documentation to see these more clearly.

[20] Examples of this disturbing behaviour, many of which target women and promote rape culture, are far too numerous. As of this writing, I read about Emily Vance who posted a video of herself urinating on an American flag. Although such an act may be deemed offensive by some, it is not illegal, and she was engaging in free expression. As a disproportionate response, angry

social media users have sent her death and rape threats, and even threatened to do harm to her family. Similar threats against women and their families have occurred in response to advocating for female empowerment or against those who have investigated the military to expose the extent of sexual assault in the ranks.

21   I draw the term 'applause' from the very poetic description Elias Canetti provides in his book, *Crowds and Power*, where he calls the breaking of windows in a riot as the encouraging applause of objects.

22   An earlier attempt to automate pre-moderation relied on keyword filters, but this provided little barrier for users to bypass by engaging in creative spelling so that certain expletives and racist terms could be posted.

23   The topic of cyberbullying is deserving of its own extended treatment, and so we can only signal its existence here as part of a broader discussion of aggressive online behaviours.

24   For a contemporary example, there is no shortage of tweets by President Donald Trump on a wide range of issues where he blatantly contradicts himself, and may have done so strategically to play to what his team recognise as his foundational support base. His pre-campaign tweets and his presidential tweets are by far the most contradictory.

25   Or, as a strategic operation that has been performed in the past, intentionally releasing 'sourceless' rumours to the media one wishes to discredit, knowing that they will print it, and then legitimising the claim that the media is 'fake news.'

26   As of this writing, Facebook's Mark Zuckerberg made a public pledge to get a billion people to buy into virtual reality devices. Such devices allow for the integration of AR (augmented reality) and may prove a much more invasive method as it colonises our sense perception of space as something that is commercially linked, in ways much more advanced than the location services of Google Maps that may privilege sites for consumption. It may not be a far step from being constantly 'logged in' to Facebook even without a device. If Facebook uses AR to deliver purely commercial experiences on a perpetual basis has very serious ideological implications on how we can understand space.

Bibliography

Abidin, Crysal. '"Aren't These Just Young, Rich Women Doing Vain Things Online": Influencer Selfies as Subversive Frivolity'. *Social Media + Society* April-June: 1–17, 2016.

Adams, Richard, John Bessant and Robert Phelps. 'Innovation Management Measurement: A Review'. *International Journal of Management Reviews* 8, no. 1: 21–47, 2006

Anderson, Chris. 'The Long Tail'. *Wired* 12, no. 10, 2004

Armitage, John. 'Resisting the Neoliberal Discourse of Technology'. *cTheory* 3, 1999.

Arthur, Charles. 'How low-paid workers at 'click farms' create appearance of online popularity'. *The Guardian*. August 2, 2013.

Associated Press. 'Facebook, Twitter Followers a Multi Million-Dollar Business'. 5 January 2014.

Baregeh, Anahita, Jennifer Rowley and Sally Sambrook. 'Towards a Multidisciplinary Definition of Innovation'. *Management Decision* 47, no. 8: 1323–39, 2009

Barnes, John Arundel. *Social Networks*. Boston, MA: Addison-Wesley, 1972.

Baudrillard, Jean. *The Ecstasy of Communication*. Trans. by Bernard and Caroline Schutze. New York: Semiotext(e), 1988.

———. *Symbolic Exchange and Death*. Trans. by Iain Hamilton Grant. London: Sage Publications, 1993.

———. *The Consumer Society: Myths and Structures*. London: Sage Publications, 1998.

Bauman, Zygmunt. *Freedom*. Minneapolis, MN: University of Minnesota Press, 1988.

Baumeister Roy F., Brad J. Bushman and W. Keith Campbell. 'Self-Esteem, Narcissism, and Aggression: Does Violence Result From Low Self-Esteem or From Threatened Egotism?' *American Psychological Society* 9, no. 1: 26–29, 2000.

Benkler, Yochai. *The Wealth of Networks: How Social Production Transforms Markets and Freedom*. New Haven, CT: Yale University Press, 2006.

Beran, Dale. '4Chan: The Skeleton Key to the Rise of Trump'. *Medium*. (https://medium.com/@DaleBeran/4chan-the-skeleton-key-to-the-rise-of-trump-624e7cb798cb), 14 February 2017.

Best, Steven and Douglas Kellner. 'Debord and the Postmodern Turn: The New Stages of the Spectacle'. *Substance*, 90: 129–156, 1999.

Boltanski, Luc and Eve Chiapello. 'The New Spirit of Capitalism'. *International Journal of Politics, Culture, and Society* 18: 161–188, 2005.

Boltanski, Luc and Eve Chiapello. *The Spirit of Capitalism*. New York: Verso, 2006.

Borgmann, Albert. 'Information, Nearness and Farness'. *The Robot in the Garden: Telerobotics and Telepistemology in the Age of the Internet*. Ed. by Ken Goldberg. Cambridge, MA: MIT Press, 2000.

Bourdieu, Pierre. *Distinction: A Social Critique of the Judgement of Taste*. Trans. R. Nice. Cambridge: Harvard University Press, 1984.

———. 'The Forms of Capital'. *Education: Culture, Economy and Society*. Eds. A. Halsey, H. Lauder, P. Brown & A. Stuart Wells. Oxford: Oxford University Press, 1997.

Bourdieu, Pierre and Loïc Wacquant. *An Invitation to Reflexive Sociology*. Chicago, IL: University of Chicago Press, 1992.

boyd, danah. 'Why Youth (Heart) Social Network Sites: The Role of Networked Publics in Teenage Social Life'. *MacArthur Foundation Series on Digital Learning – Youth, Identity, and Digital Media*. Ed by David Buckingham. Cambridge: MIT Press, 2007

Brandtzaeg, Petter Bae and Ida Maria Haugstveit. 'Facebook Likes: A Study of Liking Practices for Humanitarian Causes'. *International Journal of Web Based Communities* 10. no. 3, 258–79, 2014.

Bratton, Benjamin H. 'Black Stack'. *e-Flux* 53 (http://www.e-flux.com/journal/53/59883/the-black-stack/), 2014.

Bruns, Axel. 'From Prosumer to Produser: Understanding User-Led Content Creation'. *Transforming Audiences* 3–4, 2009.

Buffardi, Laura E. and W. Keith Campbell. 'Narcissism and Social Networking Web Sites'. *Personality and Social Psychology Bulletin* 34:1308, 2008.

Burgoon, J.K. et al. 'Testing the Interactivity Model: Communication Processes, Partner Assessments, and the Quality of Collaborative Work'. *Journal of Management and Information Systems* 16, no. 3: 33–56, 2000.

Cameron, William Bruce. *Informal Sociology: A Casual Introduction to Sociological Thinking*. New York: Random House, 1963.

Canetti, Elias. *Crowds and Power.* New York: Viking Press, 1962.

Castells, Manuel. *The Rise of the Network Society.* Oxford: Blackwell, 1996.

de Cauter, Lieven. *The Capsular Civilization: On the City in the Age of Fear.* Rotterdam: NAi Publishers, 2004.

Christensen, Henrik Serup. 'Political Activities on the Internet: Slacktivism or Political Participation by Other Means?' *First Monday* 16, no. 2: n.p., 2011.

Coleman, James S. 'Social Capital in the Creation of Human Capital.' *American Journal of Sociology* 94: S95-S120, 1988.

———. *Foundations of Social Theory.* Cambridge: Bellknap Press. 1994.

Contrera, Jessica. '13, Right Now: This is What it's Like to Grow Up in the Age of Likes, lols and longing.' *Washington Post*, 25 May 2016.

Day, Ronald E. *The Modern Invention of Information: Discourse, History, Power.* Carbondale, IL: Southern Illinois University Press, 2001.

De Graaf, Nan Dirk. and Hendrik. D. Flap. 'With a Little Help From My Friends: Social Resources as An Explanation of Occupational Status and Income in West Germany, the Netherlands, and the United States.' *Social Forces* 67: 453–472, 1988.

Dean, Jodi. 'Communicative Capitalism: Circulation and the Foreclosure of Politics.' *Cultural Politics* 1, no.1: 51–74, 2005.

———. *Democracy and Other Neoliberal Fantasies: Communicative Capitalism and Left Politics.* Durham, NC: Duke University Press, 2009.

Debord, Guy. *Society of the Spectacle.* Detroit, MI: Black & Red, 2000 [1967].

———. *Comments on the Society of the Spectacle.* New York: Verso, 1998 [1988].

Deleuze, Gilles. 'Postscript on Control Societies.' *Negotiations: 1972–1990.* Trans. by Martin Joughin. New York: Columbia University Press 177–182, 1995.

di Segna Garbasz, Yarra. 'Flame Wars, Flooding, Kicking and Spamming: Expressions of Aggression in the Virtual Community'. http://www.personal.u-net.com/~yandy/papers/PSA.html, June 1997.

Dorfman, Joseph. *Thorstein Veblen and His America.* New York: Augustus M. Kelley, [1934] 1966.

Dyer-Witheford, Nick. *Cyber-Marx: Cycles and Circuits of Struggle in High Tech Capitalism.* Chicago, IL: University of Chicago Press, 1999.

Edwards, Bob, and Michael W. Foley. 'Social Capital and the Political Economy of Our Discontent'. *The American Behavioral Scientist* 40, no. 5:. 669–78, 1997.

Ellison, Nicole B., Charles Steinfield and Cliff Lampe. 'The Benefits of Facebook Friends: Social Capital and College Students' Use of Online Social Network Sites'. *Journal of Computer-Mediated Communication* 12, no. 4: 1143–68, 2008.

Enli, Gunn S. and Nancy Thumim. 'Socializing and Self-Representation Online: Exploring Facebook'. *Observatorio* (OBS) 6, no.1, 2012.

Epstein, Robert, and Ronald E. Robertson. 'The Search Engine Manipulation Effect (SEME) and Its Possible Impact on the Outcomes of Elections'. *Pro-

ceedings of the National Academy of Sciences of the United States of America 112, no. 33: E4512-E4521, 2015.

Facebook. Open Graph. Available at: http://developers.facebook.com/docs/opengraph/ 2013

Farag, Dina, 'The Driving Force Behind the Social Networking Giant'. *Bearmun: The Official Newspaper of the Berlin Model United Nations.* 16 November 2012.

Faucher, Kane X. 'Thumbstruck: The Semiotics of Liking Via the "Phaticon"'. *Semiotic Review.* http://www.semioticreview.com/index.php/open-issues/issue-open-2013/12-thumbstruck-the-semiotics-of-liking-via-the-phaticon.html, 2013.

Fisher, Eran. *Media and New Capitalism in the Digital Age.* New York: Palgrave Macmillan, 2010.

Fisher, Eran. 'How Less Alienation Creates More Exploitation: Audience Labour on Social Network Sites'. *TripleC: Communication, Capitalism and Critique* 10, no. 2: 171–83, 2012.

Fogg B.J. 'Mass Interpersonal Persuasion: An Early View of a New Phenomenon'. *Proceedings of the Third International Conference on Persuasive Technology.* 2008.

Follows, Stephen 'How movies make money: $100m+ Hollywood blockbusters' https://stephenfollows.com/how-movies-make-money-hollywood-blockbusters, 2016

Foucault, Michel. 'The Birth of Biopolitics'. *Lectures at the College De France.* Trans. by Graham Burchell. New York: Palgrave Macmillan, 2008.

Freud, Sigmund. *Civilization and its Discontents.* Trans. by Joan Riviere. New York: Doubleday, n.d.

Fuchs, Christian 'Labor in Information Capitalism and on the Internet'. *The Information Society* 26:179–196, 2010.

———. 'Digital prosumption labour on social media in the context of the capitalist regime of time'. *Time & Society* 2(1): 97–123, 2014.

———. *Culture and Economy in the Age of Social Media.* New York: Routledge, 2015a.

Fuchs, Christian and Sebastian Sevignani. 'What is Digital Labour? What is Digital Work? What's their Difference? And why do these Questions Matter for Understanding Social Media?' *TripleC: Communication, Capitalism and Critique* 11, no. 2: 237–93, 2013.

Fukuyama, Francis. *Trust: The Social Virtues and the Creation of Prosperity.* London: Hamish Hamilton, 1995.

Gehl, Robert W. *Reverse Engineering Social Media: Software, Culture, and Political Economy in New Media Capitalism.* Philadelphia, PA: Temple University Press, 2014.

Gerlitz, Carolin and Anne Helmond. 'The Like Economy: Social Buttons and the Data-Intensive Web'. *New Media & Society* 15, no. 8: 1348–65, 2013.

Gillespie, Tarleton. The Politics of 'Platforms', *New Media and Society,* 12(3): 347–64, 2010.

Goffman, Eric. *Strategic Interaction*. Philadelphia, PA: University of Pennsylvania Press, 1969.

Granovetter, Mark. 'The Strength of Weak Ties.' *American Journal of Sociology*. 78: 1360–1380, 1973.

Grimmelman, James. 'As Flies to Wanton Boys' (Blog post retrieved: 16 May 2016: http://laboratorium.net/archive/2014/06/28/as_flies_to_wanton_boys, 2014.

Hardt, Michael, and Antonio Negri. *Empire*. Cambridge: Harvard University Press, 2000.

Harvey, David. *A Brief History of Neoliberalism*. Oxford: Oxford University Press, 2005.

———. *The Enigma of Capital: and the Crises of Capitalism*. New York: Oxford University Press, 2011.

Hassan, Robert. 'Crisis Time: Networks, Acceleration and Politics within Late Capitalism.' *cTheory*. https://journals.uvic.ca/index.php/ctheory/article/view/14767/5639, 2009.

Hearn, Alison. 'Meat, Mask, Burden: Probing the Contours of the Branded Self.' *Journal of Consumer Culture* Vol. 8, no. 2: 197–219, 2008.

Hodkinson, Paul. 'Interactive Online Journals and Individualization.' *New Media & Society* 9, no. 4: 625–50, 2007.

Huang, Jen-Hung, and Yi-Fen Chen. 'Herding in Online Product Choice.' *Psychology & Marketing* 23, no. 5: 413–28, 2006.

Jacobs, Jane. *The Death and Life of Great American Cities*. London: Cape, 1961.

Jeanes, Emma L. '"Resisting Creativity, Creating the New." A Deleuzian Perspective on Creativity'. *Creativity and Innovation Management* 15, no. 2: 127–34, 2006.

John, Nicholas A. 'Sharing and Web 2.0: The Emergence of a Keyword'. *New Media and Society* 15, no.2: 167–82, 2013.

Junker, Louis J. 'Markings on the Nature, Scope, and Radical Implications of the Ceremonial-Instrumental Dichotomy in Institutional Analysis'. *Annual Meeting of the Western Social Sciences Association*, 24 April 1980.

Kernberg, Otto. *Borderline Conditions and Pathological Narcissism*. New York: Jason Aronson Inc., 1985.

Khamis, Susie, Lawrence Ang and Raymond Welling. 'Self-branding, "Micro-celebrity" and the Rise of Social Media Influencers.' *Celebrity Studies* 8, no. 2: 191–208, 2017.

Knack, Stephen and Philip Keefer. 'Does Social Capital Have an Economic Payoff: A Cross-Country Investigation'. *The Quarterly Journal of Economics* 112, no. 4:1251–88, 1997.

Koerner, Brendan I. 'Why ISIS is Winning the Social Media War'. *Wired,* April 2016.

Kohut, Heinz. *The Analysis of the Self*. New York: International Universities Press, 1971.

Konrath, Sara, Brad J. Bushman and W. Keith Campbell. 'Attenuating the Link Between Threatened Egotism and Aggression'. *Psychological Science* 17, no. 11: 995–1001, 2006.

Krackhardt, David. 'Cognitive Social Structures'. *Social Networks* 9, no. 2: 109–134, 1987.

Kramer, Adam D., Jaime E. Guillory and Jeffrey T. Hancock. 'Experimental Evidence of Massive-Scale Emotional Contagion Through Social Networks'. *Proceedings of the National Academy of Sciences of the United States of America* 111, no. 24: 8788–8790, 2014.

Kristoffersen, Kirk, Katherine White and John Peloza. 'The Nature of Slacktivism: How the Social Observability of an Initial Act of Token Support Affects Subsequent Prosocial Action'. *Journal of Consumer Research* 40, no. 6: 1149–66, 2014.

Labonte, Ronald. 'Social Capital and Community Development: Practitioner Emptor'. *Australian and New Zealand Journal of Public Health* 23, no. 4: 430–33, 2008.

Lasch, Christopher. *The Culture of Narcissism*. London: Abacus, 1979.

Latour, Bruno. *Science in Action: How to Follow Scientists and Engineers Through Society*. Milton Keynes: Open University Press, 1987.

———. *Reassembling the Social: An Introduction to Actor-Network-Theory*. Oxford: Oxford University Press, 2005.

Law, John and Peter Lodge. *Science for Social Scientists*. London: Macmillan Press, 1984.

Lazarsfeld, Paul F., Bernard Berelson and Hazel Gaudet. *People's Choice: How the Voter Makes Up His Mind in a Presidential Campaign*. New York: Columbia University Press, 1948.

Lazzarato, Maurizo. 'Immaterial Labour'. *Radical Thought in Italy: A Potential Politics*. Eds. Michael Hardt and Paolo Virno. Minneapolis, MN: University of Minnesota Press, 1996.

Le Bon, Gustave. *Psychologie des Foules*. Alcan, 1895.

Levinson, Paul. *New New Media*. London: Pearson Publishing, 2009.

Lewis, Sinclair. *It Can't Happen Here*. New York: Penguin, 1993 [1935].

Lovink, Geert. What is the Social in Social Media? *e-flux* 40: http://www.e-flux.com/journal/40/60272/what-is-the-social-in-social-media/, 2012.

Lukács, Georg. *History and Class Consciousness*. Cambridge: MIT Press, 1972.

Lunbeck, Elizabeth. *The Americanization of Narcissism*. Cambridge: Harvard University Press, 2014.

Madge, Charles and Tom Harrisson. *Mass-Observation* (pamphlet). London: Frederick Muller, 1937.

Manzerolle, Vincent R. 'Technologies of Immediacy / Economies of Attention: Notes on the Commercial Development of Mobile Media and Wireless Connectivity'. *The Audience Commodity in a Digital Age*. Ed. by Lee McGuigan and Vincent R. Manzerolle. Peter Lang, 2014.

Marcuse, Herbert. *Negations: Essays in Critical Theory*. Trans. by Jeremy J. Shapiro. Boston, MA: Beacon Press, 1969.

Marx, Karl. *Economic and Philosophical Manuscripts of 1844*. New York City: International Publishers, 1964.

———. 'Economic and Philosophic Manuscripts of 1844', from *The Marx-Engels Reader*. Ed. Robert C. Tucker. W.W. Norton: New York, 1972.

———. 'Wages'. *Marx and Engels Collected Works* Vol. 5. Chadwell Health: Lawrence and Wishart, 1975 [1847].

———. *Capital: A Critique of Political Economy, Volume 1*. Ed by Frederick Engels. Trans. by Samuel Moore and Edward Aveling. New York: International Publishers, 1967 [1867].

———. *Capital: A Critique of Political Economy, Volume 2*. Ed by Frederick Engels. Trans. by Samuel Moore and Edward Aveling. New York: International Publishers, 1967 [1885].

———. *Capital: A Critique of Political Economy, Volume 1*. Ed by Frederick Engels. Trans. by Samuel Moore and Edward Aveling. New York: International Publishers, 1967 [1894].

Maslow, Abraham H. 'A Theory of Human Motivation'. *Psychological Review* 50, no. 4: 370–96, 1943.

Maxwell, Richard and Toby Miller. *Greening the Media*. New York: Oxford University Press, 2012.

McCullough, M.E. et al. 'Interpersonal Forgiving in Close Relationships: II. Theoretical Elaboration and Measurement'. *Journal of Personality and Social Psychology* 76: 1586–1603, 1998.

Mehdizadeh, Soraya. 'Self-Presentation 2.0: Narcissism and Self-Esteem on Facebook'. *Cyberpsychology, Behavior, and Social Networking* 13, no. 4: 357–64, 2010.

Mejias, Ulises. *Off the Network: Disrupting the Digital World*. Minneapolis, MN: University of Minnesota Press, 2013.

Merton, Robert K. 'The Matthew Effect in Science'. *Science* 159 no. 3810: 56–63, 1968.

Mestrovic, Stjepan. *Thorstein Veblen on Culture and Society*. London: Sage Publications, 2003.

Mikiewicz, Piotr. 'The Theoretical Foundations of the Concept of Social Capital and Their Implications for Educational Empirical Research'. *Kultura i Edukacja* 76–96, 2011.

Mills, Mark P. 'The Cloud Begins with Coal: Big Data, Big Networks, Big Infrastructure, and Big Power: An Overview of the Electricity Used by the Global Digital Ecosystem'. 2013.

von Mises, Ludwig. *Human Action: A Treatise on Economics*. New Haven, CT: Yale University Press, 1963.

Monbiot, George. 'The Need to Protect the Internet from "Astroturfing" Grows Ever More Urgent'. *The Guardian*, 23 February 2011.

Moore, Phoebe. *International Political Economy of Work and Employability*. New York: Palgrave Macmillan, 2010.

Moreno, J. L. *Who Shall Survive? A New Approach to the Problem of Human Interrelations*. Boston, MA: Beacon House, 1934.

Morini, Cristina. 'The Feminisation of Labour in Cognitive Capitalism'. *Feminist Review* 87: 40–59, 2007.

Morozov, Evgeny. *The Net Delusion: The Dark Side of Internet Freedom*. New York: PublicAffairs, 2012.

Mosco, Vincent. *The Digital Sublime: Myth, Power, and Cyberspace*. Cambridge, MIT Press, 2004.

Mumford, Lewis. *The Condition of Man*. London: Martin Secker & Warburg, 1944.

———. *The Pentagon of Power: The Myth of the Machine Volume Two*. New York: Harcourt Brace Jovanovich, 1970.

Neubauer, Robert. 'Neoliberalism in the Information Age, or Vice Versa? Global Citizenship, Technology, and Hegemonic Ideology'. *Communication, Capitalism and Critique* 9, no. 2: 195–230, 2011.

Noshpitz, J.D. 'Narcissism and Aggression'. *American Journal of Psychotherapy* 38, no. 1: 17–34, 1984.

Obama, Barack. 'President Obama's Farewell Address'. (https://obamawhitehouse.archives.gov/farewell), 10 January 2017.

Ong, Aihwa. 'Neoliberalism as a Mobile Technology'. *Transactions of the Institute of British Geographers* 32, no. 1: 3–8, 2007.

Papachrissi, Zizi. 'The Virtual Geographies of Social Networks: A Comparative Analysis of Facebook, LinkedIn, and ASmallWorld'. *New Media & Society*. 11, no. 1–2: 199–220, 2009.

Pariser, Eli. *The Filter Bubble: How the New Personalized Web is Changing What We Read and How We Think*. New York: Penguin, 2012.

Pasquinelli, Matteo. 'Machinic Capitalism and Network Surplus Value: Notes on the Political Economy of the Turing Machine'. (http://matteopasquinelli.com/docs/Pasquinelli_Machinic_Capitalism.pdf), 2011.

Peck, Jamie, and Adam Tickell. 'Neoliberalizing Space'. *Antipode* 34, no. 3: 380–404, 2002.

Perry, Mark et al. 'Dealing with Mobility: Understanding Access Anytime, Anywhere'. *ACM Transactions on Computer Human Interaction* 8, no. 4: 323–47, 2001.

Peters, Michael A., Rodrigo Britez and Ergin Bulut. 'Cybernetic Capitalism, Informationalism and Cognitive Labour'. *Geopolitics, History and International Relations* 2: 11–40, 2009.

Peters, Tom. 'The Brand Called You'. *Fast Company*. (https://www.fastcompany.com/28905/brand-called-you), 31 August 1997.

Portes, Alejandro. 'Social Capital: Its Origins and Applications in Modern Sociology'. *Annual Review of Sociology* 24: 1–24, 1998.

Putnam, Robert D. *Bowling Alone: The Collapse and Revival of American Community*. New York: Simon & Schuster, 2001.

Rafaeli, Sheizaf. 'Interactivity: From New Media to Communication'. In *Sage Annual Review of Communication Research: Advancing Communication*

Science, Vol. 16, eds R. P. Hawkins, J. M. Wiemann and S. Pingree, 110–134. Beverly Hills, CA: Sage, 1988.

Rawls, John. *Political Liberalism*. New York: Columbia University Press, 2005.

Read, Jason. 'A Genealogy of Homo-Economicus: Neoliberalism and the Production of Subjectivity'. *Foucault Studies* 1, no. 6: 25–36, 2009.

Retteberg, Jill W. *Seeing Ourselves Through Technology: How We Use Selfies, Blogs and Wearable Devices to See and Shape Ourselves*. New York: Palgrave Macmillan, 2014.

Rigi, Jakob and Robert Prey. 'Value, Rent, and the Political Economy of Social Media'. *The Information Society* 31(5): 392–406, 2015.

Ritzer, George, and Nathan Jurgenson. 'Production, Consumption, Prosumption: The Nature of Capitalism in the Age of the Digital "Prosumer"'. *Journal of Consumer Culture* 10, no. 1: 13–36, 2010.

Robison, Lindson J., Allen Schmid and Marcelo E. Siles. 'Is Social Capital Really Capital?' *Review of Social Economy* LX, no.1: 1–21, 2002.

Roosendaal, Arnold. 'Facebook Tracks and Traces Everyone: Like This!' *Tilburg Law School Legal Studies Research Paper*, SSRN eLibrary, 2010.

Rosen, Christine. 'Virtual Friendship and the New Narcissism'. *The New Atlantis* 15: 15–31, 2007.

Roth, Philip. *The Plot Against America*. New York: Random House, 2004.

Shannon, Claude E. 'A Mathematical Theory of Communication'. *The Bell System Technical Journal*. 27: 379–423, 623–656, 1948.

Shirky, Clay. *Here Comes Everybody: The Power of Organizing Without Organizations*. New York: Penguin, 2008.

di Segna Garbasz, Yarra. 'Flame Wars, Flooding, Kicking and Spamming: Expressions of Aggression in the Virtual Community'. June 1997: http://www.personal.u-net.com/~yandy/papers/PSA.html. Accessed: July 2016.

Senft, Theresa M. *Camgirls: Celebrity & Community in the Age of Social Networks*. New York: Peter Lang, 2008.

Srnicek, Nick. *Platform Capitalism*. Cambridge: Polity Press, 2017.

Terranova, Tiziana. 'Free Labor: Producing Culture for the Digital Economy'. *Social Text* 18, no. 2: 33–58, 2000.

———. *Network Culture: Politics for the Information Age*. London: Pluto Press, 2004.

———. 'Free Labor'. Ed. Trebor Scholz. *Digital Labor: The Internet as Playground and Factory*. New York: Routledge, 2013.

Thiry-Cherques, Hermano. 'Intranets: A Semiological Analysis'. *Journal of Information Science* 36: 705–718, 2010.

de Tocqueville, Alexis. *De la démocratie en Amérique*. London: MacMillan & Co Ltd, 1960 [1835].

Toffler, Alvin. *Powershift: Knowledge, Wealth, and Violence at the Edge of the 21st Century*. New York: Bantam Books, 1991.

Tönnies, Ferdinand. *Community and Society*. Trans. by Charles P. Loomis. New York: Dover Publications, 2002 [1887].

Turkle, Sherry. *Alone Together: Why We Expect More from Technology and Less from Each Other*. New York: Basic Books, 2012.

Turnage, A.K. 'Email Flaming Behaviors and Organizational Conflict'. *Journal of Computer-Mediated Communication* 13, no. 1:43–59, 2007.

Twenge, Jean, and W. Keith Campbell. '"Isn't it Fun to Get the Respect That We're Going to Deserve?" Narcissism, Social Rejection, and Aggression'. *Personality and Social Psychology Bulletin* 39, no. 2: 261–272, 2003.

———. *The Narcissism Epidemic: Living in an Age of Entitlement*. New York: Free Press, 2009.

Utz, Sonja. 'Show Me Your Friends and I Will Tell You What Type of Person You Are: How One's Profile, Number of Friends, and Type of Friends Influence Impression Formation on Social Networking Sites'. *Journal of Computer-Mediated Communication* 15, no. 2: 314–335, 2010.

van Dijck, Jose. *The Culture of Connectivity: A Critical History of Social Media*. Oxford: Oxford University Press, 2013.

———. 'Datafication, Dataism and Dataveillance: Big Data Between Scientific Paradigm and Ideology'. *Surveillance & Society* 12: 197–208, 2014.

Vazir, Simine, and David C. Funder. 'Impulsivity and the Self-Defeating Behavior of Narcissists'. *Personality and Social Psychology Review* 10, no. 2: 154–65, 2006.

Veblen, Thorstein. 'Why is Economics Not an Evolutionary Science?' *Quarterly Journal of Economics*, 12, no. 4: 373–97, 1898.

———. *The Theory of the Leisure Class*. N.P.: World Library Classics, 2010 [1899].

———. *The Theory of Business Enterprise*. New York: Cosimo, 2005 [1904].

———. 'On the Nature of Capital II: Investment, Intangible Assets, and the Pecuniary Magnate'. *Quarterly Journal of Economics*, 23, no. 1, 104–36, 1908.

———. 'Fisher's rate of interest'. *Political Science Quarterly*, 24: 296–303, 1909a.

———. *The Place of Science in Modern Civilization*. New York: B.W. Huebsch, 1919.

———. *The Engineers and the Price System*. New York: B.W. Huebsch, 1921.

Virilio, Paul. *The Futurism of the Instant: Stop-Eject*. Trans. by Julie Rose. New York: Polity Press, 2010.

Virno, Paolo. 'Virtuosity and Revolution. The Political Theory of Exodus'. Eds. Paolo Virno and Michael Hardt. *Radical Thought in Italy: A Potential Politics*. Minneapolis, MN: University of Minnesota Press, 2006.

Walther, Joseph B. 'Computer-Mediated Communication: Impersonal, Interpersonal, and Hyperpersonal interaction'. *Communication Research* 23: 3–43, 1996.

Wang, Shaojung Sharon and Michael A. Stefanone. 'Showing Off? Human Mobility and the Interplay of Traits, Self-Disclosure, and Facebook Check-Ins'. *Social Science Computer Review* 41, no. 4: 437–57, 2013.

Wiener, Norbert. *Cybernetics: Or Control and Communication in the Animal and the Machine*. Cambridge: MIT Press, 1948.

Index

Printed and bound by CPI Group (UK) Ltd, Croydon, CR0 4YY

08/07/2026

14916661-0001